Black Colleges

Recent Titles in
Educational Policy in the 21st Century

Educational Leadership: Policy Dimensions in the 21st Century
Bruce Anthony Jones

Community Colleges: Policy in the Future Context
Barbara K. Townsend and Susan B. Twombly, editors

Policy and University Faculty Governance
Michael Miller and Julie Caplow, editors

Black Colleges

New Perspectives on Policy and Practice

EDITED BY
M. CHRISTOPHER BROWN II
AND KASSIE FREEMAN

Dr. Mettler,
Thank you for your support of the Patterson Research Institute.
All the best,

Christopher
M/2
4/20/2002

Educational Policy in the 21st Century
Bruce Anthony Jones, Series Editor

PRAEGER

Westport, Connecticut
London

Library of Congress Cataloging-in-Publication Data

Black colleges: new perspectives on policy and practice / edited by M. Christopher
Brown II and Kassie Freeman.
     p. cm.—(Educational policy in the 21st century)
     Includes bibliographical references and index.
     ISBN 1–56750–586–4 (alk. paper)
     1. African American universities and colleges. 2. African Americans—Education
(Higher) I. Brown, M. Christopher. II. Freeman, Kassie. III. Series.
    LC2781.B444   2004
    378.73′089′96073—dc22   2003057981

British Library Cataloguing in Publication Data is available.

Library of Congress Catalog Card Number: 2003057981
ISBN: 1–56750–586–4

First published in 2004

Praeger Publishers, 88 Post Road West, Westport, CT 06881
An imprint of Greenwood Publishing Group, Inc.
www.praeger.com

Printed in the United States of America

The paper used in this book complies with the
Permanent Paper Standard issued by the National
Information Standards Organization (Z39.48–1984).

10 9 8 7 6 5 4 3 2 1

To a new generation of scholars researching black colleges

Contents

Acknowledgments

This book would not have been possible without the help of so many friends and colleagues. There are many nameless persons around the country who have aided in conceptualization, author selection, and editing. We thank each of you. While we are responsible for all errors, gaps, and inconsistencies, this volume represents a collective effort on the part of a group of authors with whom it has been a pleasure to work. Without their collective effort, this book could not have been put together.

The State of Research on Black Colleges: An Introduction

M. Christopher Brown II and Kassie Freeman

The formation of historically black colleges and universities (HBCUs) is rooted in the aspiration of African Americans to gain education during a time in which legalized racial segregation and the preclusion of African Americans from obtaining formal education endured. As remnants of a period in America's past that some would like to pretend did not exist, HBCUs have been excluded from the focus of mainstream historical and empirical higher education research. In the absence of an authentic, comprehensive body of research on HBCUs, few have accurately described or assessed the place these institutions occupy in the landscape of American higher education. "From their very beginnings," argue Allen and Jewell (2002), "HBCUs were faced with outright opposition to their existence" (p. 242). Many feared the social, economic, and political implications of an educated African American citizenry. Early opposition to these institutions was manifest in overt hostility and physical destruction (Roebuck and Murty, 1993), as well as charges that African American students were intellectually inferior. Today, HBCUs continue to be devalued and misjudged, and the label of inferiority continues to be misapplied to African American students and historically black institutions alike. Since the 1954 U.S. Supreme Court decision in *Brown v. Board of Education*, HBCUs have also been accused of being anachronisms and charged with promoting segregation. However, those who make such claims do so in direct opposition to the history that led to the development of these institutions.

Much can be learned from and about HBCUs. Although the fact is often concealed from mainstream discourse, HBCUs have a long-standing tradition of preparing their students for social, economic, and political success. Research shows that HBCUs have been the primary educators of African Americans (Akbar, 1989; Allen, 1991; Astin, 1982; Edmonds, 1984; Fleming, 1984; Garibaldi, 1984; Hytche, 1989; Jones, 1971; Stikes, 1984; Thomas, 1981). Moreover, HBCUs have historically created pools of qualified individuals who have diversified academia and corporate America. In Roebuck and Murty's (1993) *Historically Black Colleges and Universities,* Vernon Jordan notes that "it is the black colleges that have graduated 75 percent of all black Ph.D.'s, 75 percent of all black army officers, 80 percent of all black federal judges, and 85 percent of all black doctors" (p. 13). While approximately 75 percent of African American college students are now enrolled in traditionally and predominantly white colleges and universities across the country, HBCUs educate approximately one-third of the African Americans who earn baccalaureate degrees each year (Roebuck & Murty, 1993).

In an attempt to expound on the mission and goals of the predominantly black college, Roebuck and Murty (1993) state: "HBCUs, unlike other colleges, are united in a mission to meet the educational and emotional needs of black students. They remain the significant academic home for black faculty members and many black students. The goals described in black college catalogs, unlike those of white schools, stress preparation for student leadership and service roles in the community" (p. 10). Lamont (1979), in *Campus Shock,* says that for many African American students the historically black institution is "culturally more congenial" than the traditionally white mainstream university (p. 32). Moreover, "there is also a general level of satisfaction and camaraderie among black students at black schools that is not found among black students on white campuses" (Roebuck & Murty, 1993, p. 15). However, as Garibaldi (1984) indicates:

Black colleges are not monolithic. Although they are similar to predominantly White institutions in many ways, their historical traditions and their levels and types of support make them distinct. Like many other institutions of higher learning, Black colleges reflect the diversity that is so characteristic of the United States' postsecondary education system. This diversity should always be remembered when considering their past, their current conditions, and their future roles in higher education. (p. 6)

The historic successes and continuing contributions of historically black colleges and universities do not divorce higher education from its responsibility to explore the role of society in shaping the sociocultural, socioeconomic, political, and familial influences that contribute to African American student attainment (Lang & Ford, 1988). In the four decades since the enactment of the 1964 Civil Rights Act, institutions throughout the country have initiated a variety of programs and policies to promote the recruitment and retention of students from various minority groups. However, these institutions have not been particularly successful in retaining African American students. With the conservative shift of the American ideology, evidenced by the works of Allan Bloom (1987), Dinesh D'Souza (1991), Richard Herrnstein and Charles Murray (1994), Richard Bernstein (1994), and others, there has been an unrelenting erosion of policies and programs that promote recruitment and retention, particularly for African American students (Wilson, 1982). Reginald Wilson (personal communication, January 16, 1994), senior scholar at the American Council on Education, argues that during this retrenchment, only historically black colleges and/or effective retention policies safeguard minorities from the pernicious effects of institutionalized discrimination.

Ensuring the future success of African American college students requires a fundamental shift in institutional objectives, environments, and populations as we move beyond the daybreak of a new millennium. As we consider the state of research on black colleges and universities and the chasm in our current knowledge and understanding of these institutions in the broader spectrum of postsecondary education, five critical questions emerge: What is the nature and function of HBCUs in the larger context of American higher education? What are the major policy issues facing HBCUs at the beginning of a new millennium? What considerations for practice should HBCUs make in an era of accountability and retrenchment in order to sustain a competitive market advantage and enhance the success of African American students? What lessons can traditionally and predominantly white institutions learn from HBCUs about supporting African American achievement? What will HBCUs do to meet the challenges of changing national and global contexts for higher education?

These questions involve issues that have significant implications for public policy and educational planning. The pressing nature of these issues and our foray into a new millennium provide an opportune time to examine the policies and practices relating to the black college. Given the complexity and ambiguity surrounding many of the issues, it is important to employ the expertise of multiple scholars and researchers in assessing the status and future of black colleges. There are no current volumes about black colleges; however, both the '70s and '80s saw major intellectual contributions to the scholarship about these institutions. In 1978, Willie and Edmonds edited a book entitled *Black Colleges in America: Challenge, Development, Survival*. In 1984, Garibaldi edited an '80s version of the Willie and Edmonds work, titled *Black Colleges and Universities: Challenges for the Future*. The ideological reprisal of the '90s went by without any significant volume being written about these important institutions. There was only one text with a limited historical and statistical focus (Roebuck and Murty's *Historically Black Colleges and Universities: Their Place in American*

Higher Education, published in 1993). Given the changing face of American higher education, the time is ripe to reassess the position of the black college in American higher education.

Thus, the purpose of this book is threefold. First, it provides an accurate historical and contemporary analysis of historically black colleges and universities. Second, it locates their position in the higher education landscape, and the embedded notions of race and power in the policies that affect their nature and function. Third, this book provides recommendations for institutional practices and higher education policy initiatives. This volume is divided into two parts. In the first part, several contributors document the status, practices, and trends of black colleges and highlight major policy challenges facing black colleges as they approach the millennium. The second part provides constructive criticisms and recommendations for institutional practices and initiatives and includes a chapter on black colleges within an international context.

PART I

The Policy Context

CHAPTER 1

The Changing Role of Historically Black Colleges and Universities: Vistas on Dual Missions, Desegregation, and Diversity

M. Christopher Brown II, Ronyelle Bertrand Ricard, and Saran Donahoo

INTRODUCTION

The college that a student chooses to attend is an important determinant of educational satisfaction, professional development, and future success. Prior to the legal promotion of universal collegiate access, the majority of America's institutions of higher learning restricted the opportunity for African Americans to pursue education in general, and higher education in particular (Brown, 1999b; Cohen, 1998). Consequently, this population's desire to learn, develop, and attain gave rise to the birth of the nation's historically black colleges and universities (HBCUs). Black colleges were formed as an intentionally subordinate tier of mainstream higher education. They were designed to allow African Americans to replicate the existing national stratification and hierarchy within a racially enclaved context (Barrow, 1990).

Despite the narrow scope of their intended function, historically black colleges and universities grew into significant institutions in the production of research, particularly on the African diaspora. Black colleges became the primary teachers of the previously under- and/or uneducated populace, central repositories of cultural heritage, and stalwart beacons for community uplift (Brown & Freeman, 2002). The purpose of this chapter is to highlight the significance of HBCUs and their continuing contribution to higher education. The pages that follow review the historic dual mission of HBCUs as they endeavor to provide effective education for their students. Additionally, critical analysis is given to the import and impact of collegiate desegregation and the concept of diversity within this unique educational context.

EDUCATIONAL ACCESS FOR AFRICAN AMERICANS

Prior to the era of Reconstruction, very few educational opportunities existed for African Americans. The slave codes expressly prohibited any efforts to educate enslaved men, women, and children. Indeed, endeavoring to protect both the peculiar institution and the South itself, every state except Tennessee enacted laws preventing slaves from being educated. Although some slaves and masters circumvented these laws, very few African Americans were literate at the time they gained their freedom (Foner, 1988; Roebuck & Murty, 1993).

Following the end of the Civil War, many recognized the need to provide educational opportunities for freed men and women. Only two of the nation's HBCUs were founded before the advent of the Civil War—Lincoln University and Cheyney State University (both in Pennsylvania). Neither of them was located in the South, thus limiting the ability of most African Americans to make use of them (Brown & Davis, 2001; Roebuck & Murty, 1993). In order to make education more accessible to the mass population of former slaves, the American Missionary Association and the Freedmen's Bureau, as well as various philanthropists, African American churches, and communities, established institutions in the South specifically devoted to black education (Brown, 1999b; Brown & Davis, 2001; Brown, Donahoo, & Bertrand, 2001; Browning & Williams, 1978; Foner, 1988). Although Southern planters were opposed to educating their former chattel, the Morrill Act of 1890 provided the financial incentive for states in the region to establish public higher education institutions for African Americans. In addition to gaining access to federal funds, land-grant HBCUs also provided Southern whites with the means to keep white colleges and universities segregated while also maintaining some control over African American education (Brown, 1999b; Browning & Williams, 1978; Hall, 1973; Roebuck & Murty, 1993).

Armstrong, Hampton, and Early Efforts at Higher Education

The education of African Americans remained a thoroughly debated issue even as HBCUs were being established throughout the South. The social and economic instability of the South following the Civil War helped perpetuate the fear that educating freedmen would lead to racial upheaval (Bond, 1935; Clement, 1966; Roebuck & Murty, 1993). Although they did not generally support the idea of schooling for African Americans, some whites did recognize the social, political, and economic advantages these education efforts afforded them (Anderson, 1988; Engs, 1999; Spivey, 1978). As Donald Spivey (1978) suggests, maintaining control over black education helped Southern whites institute a "new slavery" during the Reconstruction era.

Viewing himself as a champion of the cause of freedmen, Samuel Chapman Armstrong was instrumental in furthering the efforts of Southern whites to control African American education. The son of Hawaiian missionaries, Armstrong served in the Union Army leading black troops. While stationed in the Sea Islands of South Carolina, Armstrong began to recognize the similarities between the circumstances confronting the former slaves and the native Hawaiian people his parents had dedicated their lives to saving. Acknowledging their eagerness to learn, Armstrong believed that freedmen needed proper training to survive in the white world (Engs, 1999; Hall, 1973).

When Armstrong founded Hampton Institute in 1868, it was the culminating event combining his Hawaiian, Civil War, and Freedmen's Bureau experiences. Constructing the new institution to resemble the Hilo Manual Labor School of Hawaii, Armstrong designed Hampton to include a labor regimen, which served two purposes. While affording some students the opportunity to use their labor as a way of offsetting the costs of their education, the work requirements placed on all Hampton students were also aimed at socializing them to accept their place in the New South (Anderson, 1978; Brown, 1999a; Hall, 1973). While serving in the Union Army, Armstrong realized that neither the South itself nor the newly emancipated were prepared for a society divorced from the socially constructed boundaries of human commodification and enslavement. In the true spirit of the term "reconstruction," Armstrong felt that the best way to save the South and all its citizens was to supply African Americans with industrial training that provided them with skills they could use to survive as skilled laborers. Concurrently, the training advocated by Armstrong silently condoned the social system of African American subordination that Southern whites so desperately needed (Anderson, 1988; Engs, 1999; Spivey, 1978).

During the early years of Reconstruction, Armstrong served as assistant subcommissioner for the Ninth District of Virginia for the Freedmen's Bureau. He settled in the town of Hampton and began plans to establish a school to educate freedmen (Engs, 1999). More than any of his other experiences, Armstrong's time with the Freedmen's Bureau directly influenced the shape of Hampton Institute and his philosophy of African American education. Like the Freedmen's Bureau itself, Armstrong actually hindered the former slaves' attempts at self-determination (Anderson, 1978; Anderson, 1988; Spivey, 1978). Despite his interactions with black soldiers during the Civil War, Armstrong was a much better friend to white property owners than he was to their former slaves. Both the Freedmen's Bureau and white property holders were more interested in bringing economic stability to the South than they were in actually making it easier for African Americans to adjust to freedom. For his part, Armstrong truly believed that the white landowners shared common goals with the freedmen and freedwomen. Using some of the same arguments presented by Southerners to justify slavery, Armstrong insisted that African Americans needed education to alter their naturally poor character and make them capable of living among whites. Ignoring the black codes and racism that limited African American social and economic mobility, Armstrong blamed the freedmen for their poor circumstances. He suggested that they could escape their natural penchant for laziness and move on to a better life only through the earnest benefits of labor (Spivey, 1978).

The Hampton-Tuskegee Idea: Perceptions and Debate

Despite its reputation and Armstrong's ideology, Hampton Institute was not initially designed to train freedmen to become laborers. Instead, Hampton was actually opened as a normal school where African American teachers could be prepared to go out and replicate Armstrong's philosophy in their education of others (Anderson, 1978; Anderson, 1988; Engs, 1999). Industrial education helped to maintain the social order by supplying the teachers being trained at Hampton with the discipline and character development they would need to help prepare their race for its subordinate role in the New South (Anderson, 1978; Anderson, 1988; Brown, 1999a). From a practical standpoint, African American teachers were also needed to replace Northern missionaries and teachers who started losing interest in the freedmen's cause in the middle of Reconstruction (Engs, 1999).

Furthermore, when Hampton began providing industrial training in 1895, these courses were offered as an addendum to its traditional teacher and leadership education focus (Anderson, 1978; Anderson, 1988). Much like the resolution of Reconstruction itself, the education model developed by Armstrong for Hampton emerged as a three-pronged compromise partially achieving the goals established by Southern whites, freedmen, and Northern whites. For Southern whites, Hampton provided a way to socialize African Americans and maintain the whites' political, economic, and social supremacy (Anderson, 1978; Anderson, 1988; Clement, 1966; Engs, 1999; Hall, 1973; Roebuck & Murty, 1993; Spivey, 1978). At the same time, Hampton and the other educational facilities left former slaves with one of the few tangible gains that remained after Reconstruction. Furthermore, Hampton also helped release increasingly disinterested Northern missionaries and teachers from their commitments to educate African Americans by providing suitable replacements (Engs, 1999). Armstrong's approach to African American education also made it easy for Northern politicians and philanthropists to assist the freedmen without jeopardizing reconciliation with the South. Indeed, Armstrong's construction of African American education helped put an end to Reconstruction by providing all parties with a way to claim victory regarding the freedmen issue.

Hampton's amalgamation of teacher preparation and industrial education programs made it easy for America's general population to ignore the freedmen issue and concentrate on rebuilding the nation as a white man's land. However, it also helped spark a debate regarding how African Americans might best respond to their new subjugation. Best known as the Washington–Du Bois debates, African American opposition to the accommodation strategy championed by Booker T. Washington and symbolized by Hampton and Tuskegee Institutes began soon after Hampton added industrial training to its curriculum (Brown, 1999a). In the 1890s, black newspapers such as the *Cleveland Gazette* and the *Washington Bee* challenged Washington's approach long before W. E. B. Du Bois spoke out on the issue (Anderson, 1988).

Even so, it is not possible to ignore the influence both Washington and Du Bois exerted over the curriculum that developed in HBCUs. In many ways, Washington and Du Bois were complete opposites. Washington was born a slave, educated at Hampton, and willing to accept the failure of black Reconstruction as an opportunity for African Americans to prove their worth as free men and women (Anderson, 1988; Washington, 1969). Conversely, Du Bois was born free in the North the same year Hampton opened, was educated at Fisk and Harvard, and was emphatically opposed to any education system devoted to the principle that African Americans had always been and would forever remain inferior (Anderson, 1988; Du Bois, 1996).

As one of Hampton's most successful graduates, Washington thoroughly exemplified and accomplished many of the goals Armstrong articulated when he founded the normal school. In 1881, Washington replicated Hampton Normal and Agricultural Institute by establishing Tuskegee Normal and Industrial Institute in Alabama (Anderson, 1988; Brown, 1999a; Hall, 1973; Spivey, 1978). In addition, Washington gave more legitimacy to the Hampton Idea by serving as the leading African American spokesperson for industrial education. Like Armstrong, Washington believed that both blacks and whites could benefit from what was renamed the Hampton-Tuskegee Idea for industrial education. Industrial training provided an education that would help blacks adapt to the work world and earn a living. It also gave whites a way to limit the criminal activity and poverty of freedmen while increasing the number of skilled laborers ready for employment (Washington, 1969). Washington, a consummate politician, had something for everyone in his presentation and description of black industrial education (Brown, 1999a).

Notwithstanding this success, it was Washington's attempt to satisfy everyone that Du Bois seemed to despise the most. Viewing him as an agent of white industrialists and supremacists, Du Bois accused Washington of sacrificing black political power, civil rights, and higher education for industrial education, wealth, and Southern reconciliation. Although Du Bois believed that Washington's efforts were noble and well intended, he was most distressed by the negative consequences of Washington's compromise. Rather than prepare blacks to simply accept what the nation was willing to give them, Du Bois advocated an education system that encouraged the pursuit of knowledge, character, and culture that would eventually elevate the entire race (Du Bois, 1996).

Although the Washington–Du Bois debates concentrated on issues affecting African American education, the question at the heart of their dispute remains a recurring theme in the field of higher education. Even though both Washington and Du Bois ultimately wanted to develop an African American elite, they devised different methods for accomplishing this goal. In the tradition of Samuel Chapman Armstrong and Hampton Institute, Washington believed that the process of developing an intelligentsia should begin by providing a basic education to the masses. Du Bois, in contrast, championed an education system similar to the one he had received at Fisk and Harvard, which could prepare an elite that would then be responsible for teaching the masses. Applying the suggestions of both Washington and Du Bois, the early curriculum at HBCUs catered to the needs of both the masses and the elite in an effort to prepare their students for life in both the present and the future.

THE DUAL MISSION OF HBCUS

The history of HBCUs reflects a unique blend of missions designed to teach students to both think and do. The design of these institutions differed from most of the colleges and universities before them in two respects: HBCUs promoted universal access and provided a curriculum designed to meet the needs of both the institution and the community. Although it is often characterized as a weakness, HBCUs have a unique tradition of providing their students with a culturally, socially, economically, and politically relevant education.

Universal Collegiate Access

Whether in New England or the New South, Americans have always struggled to determine who should have access to higher education (Brown, 2002b). Recognizing that education promotes and enables social mobility, the founders of the nation's earliest institutions limited access to a select group of people. Colleges of the Colonial era successfully controlled who enrolled by requiring students to speak Latin and Greek, pass oral examinations, and accept the discipline, structure, and religious affiliation of each institution (Cohen, 1998). As a result, the typical American college student of the period was male, white, and socially elite.

Although the development of public universities increased the number of institutions and made it easier for students to attend college, this in no way universalized education. Indeed, at the close of the Civil War, the South did not have a public education system at any level for people of any race (Anderson, 1988). Out of all of the Southern states, only Kentucky and North Carolina had anything that even resembled a public education system before 1860 (Bowles & DeCosta, 1971). Thus, when the former slaves began to demand and work to establish formal public schooling open to people of all ages, they were actually asking the South and the rest of the nation to embrace a relatively new philosophy of education. Not only were they asking white Southerners to pay for the education of people they once held as property, they were also effectively demanding rights that had not been generally available to the majority of whites who inhabited the region (Brown & Bartee, in press).

The multiple levels of education available at historically black colleges made it easier for communities to teach their citizens without having to construct and operate other educational facilities at a time when many Southern states were reluctant and slow to fund African American schools (Brown, 1999b). In addition, offering academic programs for students who possessed minimal skills or who were underprepared for college presented black colleges with a way of manufacturing a niche for their advanced curricula. Rather than expecting students to come to school already prepared to learn advanced material, HBCUs accepted them as they were and taught them as much as they could before letting them depart.

In the early years of HBCUs, the concept of universal collegiate access was broadly interpreted. Rather than following the trend of elite institutions, which limited access to only a small segment of society, HBCUs opened their doors to anyone who was interested. Indeed, the first schools that opened to educate African Americans during the Civil War were utilized by people of all races and ages who felt that freedom would not be complete until they at least learned to read and write. In many communities, the new black colleges were universities and normal schools that also housed elementary and secondary components. This caused some to criticize these institutions for not providing a truly collegiate program (Anderson, 1988; Bowles & DeCosta, 1971; Brown, 1999a; Brown & Davis, 2001; Du Bois, 1996). However, this actually proved to be a both reasonable and mutually beneficial course of action. By providing education to people at all levels, historically black colleges helped increase their chances of survival by solidifying relationships with their local communities.

Education for Survival and Salvation

An essential question for systems of higher education across their spectrum of development has been "How should the curriculum be structured?" In like vein, the central question facing the newly minted black colleges was "Should an African American–focused higher education endeavor to create good thinkers or skillful doers?" During the late nineteenth and early twentieth centuries, the founders and financial supporters of each historically black college determined the institutional response to this curricular question. Using the primary benefactors of these institutions to establish a framework, Anderson (1988) categorizes black colleges into three groups: missionary, Negro, and industrial philanthropies. Missionary institutions are those founded by the American Missionary Association and other similar organizations, while African American churches and other religious organizations sponsored Negro colleges. Rich industrialists assisted in establishing the black industrial schools (Anderson, 1988).

Although they had different founders, the missionary and Negro colleges were very much alike. Both types of institutions focused on providing students with a liberal arts curriculum designed to prepare black leaders for a life of racial and social service. Neither group of institutions expressed any real interest in promoting industrial training since they did not believe that it would assist their students in their future roles as doctors, educators, lawyers, and clergy (Anderson, 1988; Du Bois, 1996; Heintze, 1985). In contrast, the interests of their investors seemed to consume Hampton and Tuskegee, the only real industrial schools. Touted as a way to equip Negroes for freedom, philanthropists generally supported industrial education because they recognized its potential as a mechanism for social control. The only leaders they were interested in cultivating were those who would replicate the industrial model and its accommodation politics in others (Anderson, 1988; Brown, 1999a; Hall, 1973; Spivey, 1978).

The popularity of the Hampton-Tuskegee Idea for black education fostered and endorsed by Samuel Armstrong and Booker T. Washington gave many of their contemporaries the mistaken impression that all HBCUs did or should focus on industrial education. Although missionary and Negro colleges resisted pressure to convert to industrial institutions, poor revenue streams forced many of them to compromise by adding some industrial courses to their curricula to attract donations (Anderson, 1988; Richardson, 1980; Whiting, 1991). For example, even though both Fisk and Clark (Atlanta) Universities offered industrial training by 1916, neither institution made industrial education a formal part of the college curriculum. Indeed, when secondary education left Fisk in 1927, industrial education went with it (Hall, 1993). For missionary and Negro colleges, industrial and manual training were a survival adaptation rather than institutional missions and goals.

Despite their public reputations, both Hampton and Tuskegee offered more liberal arts courses than many of their industrial supporters would have imagined or approved of. Although industrial training was an element of the curriculum offered by each institution, it was not the only thing they provided. Along with their mechanical, industrial, and agricultural foci, both Hampton and Tuskegee maintained normal schools that offered traditional liberal arts classes. In 1880, Hampton's normal students had access to a variety of nonindustrial courses, including reading, rhetoric, English grammar, arithmetic, geometry, algebra, U.S. history, natural history, natural philosophy, physiology, botany, civil government, principles of business, and Bible lessons (Brown, 1999a; Engs, 1999). Similarly, Tuskegee also offered reading, grammar, algebra, geometry, and history courses along with its labor-related programs (Hall, 1973). Nevertheless, it would be erroneous to disregard the industrial and labor emphasis proffered by these and other similar institutions. The fact that both institutions required all of their students, regardless of assigned program, to participate in manual labor illustrates their commitment to practical education (Anderson, 1988; Engs, 1999; Hall, 1973).

Industrial education posed a dilemma for many of the nation's private HBCUs. For public black institutions, state control rendered the curriculum debate a moot issue. Primarily founded and supported by the Second Morrill Act of 1890, few of these public black colleges enjoyed the level of autonomy bestowed upon the private institutions. As land-grant institutions, many of the public colleges and universities were developed and expected to provide students with agricultural, mechanical, and industrial training. In 1917, the Smith-Hughes Act increased the land-grant commitment to practical education by instituting a national system for training vocational teachers (Hall, 1973; Mayberry, 1991). However, even state mandates were not enough to stop these institutions from providing an intellectually academic curriculum. Similar to other black land-grant colleges, Alcorn Agricultural and Mechanical College, the first state-supported black institution, required all trade students to complete both industrial and academic coursework. These course requirements included reading, writing, grammar, English and American literature, history, arithmetic, algebra, geometry, and philosophy as well as studies in agriculture and military tactics (Hall, 1973; Posey, 1994). Although many public HBCUs accomplished the land-grant mission by providing vocational programs, they did not allow either this mission or restricted institutional governance to dissuade them from their larger purpose of fulfilling the needs of the black community—intellectual, economic, political, or social.

The fact that the history of numerous historically black colleges includes the provision of industrial training has led some to misjudge the value of these institutions. When industrial education was at its peak, several African American leaders maligned historically black colleges for acting as agents of the white majority by offering an education that was allegedly a force in relegating freedmen to submit to a hegemonic system of domination emblematic of the conditions of enslavement (Anderson, 1988; Bond, 1935; Du Bois, 1996; Spivey, 1978; Woodson, 1998). At the same time, many black and white critics scoffed at the curricula offered by many HBCUs because they were not intellectually equal to curricula at the nation's premier white colleges and universities (Anderson, 1988; Bowles & DeCosta, 1971; Du Bois, 1996). Although correct, these assessments underestimate the real impact these historically black colleges had on the lives of their students. Though not highly regarded in modern contexts, the early curricula provided by HBCUs demonstrate their genuine interest and efforts to serve the needs of their primary constituents: the general African American population.

Recognizing that African American college students needed to be prepared to succeed in both the present and the future, black colleges crafted educational programs that trained students to work with both their bodies and their minds. In spite of the widespread interest in acquiring at least basic literacy skills, African Americans had little reason to go to college if it did not help prepare them for a career (Bowles & DeCosta, 1971). Although the traditional liberal arts curriculum taught students to think, it was not enough to shatter the racial barriers that prevented most college-educated African Americans from gaining employment commensurate with their academic skills. Likewise, even though the push to provide African Americans with industrial training may have been encouraged and financed by racist whites, this did not diminish the value of these generic education programs. Indeed, the fact that mainstream apprenticeship programs were closed to African Americans at the conclusion of the Civil War made it necessary for students interested in acquiring manual skills to locate other sources of training (Hall, 1973). Given the oppressive goals articulated by many benefactors of historically black colleges, the vocational training offered by HBCUs actually helped fulfill their commitment to serving various levels of the African American community. At the local level, vocational training helped provide students with skills that they could use both for self-sufficiency and to increase the economic capital of the African American community. The industrial courses offered by black colleges also solidified their role within the local and national landscape, hence ensuring their survival and continued ability to positively influence the lives of African Americans and others.

Mission Maintenance in Changing Contexts

In recent years, the development of a global economy has renewed debate over the functions of higher education. As illustrated by the history of the nation's HBCUs, a well-structured institution can serve the needs of both exceptional and traditional students by providing intellectual and pragmatic programs. Rather than restricting themselves to fulfilling a singular commitment, higher education institutions might do well to emulate HBCUs by adopting principles and practices that first meet students where they are, followed by the provision of the spectrum of skills that will enable them to remain successful during and after college.

In fact, the functions and goals of historically black institutions were the subject of an intense debate between W. E. B. Du Bois and Booker T. Washington. Washington believed that the primary function of HBCUs was to provide vocational training for the masses in conjunction with liberal learning (Brown, 1999a). Du Bois, in contrast, espoused the scholastic development of an elite group who would in turn influence the African American community—the Talented Tenth (Browning & Williams, 1978). Over time, historically black colleges have merged this singular ideal into a dual mission of intellectual information coupled with practical application. Charles Willie (1981) writes, "The synthesis of liberal arts and vocationally oriented courses in the curriculum of black colleges and universities . . . has placed [HBCUs] in the vanguard of higher education" (p. 74).

Contemporary discourse surrounding the aims of HBCUs has centered on taxonomical aims of these institutions (Allen, Epps, & Hanniff, 1991). Arguably HBCUs have six continuing duties: (a) the maintenance of the black historical and cultural tradition; (b) the development of key leadership in the black community; (c) the bolstering of economic sufficiency within the black community; (d) the presentation of black role models in the black community who can interpret the way in which social, political, or economic dynamics at the general society level impact black people; (e) the production of graduates with special competence to deal with the problems arising between the minority and majority population groups; and (f) the proliferation of black agents for specialized research, training, and information dissemination (Roebuck & Murty, 1993).

While there is a general consensus about the goals and functions of HBCUs, there is increasing concern about their ability to persist in the changing national context. More specifically, critical attention is being given to the effect of collegiate desegregation on the historic mission, daily operations, and overall success of HBCUs. Brown (2001) declares, "The mandate to desegregate southern higher education systems presents fundamental policy questions regarding institutional missions, curricula, admissions policies, and fiscal appropriations. Each of these issues challenges the historic mission and character of the public black college" (p. 47). Does the implementation of collegiate desegregation policies redefine the mission and role of the historically black college in American higher education?

DESEGREGATION AND THE BLACK COLLEGE

Few issues surrounding historically black colleges are as perplexing and confusing as collegiate desegregation. The differing perceptions of the courts, government administrators, and state policymakers are revealed by an examination of the legal history of desegregation (Brown, 1999b; Preer, 1982). There has been a lack of consensus on the policies, legislation, and judicial remedies necessary to overcome the continuing effects of historical segregation in higher education institutions. The judiciary is still struggling to establish a legal mandate that resolves the issues surrounding desegregation, compliance with Title VI, equality, and equity.

These questions involve issues that have significant implications for public policy and educational law. After decades of litigation and legislation, it is an appropriate time to examine the legal and educational history that affects the way in which higher education attempts to attain desegregation. Given the complexity and ambiguity surrounding any legal mandate, it is necessary to know the history of the remedy that provides the impetus for national higher education desegregation policy.

The growing possibility of financial exigency in state systems of postsecondary education illustrates the difficult economic conditions and heavy demands on public funds. The response to overall collegiate financial needs is delayed by shrinking budgets, which furthers concern about the future viability of black colleges (Brown, 1999b). The historical and current underfunding of these colleges populated predominantly by African American students only festers the existent sores of overcrowded facilities, deteriorating buildings, inadequate library facilities, lack of support for research, meager to moderate salaries, and deteriorating esprit de corps (Sudarkasa, 1992). These along with other phenomena have made the issue of collegiate desegregation as explored in the *United States v. Fordice* a national educational policy concern.

The Legal Context for Desegregation

In 1954, the United States Supreme Court's ruling in *Brown v. Board of Education of Topeka* overturned the prevailing doctrine of separate but equal introduced by *Plessy v. Ferguson* (1896) 58 years prior. By the time *Brown* was decided, many states had created dual collegiate structures of public education, most of which operated exclusively for Caucasians in one system and African Americans in the other. Although *Brown* focused the nation on desegregation in primary and secondary public education, the issue of disestablishing dual systems of public higher education had yet to come to the forefront.

The mandate of desegregation reached postsecondary education two years later. In *Florida ex rel. Hawkins v. Board of Control* (1956), the Supreme Court applied the *Brown* principle to higher education for the first time. The *Hawkins* ruling was ultimately ineffective as a result of failure to resolve the issue of remedy. Beyond the myopic response regarding remedy, both federal law and the courts remained silent on officially mandating the dismantlement of dual collegiate structures.

The pressure to dismantle dual systems of higher education was not extended to higher education until the passage of the Civil Rights Act of 1964. Title VI of this Act stated that:

No person in the United States shall, on the ground of race, color, or national origin, be excluded from participation in, or be denied the benefits of, or be subjected to discrimination under any program or activity receiving Federal financial assistance. (Pub. L. No. 88–352, 78 Stat. 241)

Although this legislation did not center on higher education desegregation, its administrative implementation guidelines declared that "in administering a program regarding which the recipient has previously discriminated . . . the recipient must take affirmative action to overcome the effects of prior discrimination" (34 C.F.R. 100.3 (6)(i)). It was this mandate that gave the federal government oversight of the desegregation of public higher education. The granting of authority was not difficult. It was the interpretation and implementation of the law that would lead to decades of litigation.

Despite Title VI, 19 states continued to operate dual systems of higher education: Alabama, Arkansas, Delaware, Florida, Georgia, Kentucky, Louisiana, Maryland, Mississippi, Missouri, North Carolina, Ohio, Oklahoma, Pennsylvania, South Carolina, Tennessee, Texas, Virginia, and West Virginia. From 1969 to the mid-'70s the Office of Civil Rights in the Department of Health, Education, and Welfare (HEW) contacted 10 of these states to notify them that they were in violation of Title VI. This compliance initiative was fueled when the National Association for the Advancement of Colored People (NAACP) Legal Defense Fund filed suit against HEW in 1970. This lawsuit, *Adams v. Richardson* (1972), asserted that 10 states still operated segregated and discriminatory higher education systems; eventually, the suit included all 19 of the southern and border states. However, the *Adams* litigation died in 1990 with the *Women's Equity Action League v. Cavazos* (1990) ruling that plaintiffs lacked a private right of action against a federal agency.

As a result of the death of *Adams*, private plaintiff litigation ensued in four states: Alabama, Louisiana, Mississippi, and Tennessee. Recently the Supreme Court and federal courts have proffered higher education desegregation decisions in Mississippi's *United States v. Fordice* (1992), *Knight v. Alabama* (1991), *United States v. Louisiana* (1989), and Tennessee's *Geier v. Alexander* (1984). Although the American legal system has spent the last 40 years tackling the issue of desegregation in elementary and secondary schools, the strategies necessary to effect change in colleges and universities have yet to be defined.

The Significant Policy Questions

Higher education policymakers are not unclear on issues regarding the legal and moral tenets of desegregation. They are, however, gray on how to interpret and/or comply with Title VI. Consequently, although questions arise about the cost effectiveness of the historically black college, rarely, if ever, are these questions raised about the historically white university. Hence, the burden of desegregation of state systems of higher education has been placed on the shoulders of historically black colleges (Brown & Hendrickson, 1997). Burdened by the onus of desegregation, public black colleges face a mandate to define institutional relevance. The federal courts, state coordinating agencies, and local institutions are all struggling with fundamental questions that will chart the future of the black college in the next century.

The historic successes and continuing contribution of HBCUs should not be disregarded in the quest to disestablish dual systems of higher education. Kenneth Tollett (1981), former director of the Institute for the Study of Educational Policy, best articulates the argument of those concerned about the future of the black college in desegregated systems of higher education. He writes:

Higher education is one of the central institutions in America. It is a major avenue for upward social mobility, to say nothing of the development of human potential and self-realization. Blacks must pursue this avenue in increasing numbers. Black institutions of higher learning have been one of the major means of reaching this position of mobility. To sacrifice this avenue in the name of integrated locomotion is to push to the wayside thousands of Blacks who could benefit from the experience. (p. 31)

Likewise, Charles Willie (1981) of Harvard University writes:

It would be a disaster to dismantle black colleges and universities, for whites would be destroying the best reflection available of the state of their own manners and morals and the innermost worth of higher education. In this new age of desegregation and integration, the value of an institution will be determined not by how well it treats the majority but by how merciful it is to the minority. In this respect, black colleges and universities can serve as a model for many by demonstrating that the way to educational enhancement for a black majority is through compassion and concern for a white minority. (p. 111)

It is in the context of the past and future that *United States v. Fordice* is best understood. The litigation brings to bear an increased awareness of the philosophical mindset and political disposition of the country at large, and of higher education specifically—similar to that of the Title VI mandate to provide equal educational opportunity to African American students enforced in *Adams*. Two examples of this appear as chapters in Gail Thomas's edited work, *Black Students in Higher Education: Conditions and Experiences in the 1970s* (1981): "The *Adams* Mandate: A Format for Achieving Equal Educational Opportunity and Attainment" (Haynes) and "Desegregation and African American Student Higher Educational Access" (Thomas, McPartland, & Gottfredson). The latter is particularly noteworthy as an assessment of higher education desegregation in the aftermath of *Adams,* focusing on access and the retention of African American students.

The disproportionately low graduation rates of African American students outside of historically black institutions are increasing, while the government and judiciary oversee collegiate desegregation (Smith, 1981). Attention to state-level involvement in higher education and the current climate and role of the historically black college in higher education serve to identify a set of conditions producing the *Adams* and *Fordice* decisions. The success of collegiate desegregation is contingent upon the willingness of higher education to (a) change the missions and institutional statements of those institutions designed to deliver inferior service, (b) redefine the financial formula whereby institutions are funded, (c) reassess the standards of institutional admission, and (d) reinterpret the possibility of educating incongruent collegiate populations.

The mandate to dismantle dual systems presents fundamental policy questions regarding institutional missions, curricula, admissions policies, and funding. These issues challenge long-standing principles of state control and governance of public higher education systems. The courts have established the doctrine of taking all reasonable and educationally sound steps to eliminate policies and practices that are traceable to the prior dual system and perpetuate segregation by race. Nevertheless, there remains considerable ambiguity regarding what is legally required and what is educationally appropriate in order to eliminate the remaining vestiges of the dual system. The political dimensions of the policy-making process are often played out between forces that advocate rational, systemic change and those that desire more incremental steps that maintain power and preserve the status quo.

An Uncertain Role for Public Black Colleges

United States v. Fordice (1992) stands as the judicial beacon for the desegregation of higher education across the country. It outlines the implications for public historically black colleges and addresses the flexibility of constitutional standards that allow the federal courts jurisdiction over the processes and justifiability of collegiate institutions' missions and traditions. *Fordice* was the first ruling since the 1954 *Brown* case in which the Supreme Court had proffered a legal standard for evaluating whether a state had addressed its affirmative duty to dismantle prior de jure segregated systems of higher education.

In the *Fordice* ruling (1992), the court held that the state of Mississippi's race-neutral policies and good faith efforts had not fulfilled its obligation to disestablish the state's dual higher education system. The court clearly set out a legal standard to address the constitutional and statutory intent of collegiate desegregation. The *Fordice* standard states:

If the State perpetuates policies and practices traceable to its prior system that continue to have segregative effects—whether by influencing student enrollment decisions or by fostering segregation in other facets of the university system—and such policies are without sound educational justification and can be practicably eliminated, the State has not satisfied its burden of proving that it has dismantled its prior system. (p. 731)

The issues surrounding collegiate desegregation and higher education offer unique perspectives on compliance and the future of public black colleges. Central to the discussion of collegiate desegregation are the legal standards set in the Supreme Court's *United States v. Fordice* decision (1992). The breakup of dual systems of higher education in the 19 southern and border states continues to be litigated and embroiled in continuing controversies over how best to comply with Title VI of the Civil Rights Act of 1964. The standard for the litigation has become the "challengeable policies and/or practices" which could be considered remnants of dual systems of higher education. This standard has been translated by some into the elimination of duplication through the closure of historically black institutions or their programs. How long before all public historically black colleges are under siege? Or, as Benjamin E. Mays (1978) posits in rhetorical fashion, "Why pick out [black] colleges and say they must die? . . . If America allows black colleges to die, it will be the worst kind of discrimination in history . . . [If these colleges are blotted out], . . . You blot out the image of black men and women in education" (pp. 19–28).

Historically black universities have been the primary educators of African Americans. Black institutions have historically created pools of qualified individuals who have traditionally been underutilized in academia and corporate America. While it is true that these black colleges are of great value, they have not convinced some in society of their importance. As a result, many questions are being raised about the need to maintain their current configuration and/or existence during this era of collegiate desegregation. Thompson (1973) writes, "Black colleges constitute an indigenous, unique, most challenging aspect of higher education in this society, and as such are still badly needed. College enrollment is expected to continue to increase for at least another generation and black colleges will be needed to participate in the education of more and more students" (p. 284).

Higher education initiatives have attempted to establish benchmarks for minority access to higher education. These benchmarks include affirmative action programs; governmental grants and incentives; offices of minority affairs; university directorships for equity; and gender, ethnic, and cultural centers (Thomas, 1981). African American student retention policies accompany the equity efforts of previous decades. However, these retention policies fall short of bringing about parity in educational attainment. Nevertheless, historically black colleges continue to produce a significant percentage of all African American baccalaureate degree recipients.

These educational attainments result from tenacity and perseverance on the part of black colleges in spite of historic underfunding. Individual states must begin to investigate the economic effects of desegregation and conduct cost analyses of unified versus dual systems, revisiting issues of "separate" and "equal." Granted, cost benefits can be realized if duplication is avoided. However, policymakers should be careful not to eliminate the potential cost benefits that result from bringing the state system into compliance with Title VI. Programs at historically black colleges may serve as models for other institutions that are striving to improve their success in retaining and graduating minority students. Justice Clarence Thomas, concurring in the *Fordice* opinion (1992), writes that "it would be ironic, to say the least, if the institutions that sustained blacks during segregation were themselves destroyed in an effort to combat its vestiges" (p. 749).

RETHINKING STUDENT DIVERSITY

The success of black colleges is often credited to the distinct campus culture that molds the academic environment. Since their inception, HBCUs have been committed to the preservation of black history, racial pride, ethnic traditions, and black consciousness (Roebuck & Murty, 1993). Naturally many African American students are drawn to these institutions because they desire a learning environment in which their identity is both appreciated and celebrated. Black colleges' commitment to this endeavor contributes to the educational experience and ultimately the resiliency of black students. Although HBCUs have been lauded for their dedication to the needs of African American students, they have also been criticized for lacking institutional diversity. The challenge, therefore, is for black colleges to maintain their cultural identity while simultaneously adhering to the pressure to make their campuses diverse.

Extant Research Findings

According to Harley (2001), "Although diversity may include a wide array of groups (e.g., race/ethnicity, age, gender, ability, language, religion, and sexual orientation), the field of public higher education usually focuses on black-white integration" (p. 152). As a result, HBCUs are placed under investigation and the need to increase the presence of white students takes precedence.

Research studies surrounding concerns of institutional diversity tend to focus on the matriculation of African American students at predominantly white institutions (PWIs). In contrast, little attention has been given to the reversed situation: white students attending black colleges. Considering the fact that whites have always had the privilege of choice, the question arises as to why they choose to attend historically black institutions where they are a racial minority. In an attempt to answer this question, Conrad, Brier, and Braxton (1997) studied factors that influence the matriculation of white students in public HBCUs. This section relies heavily on this one article and on Brown's (2002a) article on transdemographic enrollments, due to scant extant research in this area.

Conrad, Brier, and Braxton (1997) "used an open-ended, multicase study design that was anchored in the perspectives of diverse stakeholders—administrators, faculty members, and students" (p. 39). Conrad et al. selected the following five HBCUs due to their ability to attract a significant number of white students: North Carolina Agricultural and Technical State University, Winston-Salem State University, Southern University at New Orleans, Kentucky State University, and Savannah State College. The results of the research identified 14 factors that contribute to the presence of whites at HBCUs. Conrad et al. grouped the findings into three groups: (a) academic program offerings, (b) student financial support, and (c) institutional characteristics.

Academic Program Offerings

Conrad et al. (1997) ranked academic offerings in this order of importance: (a) program offerings in high-demand fields, (b) unique program offerings (programs unduplicated in PWIs/enrollment caps in PWIs), (c) alternative program delivery systems: on- and/or off-campus, (d) graduate (master's) program offerings in high-demand fields, and (e) positive reputation for quality.

The most important factor that contributes to the enrollment of white students at HBCUs is the presence of quality programs in high-demand fields such as business, engineering, and nursing (Sims, 1994). These schools have established departments with strong reputations. Through hard work and determination, these well-respected disciplines at HBCUs attract students regardless of race. For example, a white student reported that the engineering program was so strong at North Carolina A&T that he could "overlook that it's a black school" (Conrad et al., 1997, p. 43). White students found HBCUs desirable because of their unique programs. Considering that HBCUs are often located close to PWIs, the determining factor can prove to be the presence of a particular major. The study revealed that white students often chose HBCUs because they were close to their homes.

Another incentive that lured whites to HBCUs was the availability of on- and off-campus delivery systems. Whites could choose to participate through weekend and evening courses. Conrad and associates (1997) further state that "many interviewees stressed that alternative delivery systems especially appeal to nontraditional students, such as part-time, adult students attracted to institutions by the convenience of program offerings enabling them to advance their education while fulfilling work, family, and personal responsibilities" (p. 45).

It is important to note that white students reported that the reputation of the HBCU was critical. White students were deeply concerned about the quality of the programs and overwhelmingly chose institutions that were well respected nationally. Despite the fact that quality encompasses many characteristics, the interviews disclosed that "some common elements included a good faculty, small classes, and faculty members invested in students and their learning" (Conrad et al., 1997, p. 47).

Student Financial Support

Conrad et al. (1997) also ranked student financial support in the following order of importance: (a) student scholarships and (b) low cost (tuition and fees). Funding a college education can be an overwhelming task. Although financial aid is available, ideally students prefer scholarships to alleviate the cost of tuition and fees. The study showed that if HBCUs hope to continue to increase the white student population, they must provide a substantial amount of student aid in the form of scholarships. Some HBCUs initiated scholarships designed specifically for other-race students. Students, faculty, and administrators agreed that scholarships are one of the best ways to attract and retain white students. A student declared, "I am here for the money. There is no way I would be here but for the money I am getting" (Conrad et al., 1997, p. 49). Additionally, the findings show that HBCUs had another advantage over PWIs—that is, lower cost of tuition.

Institutional Characteristics

Conrad et al. (1997) ranked institutional characteristics in the following order of importance: (a) positive image as a multiracial institution, (b) supportive and inclusive campus culture, (c) white student recruitment, (d) articulation and cooperative agreements with PWIs, (e) positive external relations with community and professional constituencies, (f) safe environment, and (g) attractive campus appearance.

The results of the study included a wide range of institutional characteristics that whites found to be influential in their decision to attend an HBCU. The most important attribute was the positive image projected by the school as a multiracial institution. Conrad et al. (1997) stated, "Interviewees emphasized that this positive image can be cultivated through visible institutional leadership, effective public relations and multiracial advertising, and word-of-mouth communication between white students and alumni of HBCUs and potential white matriculants" (p. 50). Furthermore, whites wanted a sense of belonging. They desired a campus climate that was both inclusive and supportive. Although the dominant culture may prevail, HBCUs must create a learning environment attractive to all students.

In order for the number of whites to increase, HBCUs must forcefully seek and recruit these students. They must make a deliberate effort to reach out and make their facilities known and preferred. Note the finding below:

Interviewees suggested a number of ways to enhance white student recruitment, including more active faculty and student recruitment, visitations to high schools with substantial numbers of white students, targeted mailings at prospective white students, and on-campus visitations by white high school students. (Conrad et al., 1997, p. 53)

Another important factor was the cooperative agreements between HBCUs and PWIs. HBCUs and PWIs in the same state are often close to each other. Due to this proximity, HBCUs are often able to make positive impressions on white students at PWIs. Articulation and cooperative agreements with other institutions provide white students the chance to explore the black college. Perhaps white students may be curious, and these agreements allow them the opportunity to get a little taste of the campus by taking a class. White students often transfer to the HBCU as a result.

White students were also concerned about the external relations of the HBCU with both professional and community members. White students professed that it was imperative for their institution to connect with society. A safe campus environment was also a concern for whites. They

needed to feel comfortable and protected. And, finally, whites that ma-
triculated at HBCUs said that campus appearance was indeed significant.
A campus that had attractive buildings was an added incentive for whites.

Transdemography and Campus Climate

In a seminal study on transdemography at public historically black colleges, Brown (2002a) explores the implications of white students attending
public historically black institutions. An ethnographic case study was conducted at Bluefield State University in which artifact gathering, participant observation, document analysis, and informal interviews were used
to collect data. The uniqueness of Bluefield is that although by federal
regulation it is identified as an HBCU, it has the lowest African American
and highest white student enrollment of the nation's 103 HBCUs. Additionally, 92 percent of the faculty is white, and Bluefield remains the only
HBCU to have a white president.

Brown (2002a) coins the term transdemography to describe "shifts in
the statistical composition of the student population within the corre-
sponding institutions based solely on race" (p. 264). This is particularly
important for public HBCUs because they are indisputably the primary
targets of desegregation initiatives. Bluefield, however, is an example of
collegiate desegregation gone awry (Drummond, 2000; Levinson, 2000).
Brown writes: "There are no Black Greek-letter organizations on campus.
Most of the traditions typical of an HBCU have vanished. There is no
Greek life, no marching band, limited Black faculty/staff presence, and
no signs of the historic traditions of the formerly Black-populated student
body" (p. 270). While Bluefield intended to make its campus more diverse
by increasing the enrollment of white students, the black population of
students disappeared in the process. It could be argued that this transdemographic shift poses a survival conflict for public black colleges. They
have the option to comply with the desegregation mandate and risk cultural collapse, or maintain the historic enrollment patterns and risk judicial sanctions.

Although many HBCUs support and encourage diversity initiatives,
some critics express concern. Some believe that the recruitment of white
students ultimately hurts prospective black students. Scholarships, for example, are a major concern. Critics are appalled that black institutions
would provide scholarships to white students when the research shows
that blacks generally tend to be in greater need of lower tuition (Sims,
1994). According to Sims, some blacks feel that whites on their campuses
do not constitute legitimate peers. She states:

This belief might be based on the historical traditions that reserve HBCU for de-
scendents of slaves; therefore, whites and other races are not considered legitimate

in their roles. A common feeling is that whites have infiltrated HBCU in an attempt to claim yet another victory in the defeat of blacks and their cultural institutions. (p. 126)

Willie (1981) posits that to facilitate awareness, nurture understanding, and develop appreciation, it is imperative for whites to experience the role of being a minority population. He argues, "Whites can learn to overcome their enslavement to the false idea that they are supreme only if they have the privilege of living as a trusting minority" (p. 31). Attending an HBCU would allow whites the opportunity to engage in such an experience, but the problem is that many whites are opposed to attending black colleges and universities. Willie suggests:

Many people are fearful of marginality—are reluctant to live in, between, and beyond their race—because of their fear of loss of identity. They think they are maximizing their identity by relating primarily to like-minded and look-alike people when, in essence, they are limiting the range of their identity. (p. 16)

The Best Is Yet to Come

It is ironic that HBCUs have been ignored when the discussion of diversity surfaces, when in fact they were perhaps the first type of higher education institution that did not discriminate. Not only do HBCUs embrace people from different racial backgrounds, but they also reach out to those students who have been convinced that they are not college material due to their poor academic performance. PWIs can often be self-serving institutions. Some do their best to make admissions a cutthroat competition by raising the grade point average and standardized test score requirements. Freeman (1998), however, claims that HBCUs are able to successfully educate students in spite of the predictive validity of standardized tests. The strict selection process of some PWIs possibly causes more harm than good because it detours a large number of potential students. The HBCU open-door policy, however, provides more opportunity for more students. Nevertheless, black colleges have acquired a negative image because of this policy.

Black colleges literally reversed the tradition of social-class and academic exclusiveness that has always been characteristic of higher education. They invented the practice if not the concept of open enrollment. Their flexible admissions practices and academic standards have been without precedent in higher education. This is, no doubt, a fundamental reason why black colleges have been so widely criticized by leaders in higher education and why they have been largely ignored by the most prestigious honor societies (Thompson, 1978, p. 185).

The efforts of HBCUs should not only be applauded, but also envied.

It is easy to work with students who come to college academically strong. But it is a challenge to work with those students who may have low grades and test scores and, due to certain circumstances, may not be as well prepared. According to Kannerstein (1978), HBCUs are not concerned with who gets admitted, but rather with what happens to them afterward. Undeniably HBCUs have readily accepted the challenge and continue to help students to succeed and beat the odds. Zinn argues:

What is overlooked is that the Negro colleges have one supreme advantage over the others: they are the nearest this country has to a racial microcosm of the world outside the United States, a world largely non-white, developing and filled with the tensions of bourgeois emulation and radical protest. And with more white students and foreign students entering, Negro universities might become our first massively integrated, truly international educational centers. (as cited in Cook, 1978, p. 64)

CONCLUSION

Historically black colleges and universities are an indispensable part of the national higher education landscape. Despite all of the positive evidence relating to their successes and achievements, negative misconceptions and erroneous information continue to impact the image of historically black colleges and universities. An opportunity exists for higher education researchers to document, describe, and detail these unique institutions.

HBCUs are multimission, multifaceted institutions. HBCUs are the primary actors in the desegregation of statewide higher education systems. HBCUs educate, employ, and empower a diverse population of citizens and international ambassadors. Although historically black colleges and universities were created primarily for the education of African Americans, they have been successful in making collegiate participation more accessible for all.

NOTES

1. The racial classification terms used in this paper do not necessarily represent the author's position but, rather, are used to facilitate a clear and concise discussion. Although most of these terms are familiar, they carry particular historical undertones specific to the South African context. African refers to people of indigenous ancestry; coloreds are South Africans of mixed ancestry, usually Dutch, African, Malay, and Khoisan heritage; Indians/Asians are people of Indian descent; and whites are people of European descent.

2. A green paper is a government document that is the first step toward the formation of a parliamentary bill. It is followed by a white paper; then a higher education bill will be introduced and debated in parliament. A Higher Education Act will follow, pending approval by parliament.

3. In the South African academic system the rank of faculty members is as follows: professor, associate professor, senior lecturer, lecturer, and junior lecturer.

REFERENCES

Adams v. Richardson, 351 F.2d 636 (D.C. Cir. 1972).

Allen, W. R., Epps, E. G., & Haniff, N. Z. (Eds.). (1991). *College in black and white: African American students in predominantly white and in historically black public universities.* Albany: State University of New York Press.

Anderson, J. D. (1978). The Hampton Model of normal school industrial education, 1868–1900. In V. P. Franklin & J. D. Anderson (Eds.), *New perspectives on black educational history* (pp. 61–96). Boston: G. K. Hall.

Anderson, J. D. (1988). *The education of blacks in the South, 1860–1935.* Chapel Hill: University of North Carolina Press.

Barrow, C. W. (1990). *Universities and the capitalist state: Corporate liberalism and the reconstruction of American higher education, 1894–1928.* Madison: University of Wisconsin Press.

Bond, H. M. (1935). The curriculum and the Negro child. *Journal of Negro Education, 4*(2), 159–168.

Bowles, F., & DeCosta, F. A. (1971). *Between two worlds: A profile of Negro higher education.* New York: McGraw Hill.

Brown, M. C. (1999a). The politics of industrial education: Booker T. Washington and Tuskegee State Normal School, 1880–1915. *Negro Educational Review, 50,* 123–128.

Brown, M. C. (1999b). *The quest to define collegiate desegregation: Black colleges, title VI compliance, and post-Adams litigation.* Westport, CT: Bergin & Garvey.

Brown, M. C. (2001). Collegiate desegregation and the public black college: A new policy mandate. *Journal of Higher Education, 72,* 46–62.

Brown, M. C. (2002a). Good intentions: Collegiate desegregation and transdemographic enrollments. *The Review of Higher Education, 25*(3), 263–280.

Brown, M. C. (2002b). The new perennial great debate: Affirmative action in higher education (A review essay). *Educational Researcher, 31,* 30–32.

Brown, M. C., & Bartee, R. D. (in press). *Broken cisterns: African American education fifty years after Brown.* Greenwich, CT: Information Age.

Brown, M. C., & Davis, J. E. (2001). The historically black college as social contract, social capital, and social equalizer. *Peabody Journal of Education, 76,* 31–49.

Brown, M. C., Donahoo, S., & Bertrand, R. D. (2001). The black college and the quest for educational opportunity. *Urban Education, 36*(5), 553–571.

Brown, M. C., & Freeman, K. (Eds.). (2002). Research on historically black colleges. *The Review of Higher Education, 25*(3), 237–368.

Brown, M. C., & Hendrickson, R. M. (1997). Public historically black colleges at the crossroads. *Journal for a Just and Caring Education, 3,* 95–113.

Brown v. Board of Education of Topeka, 347 U.S. 483 (1954).

Browning, J. E., & Williams, J. B. (1978). History and goals of black institutions of higher learning. In C. V. Willie & R. R. Edmonds (Eds.), *Black colleges in America* (pp. 68–93). New York: Teachers College Press.

Civil Rights Act of 1964, Pub. L. No. 88-352, 78 Stat. 241.

Clement, R. (1966). The historical development of higher education for Negro Americans. *Journal of Negro Education, 35*(4), 299–305.

Cohen, A. M. (1998). *The shaping of American higher education: Emergence and growth of the contemporary system.* San Francisco: Jossey-Bass.

Conrad, C., Brier, E. M., & Braxton, J. M. (1997). Factors contributing to the matriculation of white students in public HBCUs. *Journal for a Just and Caring Education, 3,* 37–62.

Cook, S. D. (1978). The socio-ethical role and responsibility of the black-college graduate. In C. V. Willie & R. R. Edmonds (Eds.), *Black colleges in America* (pp. 51–67). New York: Teachers College Press.

Drummond, T. (2000, March 20). Black schools go white: In search of a good deal, more and more white students enroll at historically black colleges. *Time,* p. 58.

Du Bois, W. E. B. (1996). *The souls of black folks.* New York: Penguin Books. (Original work published 1903)

Engs, R. F. (1999). *Educating the disenfranchised and the disinherited: Samuel Chapman Armstrong and Hampton Institute, 1839–1893.* Knoxville: University of Tennessee Press.

Florida ex rel. Hawkins v. Board of Control of Florida, 350 U.S. 413 (1956).

Foner, E. (1988). *Reconstruction: America's unfinished business, 1863–1877.* New York: Harper & Row.

Freeman, K. (1998). African Americans and college choice: Cultural considerations and policy implications. In K. Freeman (Ed.), *African American culture and heritage in higher education research and practice* (pp. 181–194). Westport, CT: Praeger.

Geier v. Alexander, 593 F. Supp. 1263 (M.D. Tenn. 1984).

Hall, C. W. (1973). *Black vocational technical and industrial arts education: Development and history.* Chicago: American Technical Society.

Harley, D. A. (2001). Desegregation at HBCUs: Removing barriers and implementing strategies. *The Negro Educational Review, 52*(4), 151–164.

Hedgepeth, C. M., Edmonds, R. R., & Craig, A. (1978). Overview. In C. V. Willie & R. R. Edmonds (Eds.), *Black colleges in America* (pp. 17–18). New York: Teachers College Press.

Heintze, M. R. (1985). *Private Black colleges in Texas, 1865–1954.* College Station: Texas A&M University Press.

Kannerstein, G. (1978). Black colleges: Self-concept. In C. V. Willie & R. R. Edmonds (Eds.), *Black colleges in America* (pp. 29–50). New York: Teachers College Press.

Knight v. Alabama, 787 F. Supp. 1115 (D.D. Ala. 1991).

Levinson, A. (2000, January 6). As different as day and night: Missouri's historically black Lincoln University, now predominantly white, searches for a way to bring its two divergent populations together. *Black Issues in Higher Education, 16*(23), 30–31.

Mayberry, B. D. (1991). *A century of agriculture in the 1890 land-grant institutions and Tuskegee University, 1890–1990.* New York: Vantage Press.

Mays, B. (1978). The black college in higher education. In C. V. Willie & R. R. Edmonds (Eds.), *Black colleges in America* (pp. 19–28). New York: Teachers College Press.

Plessy v. Ferguson, 163 U.S. 537 (1896).

Posey, J. M. (1994). *Against great odds: The history of Alcorn State University.* Jackson: University Press of Mississippi.

Preer, J. L. (1982). *Lawyers v. educators: Black colleges and desegregation in public higher education.* Westport, CT: Greenwood Press.

Richardson, J. M. (1980). *A history of Fisk University, 1865–1946.* University: University of Alabama Press.

Roebuck, J. B. & Murty, K. S. (1993). *Historically black colleges and universities: Their place in American higher education.* Westport, CT: Praeger.

Sims, S. (1994). *Diversifying historically black colleges and universities: A new higher education paradigm.* Westport, CT: Praeger.

Smith, J. (Ed.). (1981). *The impact of desegregation on higher education.* Raleigh: North Carolina Central University Press.

Spivey, D. (1978). *Schooling for the new slavery: Black industrial education, 1868–1915.* Westport, CT: Greenwood Press.

Sudarkasa, N. (1992). Black colleges: Over a century old and still strong. *The Philadelphia Tribune Magazine,* pp. 12–18.

Thomas, G. E. (Ed.). (1981). *Black students in higher education: Conditions and Experiences in the 1970s.* Westport, CT: Greenwood Press.

Thompson, D. C. (1973). *Private black colleges at the crossroads.* Westport, CT: Greenwood Press.

Thompson, D. C. (1978). Black college faculty and students: The nature of their interaction. In C. V. Willie & R. R. Edmonds (Eds.), *Black colleges in America* (pp. 180–194). New York: Teachers College Press.

Tollett, K. S. (1981). *Black institutions of higher learning: Inadvertent victims or necessary sacrifices?* Washington, DC: Institute for the Study of Educational Policy.

United States v. Fordice, 505 U.S. 717 (1992).

United States v. Louisiana, 718 F. Supp. 525 (E.D. La.1989).

Washington, B. T. (1969). *My larger education.* Miami, FL: Mnemosyne.

Whiting, A. N. (1991). *Guardians of the flame: Historically black colleges yesterday, today and tomorrow.* Washington, DC: American Association of State Colleges and Universities.

Willie, C. V (1981). *The ivory and ebony towers.* Lexington, MA: Lexington Books.

Women's Equity Action League v. Cavazos, 906 F.2d 742 (D.C. Cir. 1990).

Woodson, C. G. (1998). *The mis-education of the Negro* (10th ed.). Trenton, NJ: Africa World Press.

CHAPTER 2

The Significance of Historically Black Colleges for High Achievers: Correlates of Standardized Test Scores in African American Students

Jacqueline Fleming

INTRODUCTION

On the verge of the new millennium, historically black colleges can look back at the very different views that have characterized them in academic literature. The historical accomplishments of black colleges in serving an outcast population and single-handedly creating a black middle class are rarely remembered (Gurin & Epps, 1975). Instead, the question most often asked is why we need such colleges today, when integration is a pervasive fact of college life. Earlier in the century, black colleges were assailed by a number of authors as being unable to assume the intellectual responsibility for educating black students because of their inadequate financial and physical resources, and because of authoritarian or ineffective management styles (e.g., McGrath, 1972; Jencks & Riesman, 1968; Sowell, 1972). Then a series of studies that focused on student outcomes rather than institutional characteristics found that black colleges promoted better academic and intellectual development and better social adjustment than their white counterparts (Fleming, 1984; Allen, Epps, & Haniff, 1991; Nettles, 1988).

Today, the problematic academic adjustment issues for minority students in white colleges command considerable research attention and thereby raise questions as to the adjustment of black students in black colleges. An ever-growing number of studies provides evidence that black students adjust better to predominantly black schools than to predominantly white schools. Black students who attend predominantly black schools tend to have higher average grades, a richer learning environment, better relationships with faculty members, and better cognitive development, as well as displaying greater effort and engaging in more academic activities than black students who attend white schools (Berry & Asamen, 1989; Bohr, Pascarella, Nora, & Terenzini, 1995; DeSousa & Kuh, 1996; Ford, 1996; Kraft, 1991). When they attend black schools, black students are better socially adjusted, have greater social support networks, show greater social involvement, and engage in more organizational activities (Allen, 1985; Cheatham, Slaney, & Coleman, 1990; D'Augelli & Herschberger, 1993; Jay & D'Augelli, 1991; Nottingham, Rosen, & Parks, 1992; Schwitzer, Griffin, Ancis, & Thomas, 1999).

The previous research speaks to the effects of black colleges on students in general but does not attempt to determine the nature of the college experience for high achievers. The vast majority of black students attend predominantly white colleges. But among the higher achievers on both kinds of college campuses, what are the consequences of being in a black or white college? If higher SAT scores upon entry define higher achieving, then previous research on the predictive validity of the SAT among black students suggests that college academic performance is a problematic issue for those in white but not black colleges. In contrast to reports on majority students, many studies show that for blacks in white colleges, test scores overpredict academic performance, underpredict performance, or predict not at all (Houston, 1983; Nettles, Thoeny, & Gosman, 1986; Sowa, Thompson, & Bennet, 1989; Tracey & Sedlacek, 1985). Crouse and Trusheim (1988) report that in 25 of 30 cases, test scores for blacks overpredict academic performance, which means that students perform *lower* than their test scores would predict. The reasons for overprediction are not known with any precision. Similarly, SAT predictive validity studies for black students in white colleges that concentrate on the size of the correlation coefficient between SAT scores and college grades find that predictive validity estimates are lower for black than white students, averaging 11 percent versus 9.9 percent of variance accounted for (Fleming, 1990). However, prediction appears to be better in black schools, even though estimates of the degree of the difference vary (Fleming, 1990; Fleming & Garcia, 1998; Ramist, Lewis, & McCamley-Jenkins, 1994). The differences in predictive validity suggest that adjustment factors related to race may affect how test scores translate into academic performance (Nettles, Thoeny, & Gossman, 1986). However, systematic studies of a wide range of correlates of standardized tests that might inform the nature of student adjustment to college are rarely if ever conducted.

The purpose of this study is threefold. First, the study attempts to determine correlates that are similar across institutions, as well as those that differ in historically black and predominantly white colleges. Second, it attempts to fill a void in the literature with respect to African American students by going beyond the usual preoccupation with the predictive validity of the SAT with regard to academic performance, to examine the wide-ranging consequences of SAT scores on academic adjustment and psychosocial functioning. Third, this look at SAT correlates provides a view of SAT consequences within institutions, rather than across institutions. It thus treats the college environment as a moderator variable that affects how the SAT will influence college functioning. Previous analyses of correlates of the SAT looked at correlations with social class and other background variables *across institutions,* and conclude that SAT scores increase with social advantages. The present study, however, looks at correlates *within colleges* where the SAT scores are more similar than different, and where the range of socioeconomic status scores is more restricted than in the general population of test takers. It was expected that like African American students on average, high achievers would also exhibit better adjustment in predominantly black than white colleges.

METHOD

Rationale

Correlates of the SAT were examined in 15 samples (7 samples from predominantly black colleges and 8 samples from predominantly white colleges) where the students were administered the same instruments. The primary purpose of the investigation was to determine the frequency with which variables or categories of variables were consistently correlated with the SAT.

Study Participants

Study participants for the study were students in Fleming's (1984) study *Blacks in College,* recruited by a series of procedures designed to produce a high volunteer rate. Both standardized test scores and transcripts were available for 1,485 freshmen and seniors out of the 2,979 students in the original subject pool. There were 746 black students in 7 black schools, including 543 freshmen (229 males and 314 females) and 203 seniors (85 males and 118 females); 739 black students in 8 white schools, including 526 freshmen (200 males and 326 females) and 213 seniors (88 males and 125 females). Table 2.1 presents a breakdown of participants by school, class, and sex.

The students were enrolled in 14 colleges, 6 predominantly black and 8 predominantly white, in four states: Georgia, Texas, Mississippi, and Ohio. In Georgia, no attempt was made to match institutional characteristics, but only to recruit from schools where sufficient numbers of black students were enrolled. In the other states, attempts were made to match the institutional characteristics of the black and white colleges as closely as possible. Thus, there were two large urban universities in Texas, two small private colleges in Mississippi, and four colleges in Ohio (two state schools and two private schools).

At each college, students were recruited by obtaining lists of students

Table 2.1
Subject Breakdown by School, Class, and Sex

	Males		Females		
Black Students in Black Schools:	Freshman	Senior	Freshman	Senior	Total N
Spelman	0	0	68	40	108
Morehouse	78	31	0	0	109
Clark	20	2	69	12	103
Texas Southern	57	22	68	22	169
Tougaloo	19	6	52	14	91
Wilberforce	33	7	46	7	93
Central State	22	17	11	23	73
Total					
	229	85	314	118	746
Black Students in White Schools:					
Emory	5	6	13	12	36
University of Georgia	22	11	41	15	89
Georgia Tech	39	11	21	0	71
Georgia College	6	6	36	19	67
University of Houston	37	15	93	30	175
Millsap	10	12	17	7	46
University of Dayton	27	22	42	23	114
Ohio State University	54	5	63	19	141
Total	200	88	326	125	739
Grand Total	429	173	640	243	1485

from the administration. Letters were sent encouraging students to participate in a study of their adjustment to college life. In most cases, the letters were followed by phone calls, except where administrators themselves encouraged students to participate. In the predominantly white schools, more personal contact was necessary to recruit substantial numbers of the small black student populations. See Fleming (1984) for further details of the recruiting effort.

Procedure

Students came to a group testing session always conducted by a male and a female experimenter (both African American). The students received the instruments in the following order:

(1) a study participation consent form;

(2) a registrar release form for grades and standardized test scores;

(3) a Thematic Apperception Test, consisting of six pictures;

(4) a 32-page questionnaire consisting of paper and pencil measures of academic and psychosocial variables. Subsamples of students participated in experimental conditions and took four tests of cognitive skill.

Measures

Standardized Test Scores

Standardized test scores were obtained from the college's official records. In some colleges, primarily in Texas and Mississippi, both SAT and ACT scores were used. Therefore, ACT scores were converted to their SAT equivalents according to a formula made available by Marco and Abdel-Fattah (1991). Approximately 29 percent of the scores in these two states required conversion.

Socioeconomic Status

Socioeconomic status was scored according to procedures given in Hamburger's (1971) *Revised Occupational Scale for Rating Socio-economic Status*. Hamburger's procedure allows for the computing of a continuous vertical scale as well as seven horizontal occupational categories. The vertical scale was used as the primary measure of social class, with 1 being the highest score and 7 being the lowest. The horizontal categories were retained as additional background variables. The convention was to use the vertical scale as applied to the father's job (including education and income data), and to substitute the mother's data on this variable when the father was absent.

Academic Performance

The college registrar provided official transcripts for each student. From the transcripts, 10 measures of academic performance were extracted: (a) cumulative GPA; (b) GPA for the semester of the study; (c) cumulative GPA in the major, when a major was declared by the student; (d) GPA in the major for the semester of the study; (e) cumulative GPA in math; (f) cumulative GPA in the sciences; (g) cumulative GPA in English; (h) cumulative GPA in foreign language; (i) honors status for the semester of the study; and (j) probation status for the semester of the study.

Math and Verbal Performance

Four measures of cognitive skill were administered to students in Texas and Mississippi:

(1) Concept Formation (Heidbreder, 1948),

(2) Test of Thematic Analysis (Winter & McClelland, 1978),

(3) Analysis of Argument (Winter, McClelland, & Stewart, 1981), and

(4) Self-Definition (Stewart, 1992a; Stewart & Winter, 1974).

Students in Texas received only three measures of math and verbal performance:

(1) Generation Anagram Test (McClelland, Atkinson, Clark, & Lowell, 1958),

(2) Scrambled Words Test (Lowell, 1952), and

(3) Two-Step Arithmetic Test (McClelland, Atkinson, Clark, & Lowell, 1958).

On the Thematic Apperception Test, the numbers of words produced in response to each picture, as well as to the total of six stories, were used as a measure of verbal fluency.

Academic Adjustment

Three categories of variables were classified as academic adjustment variables. Perceived college climate was assessed by the open-ended method used by Stewart (1975) in her longitudinal follow-up of college-educated women. From several questions about the best aspects of college, the worst aspects of college, and the influence of college, 35 categorical variables were extracted. In addition, a series of 24 questions was designed to probe the nature of students' adjustment to academic life in college. These questions were concerned not with the specifics of what students were studying but with their feelings about the course of instruction, their satisfaction with their academic performance, their perception of the faculty responsiveness to their needs, and their degree of participation in academic and campus activities. In addition, nine composite factors were extracted from these variables, including academic effort, extracurricular involvement, importance of grades, satisfaction with teaching methods, involvement with faculty, adjustment problems, career involvement, satisfaction with major, and general academic adjustment.

Major Subject

Several questions probed the nature of student majors. From these questions, 15 college majors and 16 reasons for choosing the major were extracted.

Career Plans

From a series of open-ended questions, the following were extracted: 10 graduate school plans, 7 non-graduate–school plans, 11 specific graduate school aspirations, 23 career choices, a traditionality of career choice scale, and an educational aspirations scale.

Psychosocial Adjustment

A series of paper and pencil measures, as well as measures derived from a Thematic Apperception Test (TAT), assessed aspects of psychosocial functioning. The measures were grouped into the following categories.

Personality

The personality category included the following:

(1) Sex Role Orientation was derived from a series of 11 items chosen to determine the extent to which students were oriented toward marriage/family/home as opposed to career, and the extent of perceived conflict or compatibility between the two sets of goals. Three of the items were combined into a Role Preference Scale, three were combined into a Career Orientation Scale, and one with five options was converted to an Effect of Marriage on Career Scale.

(2) Vocational Interests were measured by a modified version of the Holland Self-Directed Search (Holland, 1997). The instrument consists of 200 yes/no questions which assess a person's interests, competencies, and vocational interest and yield six personality types—Realistic (mechanical), Investigative (scientific), Artistic, Social, Enterprising (business), and Conventional (clerical).

(3) A rank order scale was developed to measure 10 traits perceived by the student as important in getting ahead, such as persistence and intelligence. A rank order scale was developed to measure 10 advantages perceived by the student as likely to be gained from college, such as friends, social position, contacts, and so on.

(4) Stages of psychological maturity, including oral, anal, phallic, and genital stages, were measured by an empirically derived scoring system for the TAT (Stewart, 1992b; Stewart & Healy, 1992).

Motivation

From the TAT, the following measures were scored: (a) need for achievement (McClelland, Atkinson, Clark, & Lowell, 1992); (b) need for power, including hope for power and fear of power (Winter, 1973); (c) need for affiliation (Shipley & Veroff, 1992); and (d) fear of success (Horner & Fleming, 1992). In addition, the Mandler-Sarason Test Anxiety Questionnaire was used as a measure of (e) fear of failure (Atkinson & Litwin, 1960).

Self-Concept

The self-concept measure utilized was a modification of the Adjective Checklist (Wylie, 1974); participants were instructed to indicate on a 6-point Likert-type scale the extent to which each of 36 adjectives or phrases described them. The following factors were also used: social decorum (i.e., well-mannered), intellectual incompetence, ambition, fatigue, and extroversion.

Life Changes

An adaptation of the Life Adjustment Scale developed by Holmes and Rahe (1967) assessed the number and significance of life changes, or alterations in lifestyle. The 21 items ranged from changes in achievement to personal relationships. For each item and the total score, measures were possible for number of life changes and an average life adjustment score indicating the degree of adjustment. From these items, three factors were extracted: academic stress, personal stress, and personal threat (e.g., change in experience of physical attack).

Physical Symptoms

Three categories of items were included in an assessment of physical symptoms.

(1) Illness Report. Students were asked to list the illnesses they had had since entering college and to indicate additional information permitting the extraction of the following measures: (a) absolute number of illnesses experienced since college, (b) average severity of illnesses, and (c) average length of illnesses.

(2) Psychosomatic Symptoms. Students were asked to indicate whether they were currently experiencing any of a list of 19 "common complaints" that are commonly diagnosed as having psychosomatic origins. The list included disturbances such as migraine headaches and insomnia, and provided for the following measures: (a) absolute number of psychosomatic complaints, (b) number of symptoms onset since college, (c) average severity of symptoms, and (d) number of times medical assistance was sought for symptoms.

(3) Hypochondriasis Scale. Twenty-three items from the MMPI (Hathaway & McKinley, 1943) were extracted from the larger inventory as a stress indicator because the items focus on bodily disturbance; these items comprised the Hypochondriasis Scale.

Social Assertiveness Scale

The Rathus (1973) Social Assertiveness Scale consisted of 36 Likert-type items assessing assertiveness or social boldness. In addition, the following five factors were extracted: fear of confrontation, emotional suppression, openness, shyness, and submissiveness.

Black Ideology Scale

The Ramseur (1975) Black Ideology Scale consisted of 25 Likert-type items assessing the salience of blackness and black issues. Also, six factors were extracted from the items: black heritage, identity integration, white culture, black defensiveness, acceptance of white authority, and black militancy.

Background Factors

In addition to the Hamburger Scale of Socio-Economic Status, a series of questions asked students to provide information on parents' education and on their own secondary school education.

Treatment of Data

For each of the 15 samples, the SAT (or its ACT equivalent) was correlated with each variable or measure in the study. Correlates that were statistically significant at or beyond the .05 level of significance, and that produced correlation coefficients of .30 or higher (i.e., a moderate effect size, visible to the naked eye), were selected for further analysis (Cohen, 1988). Significant correlates were controlled for social class by means of partial correlations. Correlates that survived the partial correlations at significant levels were entered into a stepwise multiple regression equation. Only variables contributing unique variance in the regression equation were considered for discussion. Thus, the analysis describes trends in important correlates of standardized tests. Note that socioeconomic status did not show first-order correlations with SAT scores in any of the samples.

Correlations were rarely produced for the same variable in more than a few colleges, even in instances in which a substantial number of correlations were produced in the same category of variables. In order to fully utilize all 15 samples or cases, significant regressed variables were converted to present/absent categorical variables for later groupings.

Significant regressed variables were grouped in the following ways. Variables were categorized as GPA variables, math and verbal performance variables, academic adjustment variables (further broken down into general academic adjustment, major-related variables, and career-related variables), psychosocial adjustment variables (personality, motivation, self-concept, intellectual self-concept, black ideology, life changes, physical—i.e., psychosomatic—complaints, and social assertiveness), and background variables (general background, mother-related variables, father-related variables, and school-related variables).

Three methods of tabulation were used. First, the total number of variables within a category per school was determined (i.e., a continuous variable). Second, the number of schools with correlates in a given category, or the presence or absence of variables in a given category (i.e., a categorical variable with orthogonal coding) were assessed. Third, for selected variables for which the direction of the underlying dimension was critical, scores ranged from +1 to –1 to indicate the direction of the dimension in question and produced continuous variables with negative to positive ranges. Examples of variables converted to indicate direction: social assertiveness (high to low), black ideology (high to low), career orientation (positive outlook to negative outlook), major orientation (satisfaction to dissatisfaction), and sex-role orientation (family orientation to career orientation). In such cases, some loss of information resulted when variables indicating positive and negative poles occurred within the same sample. The convention employed was to code conflicting directions as 0.

Descriptive statistics were used to report trends in patterns of correlates. The chi-square (or Fisher Exact) test was used when both variables were categorical. *T* tests were used to determine differences in the distribution of continuous variables.

RESULTS

Strongest Correlates of the SAT

The strongest correlates of the SAT are determined by the variable loading first in each of the 15 regression equations (see also Table 2.2). Overall, 40 percent of the strongest correlates were categorized as psychosocial variables, 83 percent of which indicated positive psychological attributes such as higher estimates of general ability, need for power, absence of depression, and interest in white culture. Thirty-three percent of the strongest correlates were GPA variables indicating better academic performance. Twenty percent of the variables were academic adjustment variables, 67 percent of which indicated academic orientations such as enrollment in special programs and majoring in engineering. Seven percent of the strongest correlates were math and verbal performance variables (e.g., better concept formation). Background correlates never loaded first in the regression equations. There were no significant differences in the pattern of variables between black students in black and white colleges. However, the strongest nonsignificant trend showed that while only 14 percent of the strongest correlates were psychosocial in black schools, 63 percent were psychosocial in white schools. This difference changed

Table 2.2
Distribution of SAT Correlates for Whole Sample and by Race of College Environment

	All Schools		Black Schools		White Schools	
	Mean	%	Mean	%	Mean	%
STRONGEST CORRELATES OF THE SAT						
Psycho-Social	0.40	33%	0.14	14%	0.63	63%
GPA	0.33	33%	0.43	43%	0.25	25%
Academic Adjustment	0.20	20%	0.29	29%	0.13	13%
Math/Verbal Performance	0.07	7%	0.14	14%	0.00	0%
Background	0.00	0%	0.00	0%	0.00	0%
REGRESSED CORRELATES OF THE SAT						
Psycho-Social	**2.93**	**100%**	**2.29**	**100%**	**3.50**	**100%**
Black Ideology	0.80	53%	0.43	43%	1.13	63%
Self-Concept	0.73	53%	0.71	57%	0.75	50%
Intellectual Self Concept	0.60	47%	0.71	57%	0.50	38%
Personality	0.60	47%	0.57	43%	0.63	50%
Physical Complaints	0.27	27%	0.29	29%	0.25	25%
Life Changes	0.20	20%	0.14	14%	0.25	25%
Social Assertiveness	0.13	13%	0.14	14%	0.13	13%
Motivation	0.13	13%	0.00	0%	0.25	25%
Self Concept (non-iq)	0.13	13%	0.00	0%	0.24	25%
Other:						
Physical Complaints (w direction)		0.0	-0.29	0.25	$t = 2.18**$	
Academic Adjustment	1.47	87%	1.57	100%	1.38	75%
Career-Related	0.67	60%	0.43	43%	0.88	75%
Major-Related	0.47	33%	0.57	43%	0.38	25%
General Adjustment	0.33	27%	0.57	43%	0.13	13%
Other:						
Positive Career Outlook		0.0	0.43	-0.38	$t= 1.89*$	
Grade Point Averages	**1.13**	**80%**	**1.43**	**100%**	**0.88**	**63%**
GPA in math/science						
Background	**0.67**	**53%**	**0.57**	**57%**	**0.75**	**50%**
Father-Related	0.27	27%	0.42	43%	0.13	13%**
Education-Related	0.20	20%	0.14	14%	0.25	25%
Mother-Related	0.13	13%	0.00	0%	0.25	25%
Other:						
Positive father-related	0.13	0.43	-0.13	$t= 2.33**$		

(continued)

Table 2.2
(Continued)

	Mean	%	Mean	%	Mean	%
ALL CORRELATES OF THE SAT						
Psycho-Social	**9.0**	**100%**	**7.14**	**100%**	**10.63**	**100%**
Self-Concept	2.20	80%	1.86	86%	2.50	75%
Incompetence Factor	0.73	53%	0.86	71%	0.63	38%
SocialDecorum Factor	0.20	13%	0.00	0%	0.38	25%
Estimate of General ability	0.67	67%	0.86	86%	0.50	50%
Stereotypically Negative (w/dir)	-0.67	67%	-1.00	86%	-0.38	50%
Negative endorsement of incompetence items	0.73	53%	-1.00	86%	-.50	25% Fisher**
Personality	1.80	80%	1.43	86%	2.13	75%
Perception of What You Gain From College	0.53	47%	0.29	29%	0.75	73%
Vocational Interests	0.47	40%	0.43	43%	0.50	38%
Perception of What It Takes To Get Ahead	0.33	27%	0.43	29%	0.25	25%
Sex Role Preference	0.27	20%	0.14	14%	0.38	25%
Anal Stage of Maturity	0.20	7%	0.00	0%	0.38	13%
Black Ideology	1.27	60%	0.57	57%	1.87	63%
Low Black Ideology	0.93	60%	0.57	57%	1.25	63%
High Black Ideology	0.33	13%	0.00	0%	0.63	25%
Motivation	0.67	40%	0.57	14%	0.75	63%
Physical Complaints	1.80	33%	1.86	29%	1.75	38%
Balance of Positive/ Negative Complaints	0.07		1.86		-1.50	
Life Changes	1.13	33%	0.71	29%	1.50	38%
Balance of Positive Versus Negative Changes	0.60		0.43		0.75	
Social Assertiveness	0.27	27%	0.29	29%	0.25	25%
High Versus Low Assertiveness	-0.13		0.00		-0.25	
Academic Performance	**4.0**	**100%**	**5.14**	**100%**	**3.0**	**100% t = 1.83***
Academic Adjustment	**5.33**	**93%**	**4.86**	**100%**	**5.75**	**88%**
Career-Related	2.67	80%	2.57	71%	2.75	88%
General Adjustment	1.67	60%	1.29	71%	2.00	50%
Major-Related	1.00	53%	1.00	57%	1.00	50%

Table 2.2
(Continued)

	Mean	%	Mean	%	Mean	%
Other:						
Negative General Adjustment	0.80	60%	0.29	29%	1.25	38%
Positive General Adjustment	0.87	53%	1.00	57%	0.75	50%
Sum of Positive Versus Negative Adjustment	0.07	0.71	-0.50			
Background	**2.40**	**87%**	**2.14**	**100%**	**2.63**	**75%**
Father-Related	1.13	53%	0.86	43%	1.38	63%
Education-Related	0.67	53%	0.86	71%	0.50	38%
Mother-Related	0.40	27%	0.29	29%	0.50	25%
General Background	0.20	13%	0.14	14%	0.25	25%
Math & Verbal Performance	**0.40**	**27%**	**0.71**	**43%**	**0.13**	**13%**

$* p < .10$ $** p < .05$ $*** p < .01.$

the rank ordering of categories, such that in black schools the largest category of variables was GPA in 43 percent of the schools.

Regressed Correlates of the SAT

All correlates contributing unique variance in a regression equation: (1) Psychosocial correlates contributed unique variance in 100 percent of the colleges, with an average of 2.93 correlates per college. Psychosocial variables included the following: (a) black ideology correlates in 47 percent (7) of the colleges (M = 0.80), 75 percent of which indicated low black ideology, including 100 percent of the correlates in black colleges and 67 percent of the correlates in white colleges; (b) self-concept variables in 53 percent (8) of the colleges (M = 0.73), 82 percent of which indicated positive intellectual self-conceptions such as a higher estimate of general ability, and 18 percent of which indicated low endorsement of conformity attributes such as obedience and being a lady or a gentleman; (c) intellectual self-concept correlates, a subcategory of self-concept, in 47 percent (7) of the colleges (M = 0.60), which describe positive intellectual self-concepts or negative endorsement of intellectual incompetence items; (d) personality correlates in 47 percent (6) of the colleges (M = 0.60), which described positive personality attributes such as investigative (i.e., scientific) vocational competencies, a belief in persistence in getting ahead, and working well under pressure; (e) physical or psychosomatic complaints in 27 percent (4) of the colleges (M = .27), 67 percent of which indicated absence of physical problems such as depression, but 33 percent of which indicated physical problems such as overactivity; (f) life changes correlates in 20 percent (3) of the colleges (M = .20), 67 percent of which indicated life change problems such as violation of the law and personal threat, and 33 percent of which indicated lower average life changes scores, which are counterindicative of stress; (g) motivational correlates in 13 percent (2) of colleges (M = 0.13), which indicated positive motivational attributes such as power motivation and low fear of failure (test anxiety); (h) social assertiveness variables in 13 percent (2) of colleges (M = 0.13), indicating low assertiveness responses such as avoiding complaining about service.

(2) Academic adjustment correlates contributed variance in 87 percent (13) of the schools, with a mean of 1.47 correlates per school. Academic adjustment variables were composed of the following: (a) career-related correlates in 60 percent (9) of the colleges (M = 0.67), 50 percent of which indicated positive career choices (such as medicine and engineering) and positive career outlook (e.g., lack of career indecision), and 50 percent of which indicated career conflicts such as race being an obstacle to career choice; (b) major-related correlates of the SAT in 33 percent (5) of the colleges (M = 0.47), 43 percent of which described majoring in engineering and 29 percent described satisfaction or dissatisfaction with the major subject; (c) general adjustment correlates in 27 percent (4) of the colleges (M = 0.43), 60 percent of which described course or program status (e.g., enrolled in a special program) and 40 percent of which described positive adjustment to college (e.g., number of offices held in extracurricular activities).

(3) GPA variables contributed variance in 80 percent (12) of the schools (M = 1.13), including cumulative GPA in 27 percent, GPA in science in 27 percent, semester GPA and GPA in math and English each in 13 percent, GPA in the major (both semester and cumulative) and GPA in language courses each in 7 percent of the colleges.

(4) Background correlates contributed variance in 53 percent (8) of the colleges, with a mean of 0.67 correlates per college. Background correlates were composed of the following: (a) father-related correlates of the SAT in 27 percent (4) of the colleges (M = 0.27), 75 percent of which described fathers with college or graduate school educations; (b) education-related correlates in 20 percent (3) of the colleges (M = 0.20), which described secondary school advantages (e.g., good high school preparation); (c) mother-related correlates in 13 percent (2) of the colleges (M = 0.13),

which described educational and social class advantages (e.g., mother had B.A.).

(5) Math and verbal performance correlates of the SAT were found in 27 percent (4) of the colleges (M = 0.27), indicating better performance on tests of arithmetic, concept formation, thematic analysis, and verbal fluency, i.e; number of words, to Thematic Apperception Test Starter.

There were no significant differences in the patterns of correlates for black students in black and white colleges for absolute numbers of re-gressed correlates. However, high SAT scores in black colleges were more often, than low scores, associated with father-related educational advan-tages (t = 2.33, p < .05), the presence of psychosomatic complaints (t = 2.18, p < .05), and positive career choices and outlook (t = 1.89, p < .10).

All Correlates of the SAT

When all significant correlates of the SAT that survived a control for social class were considered, *psychosocial* correlates occurred in 100 percent of the colleges with a mean of 9.0 correlates per college distributed across the following categories (see Table 2.2).

(1) *Self-concept* correlates occurred in 80 percent (12) of the colleges (M = 2.20). The largest subcategory of self-concept items included 11 corre-lations (10/11 negative) with items of the intellectual incompetence factor in 53 percent (8) of the colleges (M = 0.73). There were 11 correlations with (higher) estimate of general ability in 67 percent (10) of the colleges (M = 0.67). There were also 3 negative correlations with items of the social decorum factor in 13 percent (2) of the colleges (M = 0.20).

(2) *Personality* correlates occurred in 80 percent of the schools (M = 1.80), including: (a) perception of "what you expect to gain from college" in 47 percent (7) of the schools (M = 0.53). Of the eight correlations produced, the most frequent expectations were to gain friends and gain direction; (b) vocational interests, according to the Holland Vocational Interest Inven-tory, in 40 percent (6) of the schools (M = 0.47). Investigative or scientific interest were most frequently associated with test scores, in three colleges, while correlations were also found with Enterprising (business) interests in two colleges and with Realistic (mechanical) interests in one college. Test scores were negatively correlated with social interests in one college; (c) perception of "what it takes to get ahead" in 27 percent (4) of the colleges (M = 0.33). Of the five correlations produced, persistence was the most frequently endorsed attribute, in three colleges, followed by as-sertiveness in two colleges; (d) sex-role-related variables in 20 percent (3) of the colleges (M = 0.27), indicating stronger marriage/family values over career values; (e) anal (i.e., anxious) stage of psychosocial develop-ment in 6 percent (1) of the colleges (M = 0.20).

(3) *Black ideology* correlates occurred in 60 percent of the colleges (M = 1.27). Test scores were not correlated with the total Ramseur (1975) Black Ideology Scale. However, significant correlations with items of the scale were surprisingly widespread—that is, in 60 percent (9) of the schools. The pattern of correlates was also provocative. Of 19 correlations, 14, or 74 percent, were indicative of low black ideology: that is, low endorsement of such items as "community stores should be black owned," importance of what happens in Africa, and "blacks should wear naturals." Only 2 of the 15 schools produced correlations indicative of high black ideology, and both were predominantly white schools. Of the 14 items, only 3 were correlated with test scores in more than one school.

(4) *Motivation* correlates occurred in 40 percent (6) of the colleges (M = 0.67); 80 percent of the 10 correlates indicated positive motivational attributes such as need for achievement, need for power, and low fear of failure, while 20 percent of the correlates indicated avoidance motives such as fear of power. Power-motivation-related variables comprised 50 percent of the correlations.

(5) *Physical (or psychosomatic) complaints* occurred in 33 percent (5) of the colleges (M = 1.80); all of the correlations in black schools were positive, indicating more vaginal infections, depression, fatigue, overactivity, and nail biting, while all but one of the correlations in white schools were negative, indicating less depression, fatigue, and diarrhea, a lower number of physical complaints, fewer physical complaints onset since college, and less medical assistance sought for physical symptoms.

(6) *Life changes* correlates occurred in 33 percent of the colleges (M = 1.13), with 76 percent (13/17) describing greater change in student lives, either positively or negatively, and with two-thirds of the variables describing changes in significant relationships and one-third describing personal threat. Of the correlations describing relationships with teachers, 50 percent described difficult relationships.

(7) *Social assertiveness* correlates occurred in 27 percent of the colleges (M = 0.27), 75 percent of which were in a nonassertive direction, with low endorsement of: complaining about poor service in a restaurant; when asked to do something, insisting on knowing why; and "if someone spreads false stories, I see him/her to have a talk."

(8) *Academic performance* correlates occurred in 100 percent of the colleges (M = 4.0). Test scores were correlated with at least one of the nine measures of academic performance in all of the 15 colleges. Cumulative grade point average was a significant correlate in 80 percent (12) of the schools, semester GPA in 53 percent (8) of the schools, GPA in math in 53 percent (8) of the schools, GPA in science in 53 percent (8) of the schools, GPA in English in 40 percent (6) of the schools, GPA in the major subject (both cumulative and semester grades) in 33 percent (5) of the schools,

GPA in language courses in 27 percent (4) of the schools, and academic honors in the semester of the study in another 27 percent (4) of the schools.

(9) *Adjustment to college* correlates occurred in 93 percent (14) of the schools (M = 5.33), including the following categories: (a) career-related correlates in 80 percent of the colleges (M = 2.67), indicating the most frequent graduate school choices in engineering and science, and a wide range of careers from medicine to the arts, with no clearly preferred career; (b) general academic adjustment correlates in 60 percent (9) of the colleges (M = 1.67). However, positive academic adjustment correlates were found in 53 percent (8) of the colleges, such as satisfaction with the quality of instruction (M = 0.87), while negative academic adjustment correlates were found in 60 percent (9) of the schools, such as less satisfaction with the college choice and lack of interest in achieving good grades (M = 0.80); (c) correlates describing college majors in 53 percent (7) of the colleges (M = 1.00). The most frequent major subject significantly associated with higher test scores was engineering, in three colleges, while the most frequently *avoided* major was business, in two colleges. Other choices associated with higher test scores ranged widely from science to communications and the arts, disallowing generalizations.

(10) *Background characteristics* were correlated with test scores in 87 percent (11) of the colleges (M = 2.40), which were distributed across four categories: (a) father-related background correlates in 53 percent of the colleges (M = 1.13), largely describing educational advantages such as father attended a predominantly white college in the Midwest, in three (white) schools; and father attended college, in two (black) schools; (b) education-related background correlates in 53 percent of the colleges (M = 0.67), indicating advantages such as good high school preparation; (c) mother-related correlates in 27 percent of the colleges (M = 0.40), indicating education-related advantages; (d) general background correlates in 13 percent of the colleges (M = 0.20), describing religious preferences (e.g., Catholic) and neighborhood racial composition (e.g., predominantly white). Note that in the 15 samples, test scores were never correlated with socioeconomic status.

As a function of race of college environment, the following differences were observed: (a) black schools more often produced negative correlations with incompetence self-descriptions, compared to white schools (Fisher = .041, p < .05); (b) black schools produced more academic performance correlates than white schools: 5.41 compared to 3.00, respectively (t = 1.83, p < .10); and (c) there were no significant differences between black and white schools in the number of black ideology correlates, despite trends in favor of white colleges. However, the standard deviation, i.e., variability, of the number of low and high black ideology correlates was greater in white colleges (.025 < p < .027).

DISCUSSION

The preceding analysis of correlates of standardized test scores was performed in order to determine the consequences of higher SAT scores for high-achieving black students in black and white colleges. It was expected that an examination of correlates would shed light on differential adjustment issues for black students, as well as the higher predictive validity estimates for black students in black colleges previously reported in the literature. The results show that, in general, higher test scores are most strongly associated with a preponderance of psychosocial attributes as opposed to academic attributes, and that high SAT scorers in black colleges do indeed exhibit a better academic adjustment than their counterparts in white colleges.

The analysis distinguished between all first-order correlates of the SAT in 15 colleges, correlates that contribute unique variance in regression equations for the 15 colleges, and correlates loading first in regression equations for each college. All analyses employed correlates that survived a control for social class, although social class was never correlated with the SAT in any of the samples. The profile of the African American high SAT scorer gleaned from all first-order correlates showed that test scores were associated with:

(1) a host of psychosocial attributes across seven categories, averaging 9.0 per college in 100 percent of the colleges, the most frequent of which were: (a) self-concept in general and positive intellectual self-concept in particular; (b) personality attributes, including an orientation to knowledge and a scientific orientation; and (c) a largely low black ideological orientation incompatible with interest in the black community or the endorsement of pro-black issues and statements;

(2) measures of academic adjustment averaging 5.3 per college in 93 percent of the colleges, including career-related aspirations and related perceptions which revolved largely around engineering, science, and a positive career outlook; and general academic adjustment issues, about 60 percent of which described negative adjustment to college;

(3) better academic performance, especially on cumulative GPA measures averaging 4.0 per college in 100 percent of the colleges; and

(4) education-related background advantages averaging 2.40 correlates per college in 87 percent of the colleges, including (a) father-related background advantages, virtually all of which were education-related (e.g., father attended college/graduate school), and (b) specifically education-related background advantages, such as good high school preparation.

It appears that higher SAT scores are no guarantee of a completely happy adjustment to college. High scorers could be described as intellectually confident, focused on both positive and negative academic adjustment issues, better academic performers, and possessed of backgrounds richer in educational advantages.

When the most important correlates of the SAT were considered—that is, correlates contributing variance in regressions equations—psychosocial attributes were most likely to contribute unique variance, averaging 2.93 correlates per school in 100 percent of the colleges. The largest category of regressed psychosocial correlates was black ideology, 75 percent of which indicated low black ideology, including 100 percent of the correlates in black colleges and 67 percent of the correlates in white colleges. The only other major category was positive self-concepts, the vast majority of which were positive intellectual self-concepts. Psychosocial correlates were followed in frequency by academic adjustment correlates averaging 1.47 per college in 87 percent of the colleges; largely career-related, academic performance correlates averaging 1.13 per college in 80 percent of the colleges; and education-related background correlates averaging 0.67 per college in 53 percent of the colleges. In terms of regressed correlates, the profile of the African American SAT scorer is similar to that derived from all first-order correlates. The major difference in profiles is the greater frequency of (low) black ideology correlates in the regressed profile that supersedes personality attributes.

Consideration of variables that loaded first in each regression equation confirms the importance of psychosocial variables for African American students. In order of frequency, 40 percent of the strongest correlates were psychosocial, 33 percent were academic performance correlates, 23 percent were academic adjustment correlates, and 7 percent were math and verbal performance correlates. Background correlates never loaded first in regression equations.

Previous studies of the SAT and black students have been narrowly focused on the prediction of academic performance or closely related variables. Although the SAT is designed to predict performance, a fact that accounts for this focus in validity studies, it appears that at least for African American students the SAT is associated with a wide range of psychological characteristics.

In previous research, predictive validity estimates were higher for black students in black colleges than for those in white colleges. Therefore, it is logical to ask whether the pattern of SAT correlates might also differ for students in black and white colleges. Three categories of differences were explored. Considering all correlates, high SAT scorers in predominantly white colleges exhibited less-positive intellectual self-concepts and less widespread evidence of better academic performance. In black schools, test scores were more than three times as likely to correlate significantly with positive intellectual self-concepts, or, in other words, black students were much less likely to endorse stereotypically nonintellectual images of themselves than did their counterparts in white schools. While the number of black ideology correlates was more frequent in white colleges, the difference was short of statistical significance. However, the variability in numbers of correlates was greater in white colleges.[1] Considering regressed correlates, students in white colleges exhibited fewer father-related background advantages and a less positive career outlook but more physical/psychosomatic correlates indicative of a relative lack of symptomatology. When the strongest correlates of the SAT were considered, there were no statistically significant differences as a function of race of college environment. However, in white colleges psychosocial correlates were most likely to load first in 63 percent of the schools, but in black colleges GPA correlates were most likely to load first in 43 percent of the colleges. Thus, for black students in white colleges, higher SAT scores were less likely to be associated with an intellectual self-image, a performance edge, career optimism, or even the advantages associated with educated fathers. Since high SAT scoring blacks in white colleges appear to suffer compromised intellectual and academic consequences, their similarly compromised SAT predictive validity appears consistent with the findings.

The results of this study have a number of implications for predominantly black colleges and universities. First, in addition to the previous literature, which convincingly documents better academic and social adjustment for African American students in general in black colleges, the present research confirms advantages for high achievers in black colleges as well. In black colleges, high achievers can more often look forward to higher self-esteem and enjoy the better performance consistent with their abilities. Second, the greater occurrence of psychosocial correlates of the SAT in predominantly white colleges suggests that such issues are more often activated in white colleges and appear to act as an interference with the academic issues that occur more often for high scorers in black colleges. The psychosocial issues that have been documented in the literature suggest a psychosocial challenge for black students in white colleges that, at least for high scorers, appears to divert attention away from academics. Third, it becomes clear that the question of whether black colleges fit with the democratic value placed on integration is a political one. If an answer to it were fashioned from social science evidence, the burden of proof would shift dramatically. While black colleges were once charged with being unable to fulfill the intellectual responsibility of educating black students, the present research, in conjunction with a considerable body of past research, suggests that it is predominantly white colleges that have failed to nurture the intellectual confidence and performance of African Americans. If the persistent debate over the value of black institutions seriously considers the research evidence relating to black student well-being, black institutions would enter the new age with a renewed sense of their own confidence and uniqueness.

NOTE

1. In a preliminary analysis of this data, Fleming (2000) reported that (low) black ideology correlates of the SAT were significantly more frequent in predominantly white than black colleges. However, a coding error was discovered that rendered the substantial differences just short of statistical significance. More recent research nonetheless still supports the arguments advanced in this work (see Fleming 2002).

REFERENCES

Allen, W. R. (1985). Black student, white campus: Structural, interpersonal and psychological correlates of success. *Journal of Negro Education, 54*(2), 135–147.

Allen, W. R., Epps, E. G., & Haniff, N. Z. (1991). *College in black and white.* Albany: State University of New York Press.

Atkinson, J. W., & Litwin, G. H. (1960). Achievement motive and test anxiety as motive to approach success and motive to avoid failure. *Journal of Abnormal and Social Psychology, 60,* 52–63.

Berry, G. L., & Asamen, J. L. (1989). *Black students.* Newbury Park: Sage.

Bohr, L., Pascarella, E. T., Nora, A., & Terenzini, P. T. (1995). Do black students learn more at historically black or predominantly white colleges? *Journal of College Student Development, 36*(1), 75–85.

Cheatham, H. E., Slaney, R. B., & Coleman, N. C. (1990). Institutional effects on the psycho-social development of African American college students. *Journal of Counseling Psychology, 37*(4), 453–458.

Cohen, J. (1988). *Statistical power analysis in the behavioral sciences.* New York: Academic Press.

Crouse, J., & Trusheim, D. (1988). *The case against the SAT.* Chicago: University of Chicago Press.

D'Augelli, A. R., & Herschberger, S. L. (1993). African American undergraduates on a predominantly white campus: Academic factors, social networks, and campus climate. *Journal of Negro Education, 62*(1), 67–81.

DeSousa, D. J., & Kuh, G. D. (1996). Does institutional racial composition make a difference in what Black students gain from college? *Journal of College Student Development, 37*(3), 257–267.

Fleming, J. (1984). *Blacks in college: A comparative study of student's success in black and in white institutions.* San Francisco: Jossey-Bass.

Fleming, J. (1990). Standardized test scores and the black college environment. In K. Lomotey (Ed.), *Going to school: The African American experience.* Albany: State University of New York Press.

Fleming, J. (2000). Affirmative action and standardized test scores. *Journal of Negro Education, 69*(1/2), 27–37.

Fleming, J. (2002). Identity and achievement: Black ideology and the SAT in African American college students. In W. R. Allen, M. B. Spencer, & C. O'Conner (Eds.), *African American education: Race, community, inequality and achievement* (pp. 77–92). New York: Elsevier Science.

Fleming, J., & Garcia, N. (1998). Are standardized tests fair to African Americans: Predictive validity of the SAT in black and white colleges. *Journal of Higher Education, 69*(5), 471–495.

Fleming, J., Garcia, N., & Embaye, F. (1997). The approach to college of the high SAT scorer: An analysis of correlates in minority students. *Texas Southern University Research Journal, 5*(1), 54–75.

Fleming, J., & Morning, C. (1998). Correlates of the SAT in minority engineering students: An exploratory study. *Journal of Higher Education, 69*(1), 89–108.

Ford, C. A. (1996). *Student retention: Success models in higher education.* Tallahassee, FL: CNJ Associates.

Gurin, P., & Epps, E. G. (1975). *Black consciousness, identity and achievement.* New York: Wiley.

Hamburger, M. A. (1971). *A revised occupational scale for rating socioeconomic status.* Unpublished manuscript, New York University.

Hathaway, S. R., & McKinley, J. C. (1943). *Minnesota multiphasic personality inventory.* Minneapolis: University of Minnesota Press.

Heidbreder, E. (1948). The attainment of concepts: VI. Exploratory experiments on conceptualization at perceptual levels. *Journal of Psychology, 26*(6), 193–216.

Holland, J. L. (1997). *Making vocational choices.* Odessa, FL: Psychological Assessment Resources.

Holmes, T. H., & Rahe, R. H. (1967). *Life crisis and disease onset-I. Qualitative and quantitative definition of life events composing the life crisis,* (1). Unpublished manuscript, Navy Medical Neuropsychiatric Research Unit, San Diego, California.

Horner, M., & Fleming, J. (1992). A scoring manual for the success motive. In C. P. Smith (Ed.), *A handbook of thematic analysis.* New York: Cambridge University Press.

Houston, L. N. (1983). The comparative predictive validities of high school rank, the Ammons Quick Test, and two Scholastic Aptitude Test measures for a sample of Black female college students. *Educational and Psychological Measurement, 43,* 1123–1126.

Jay, G. M., & D'Augelli, A. R. (1991). Social support and adjustment to university life: A comparison of African American and white freshmen. *Journal of Community Psychology, 19,* 95–108.

Jencks, C., & Riesman, D. (1968). *The academic revolution.* New York: Doubleday.

Kraft, C. L. (1991). What makes a successful black student on a predominantly white campus? *American Research Journal, 28*(2), 423–443.

Lowell, E. L. (1952). The effect of need for achievement on learning and speed performance. *Journal of Psychology, 33,* 31–40.

Marco, G. L., & Abdel-Fattah, A. A. (1991). Developing concordance tables for scores on the enhanced ACT assessment and the SAT. *College & University, 66*(4), 187–194.

McClelland, D. C., Atkinson, J. W., Clark, K. R., & Lowell, E. L. (1958). *The achievement motive.* Princeton: Van Nostrand Reinhold.

McClelland, D. C., Atkinson, J. W., Clark, K. R., & Lowell, E. L. (1992). A scoring manual for the achievement motive. In C. P. Smith (Ed.), *A handbook of thematic analysis.* New York: Cambridge University Press.

McGrath, E. J. (1972). *The predominantly Negro colleges and universities in transition.* New York: Teachers College Press.

Miller, D. M., & O'Connor, P. (1969). Achiever personality and academic success among disadvantaged college students. *Journal of Social Issues, 25*(3), 193–216.

Nettles, M. T. (Ed.). (1988). *Toward black undergraduate student equality in American higher education.* New York: Greenwood Press.

Nettles, M. T., Thoeny, A. R., & Gosman, E. J. (1986). Comparative and predictive analyses of black and white students' college achievement and experience. *Journal of Higher Education, 57,* 289–318.

Nottingham, C. R., Rosen, D. H., & Parks, C. (1992). Psychological well-being among African American university students. *Journal of College Student Development, 33,* 356–362.

Pelavin, S. H., & Kane, M. (1990). *Changing the odds: Factors increasing access to college.* New York: College Entrance Examination Board.

Ramist, L., Lewis, C., & McCamley-Jenkins, L. (1994). *Student group differences in predicting college grades: Sex, language, and ethnic groups* (College Board Report No. 93–1, ETS RR No. 94–27). New York: College Entrance Examination Board.

Ramseur, H. (1975). *Continuity and change in black identity: A study of black students at an interracial college.* Unpublished doctoral dissertation, Harvard University.

Rathus, S. A. (1973). A thirty-item schedule for assessing assertive behavior. *Behavior Therapy, 4,* 398–406.

Schwitzer, A. M., Griffin, O. T., Ancis, J. R., & Thomas, C. R. (1999). Social adjustment experiences of African American college students. *Journal of Counseling and Development, 77,* 189–197.

Shipley, T. E., & Veroff, J. (1992). A scoring manual for the affiliation motive. In C. P. Smith (Ed.), *A handbook of thematic analysis.* New York: Cambridge University Press.

Sowa, C. J., Thompson, M. M., & Bennet, C. T. (1989). Prediction and improvement of academic performance for high risk black college students. *Journal of Multicultural Counseling and Development, 17,* 14–22.

Sowell, T. (1972). *Black education: Myths and tragedies.* New York: McKay.

Stewart, A. J. (1975). *Longitudinal prediction from personality to life outcomes among college-educated women.* Unpublished doctoral dissertation, Harvard University.

Stewart, A. J. (1992a). Scoring manual for psychological stances toward the environment. In C. P. Smith (Ed.), *Motivation and personality: Handbook of thematic content analysis* (pp. 451–480). New York: Cambridge University Press.

Stewart, A. J. (1992b). Revised scoring manual for self-definition and social definition. In C. P. Smith (Ed.), *Motivation and personality: Handbook of thematic content analysis* (pp. 489–499). New York: Cambridge University Press.

Stewart, A. J., & Healy, J. M., Jr. (1992). Assessing adaptation to life changes in terms of psychological stances toward the environment. In C. P. Smith (Ed.), *Motivation and personality: Handbook of thematic content analysis* (pp. 440–450). New York: Cambridge University Press.

Stewart, A. J., & Winter, D. G. (1974). Self-definition and social definition in women. *Journal of Personality, 42,* 238–259.

Tracey, T. J., & Sedlacek, W. E. (1985). The relationship of noncognitive variables to academic success: A longitudinal comparison by race. *Journal of College Student Personnel, 26,* 405–410.

Winter, D. G. (1973). *The power motive.* Glencoe, IL: Free Press.

Winter, D. G., & McClelland, D.C. (1978). Thematic analysis: An empirically derived measure of the effects of the liberal arts education. *Journal of Educational Psychology, 70,* 8–16.

Winter, D. G., McClelland, D. C., & Stewart, A. J. (1981). *A new case for the liberal arts: Assessing institutional goals and student development.* San Francisco: Jossey-Bass.

Wylie, R. C. (1974). *The self-concept: A review of methodological considerations and measuring instruments. Vol. 1.* Lincoln: University of Nebraska Press.

CHAPTER 3

Attracting the Best and Brightest: College Choice Influences at Black Colleges

Kassie Freeman and Nicole McDonald

INTRODUCTION

Like all colleges, historically black colleges and universities (HBCUs) increasingly have to compete to lure the top African American high school graduates. Once the exclusive providers of higher education for African Americans, these institutions, often shorter of funding than predominantly white institutions (PWIs), face challenges in their recruitment, particularly of the best and brightest African American high school graduates. However, considering many African American students' desire to reconnect to their history and roots, HBCUs in this millennium have enormous opportunities to lure the top African American high school graduates.

In a quest to better understand the considerations of high-achieving African American high school graduates in choosing to attend HBCUs, this chapter examines several questions: (a) What are the background characteristics of those high-achieving African American students who choose to attend HBCUs? (b) Who and/or what are the influences on African American high school students' considerations to attend HBCUs? (c) What challenges and opportunities do HBCUs face in attracting high-achieving African American students?

Surprisingly, little is known about the influences on African American students' decisions to attend HBCUs. More recently, HBCUs have been seeking ways to lure the top African American high school graduates to their institutions. This is especially important in light of articles in the popular press (Benavides, 1996) that indicate that some HBCUs have a goal of increasing their enrollments and an article in *Black Issues in Higher Education* (Roach, 2000) stating that HBCUs are battling for the best. To better understand the experiences of high-achieving African American students at various higher education institutions, it is helpful to understand how students made their selections in the first place.

AFRICAN AMERICAN PARTICIPATION PATTERNS IN HBCUS: AN OVERVIEW

According to Davis (1998), it is very important to understand the historical context of HBCUs because "the present situation of these schools and their students cannot be understood and appreciated without some knowledge of historical events that influenced the development and current state of these institutions" (p. 144). When the first black colleges were founded more than 150 years ago, they filled an important void that existed in the educational terrain of black America (Willie & Edmonds, 1978). According to researchers such as Murty and Roebuck (1993), these institutions demonstrated as early as 1837 a remarkable capacity to survive and serve as a cultural and intellectual enclave for America's black populace.

In the decade following the Emancipation Proclamation (1863), it became evident that a system of formal education must be established for the sole purpose of directly addressing the relevant needs and conditions of the newly freed black citizens (Bullock, 1967). As Anderson (1988) explains, "Education, then, according to the more liberal and dominant segments of missionary philanthropists, was intended to prepare a college-bred black leadership to uplift the black masses from the legacy of slavery and the restraints of the postbellum caste system" (pp. 240–241). Although, according to Anderson, there may have been a difference of opinion as to the type of education that blacks should receive while attending HBCUs, there was little doubt that HBCUs should serve the central role of uplifting black people. Anderson stated it in this way: "At the core of different educational ideologies and reform movements [the role of higher education] in the overall scheme of black education lay the central goal of preparing black leaders or 'social guides', as they were sometimes called, for participation in the political economy of the New South" (p. 239).

As recently as two decades ago, the majority of African Americans in college were attending HBCUs (Wilson, 1994). African Americans were limited in their choice of higher education institutions. This was partially because the majority of African Americans of college age resided in the South where segregation barriers made it impossible to select PWIs and also because admissions barriers at northern PWIs limited access to African Americans (Gurin & Epps, 1975).

Wilson (1994) describes two revolutions in federal initiatives, Supreme Court actions, and congressional laws that dramatically changed both the number of African American participants and their geographic distribution throughout American higher education institutions. The first initiative was the passage of the G.I. Bill, which increased by the thousands the number of African American veterans able to attend college. The second initiative was the 1964 Civil Rights Act. As a result, particularly of the 1964 Civil Rights Act, more African Americans had increased opportunities to select PWIs. However, it was not until the 1970s that more African Americans began to attend PWIs, and by 1980, only 20 percent of African American students who were enrolled in higher education were attending HBCUs. In spite of these decreased numbers, HBCUs still continue to play a unique role in American higher education. These institutions have been extraordinary in their achievement of producing an overwhelming percentage of African American leaders "in the face of considerable obstacles, such as discriminatory public funding, hostility of the white power structure, low church support, minimal response from the white philanthropic community and foundations" (p. 198).

Although in the 1980s more African Americans elected to attend PWIs, in the 1990s many African American students reconsidered HBCUs because of their interest in embracing history and tradition (Benavides, 1996). Additionally, studies of African American student experiences at HBCUs and PWIs suggest that many blacks have negative experiences at PWIs and that they suffer lower achievement and higher attrition than do white students (Allen, 1992; Nettles, 1988). In contrast, studies suggest that African American students who attend HBCUs experience higher intellectual gains and have more favorable psychosocial adjustment, more positive self-images, stronger racial pride, and higher aspirations (Fleming, 1984; Gurin & Epps, 1975).

EARLY CHARACTERISTICS OF AFRICAN AMERICANS CHOOSING HBCUS

In the 1970s, according to Gurin and Epps (1975), approximately 60 percent of African Americans who attended black colleges and approximately 45 percent of African Americans who attended PWIs had fathers who had not graduated from high school. Because, according to Gurin and Epps, many African Americans' occupations have been in semiskilled or unskilled jobs, a significant difference between African Americans who selected HBCUs and PWIs was based on patterns of financial support. That is, according to Gurin and Epps, "Only one-third of Black students in Black colleges but one-half of those in White colleges held scholarships or grants that covered most of their college expenses" (p. 29). Therefore, the extent to which financial aid is available to African American students has likely influenced their selection of higher education institutions. Financial considerations have also tended to influence African Americans' consideration of colleges close to home. Therefore, for example, Gurin and Epps estimated that 90 percent of students attending HBCUs in the South were Southerners.

In Thomas's edited volume, Astin and Cross (1981) reported on the characteristics of blacks choosing to attend HBCUs. In contrast to the findings of Gurin and Epps (1975), Astin and Cross found, contrary to popular beliefs, that black students who choose to attend black colleges "tended to have somewhat better educated fathers than the latter [those who chose to attend PWIs]" (p. 36). They also reported that "the mothers of black men and women attending black schools tended to be better educated than the mothers of blacks at white institutions" (p. 36). Although Astin and Cross indicated that blacks attending white institutions "tended to have made better grades in high school and to have applied to and been accepted by more postsecondary institutions," they also found that black students attending HBCUs aspired more often to a Ph.D. or Ed.D. degree (p. 43). Another noteworthy characteristic that Astin and Cross found about black students choosing black colleges in the 1970s was that black students in black institutions "were more concerned about the political structure and community action, whereas those attending white institutions gave higher priority to financial and status goals" (p. 43).

African Americans who attend HBCUs are generally thought to have worse high school records and lower standardized test scores. Additionally, literature usually indicates that African Americans who choose to attend HBCUs select these colleges because they want to stay close to home (Allen, 1992). However, Allen cautions that assumptions about the capabilities of African American students who choose to attend HBCUs have to be questioned. Allen (1992) and Davis (1998) assert that students attending HBCUs have to be studied by the type of institution they select, just as do students attending PWIs. There are differences in the selectivity of the colleges and the socioeconomic status of students attending different types of HBCUs—for example, private and public HBCUs. Therefore, caution should be used in making general statements about the background characteristics of all students attending HBCUs.

PROFILE OF HIGH-ACHIEVING AFRICAN AMERICAN STUDENTS CHOOSING HBCUS

What is the profile of the best and brightest African American students choosing HBCUs? Are the influences on high-achieving students choosing to attend HBCUs similar or different from the influences on the general population of African Americans choosing HBCUs?

The profile of students who currently choose to attend HBCUs is varied, yet there are common characteristics of current students and students who have historically chosen to attend HBCUs. In a recently completed qualitative longitudinal study of high-achieving African American students, Freeman (1999a) found that the profile of those students choosing HBCUs was not discernibly different from that of students choosing PWIs. That is, the background characteristics of students choosing HBCUs were similar to those choosing PWIs. For example, since all the students in her sample were designated as high achievers, their academic achievements were similar. They all grew up in predominantly black environments and attended predominantly black high schools. Only 5 of the 21 students had parents who were college graduates. According to Freeman's research, contrary to much of the previous literature (Astin & Cross, 1981), current students choosing to attend HBCUs are not necessarily students who are limited in their choices because of their academic abilities or their socioeconomic background.

Regardless of institution type selected (HBCU or PWI), all the students indicated that financial aid was one of the biggest considerations in their choice among higher education institutions. In fact, the often limited financial resources of HBCUs could limit their ability to attract a broader range of students. For example, it is understandable that among the United Negro College Fund (UNCF) schools (as Figure 3.1 indicates), the highest percentage of students attending come from families that earn less than $25,000 because in reality the highest percentage of African Americans in this country are concentrated in the lowest income brackets. However, it is interesting to note that at the high end—families with incomes greater than $75,000—the gap narrows between UNCF school participants and students attending other types of higher education institutions. What these UNCF figures indicate is that as the UNCF report stated, "College Fund institutions serve students from various socioeconomic backgrounds" (Freeman, Perna, & King, 1998, p. 17).

In summary, the characteristics of African Americans choosing to attend HBCUs have been somewhat consistent over time. In reality, based on the educational experiences of African Americans in this country, it should be assumed that the profile of African American students (including the best and brightest) attending institutions of higher education would remain similar. Based on recent qualitative findings (Freeman, 1999a), HBCUs more recently have been attracting more academically capable students. However, when making judgments about African American students choosing HBCUs, it is necessary to disaggregate the data by type, just as with any other type of institution of higher education. The most consistent finding about African American students across institution type and academic ability continues to be the importance of financial aid, as many African American families are still earning salaries too low to be

Figure 3.1
Estimated Family Income of UNCF Students, Fall 1997

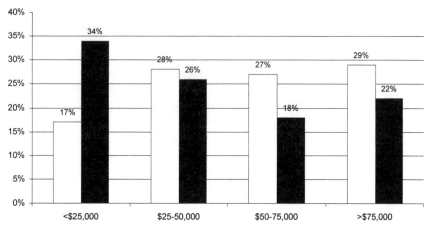

Family Income in $000s
☐ 4-year colleges
■ UNCF institutions

Source: Freeman, Perna, & King, 1998.

able to finance higher education (as demonstrated by the UNCF data in Figure 3.1).

INFLUENCES ON HIGH-ACHIEVING STUDENTS CHOOSING HBCUS

Once students move beyond the search phase, they begin to focus on decisions related to their higher education choices. Hossler and Gallagher (1987) describe this phase as a courtship between the preferences of the applicant and the attributes of the college or university.

As Table 3.1 indicates, Astin and Cross's (1981) findings suggest that in the 1970s black students' reasons for attending black colleges primarily related to relatives, a teacher, or someone who had attended HBCUs. Also, the academic reputation of the institution influenced students' selection of higher education institutions. Although black students selected PWIs for financial assistance, they selected HBCUs for their low tuition.

Therefore, it can be concluded that financial considerations have been and continue to be an important consideration in choosing a higher education institution. Hossler and Gallagher's (1987) findings supported the importance of financial aid, particularly for African Americans, but found that for white students the increase in financial aid would have to be large

Table 3.1
Reasons for Black Students' Choice of HBCU or PWI

Reasons	Blacks in White Institutions		Blacks in Black Institutions	
	Men	Women	Men	Women
My relatives wanted me to come here.	15.8[a]	13.6	9.3	8.6
My teacher advised me.	10.9	4.3	5.0	8.4
This college has a very good academic reputation.	51.9	56.4	48.3	59.1
I was offered financial assistance.	28.0	24.5	32.1	34.1
I was not accepted anywhere else.	5.3	3.3	2.9	2.4
Someone there before advised me to go.	20.7	18.5	12.8	10.1
This college offers special educational programs.	35.0	30.1	25.6	33.7
This college has low tuition.	18.2	12.6	10.8	16.2
My guidance counselor advised me.	11.7	8.8	9.8	12.1
I wanted to live at home.	11.5	11.8	7.3	4.0
A friend suggested attending.	12.6	10.5	7.7	4.2
A college representative recruited me.	10.0	7.1	15.1	9.2

Note: Percentages represent the proportion of students who checked the response category "very important."

Source: Astin & Cross, 1981, pp. 11–17.

to move students from first-choice to second-choice schools. The socio-economic composition of the school attended also tends to influence students' selectivity. That is, according to Hanson and Litten (1989), higher socioeconomic status of a secondary school's student body contributes to the selection of more selective higher education institutions.

The most recent studies on African American students' choices of higher education institutions have been conducted by Freeman (1999a); McDonough, Antonio, and Trent (1995); and Hearn, Griswold, Marine, and McFarland (1995). In the latter study, the researchers indicate that African American students' socioeconomic status (SES) and background, as well as their academic ability, high-school track, 10th-grade expectations, and having siblings in college, were positive influences on 12th-grade expectations about college matriculation. One of the researchers' findings, which they indicate requires further study, is that the percentage of whites, the percentage of disadvantaged, the high student/teacher ratio, and the high student/counselor ratio had negative effects on African American students maintaining high expectations about college matriculation. They further explain, "The more a school is populated by those from backgrounds socioeconomically disadvantaged in one respect or another, the more likely aspiring [high-achieving] lower-SES students are to receive support and encouragement they need to fulfill their dreams" (pp. 15–16).

McDonough, Antonio, and Trent (1995), in their quantitative study specific to African Americans' choosing HBCUs, suggest that students' religion (e.g., being Baptist), the school's reputation, and relatives' desire are the top reasons they choose to attend HBCUs. In that same study, they found that African Americans choose PWIs because they "are recruited by an athletic department, they wish to live near home, and they value the college's academic reputation" (p. 27).

Also, researchers (McDonough, Antonio, & Trent, 1995) have indicated that most African American students apply to only a small number of colleges (three or less) and that about three-quarters of them are accepted at their first-choice school. However, they indicate that African American students get into their first-choice school less often than the national average. According to these researchers, approximately 70 percent of first-time freshmen get into their first-choice school, while only 55 percent of African American students get into their first-choice school; 59 percent of African American students get into their first-choice HBCUs.

Freeman's (1999a) qualitative study more specifically suggested that having an HBCU connection (cultural affinity), seeking their roots, and a lack of cultural awareness were influences on African American students choosing to attend HBCUs. For African American students, regardless of the type of high school attended or the student's academic ability, having an HBCU connection through a family member, a teacher/counselor, or a friend still greatly influences their consideration of attending HBCUs. A comparison to the findings of Astin and Cross (1981) shows that the effect of having an HBCU connection has remained consistent since the 1970s (see Table 3.1).

However, after probing deeper into African American students' perceptions about why they consider HBCUs, Freeman (1999a) reports that the more African American students were isolated from their culture (e.g., those attending private schools) the more they longed to have a deeper understanding of their cultural heritage, which they perceived they could get by attending an HBCU. Freeman indicates that students who attended predominantly white private high schools were, in addition to considering prestigious PWIs, also more likely to consider HBCUs. These were the students who most often described a process of searching for their roots or a connection to the African American community.

Freeman (1999a) reports that students attending predominantly black high schools, in contrast, strongly favored considering PWIs. These students' rationale for considering PWIs included such issues as the need to share their culture with other groups and the idea that "the real world is not black."

In other more specific findings related to high-achieving African American students, Freeman (1999a) found that the students' mothers had a greater influence on their choice than other family members did. Freeman reports that regardless of whom or what else students in her sample discussed as influences on their college choice process, it almost always came back to their mothers.

The high-achieving students in Freeman's (1999a) sample also indicated that they were influenced by economic expectations. That is, they also considered schools for the perceived return on their investment in attaining higher education. This finding was consistent with common understanding of high achieving students which indicated that trying to separate these students' desire to give back to their families from their economic expectations for themselves would be difficult.

One area that is generally unexplored in terms of its influence on high-achieving students choosing to attend HBCUs is the role of the institution's leadership. As Roach (2000) points out in the article "Battling for the Best," the HBCUs that have been most successful in luring high-achieving students are those institutions whose leaders have been actively engaged in the recruiting process—for example, Humphries at Florida A&M University.

Although the influences on the best and brightest African American students include mother's wishes, cultural affinity, and family and/or school connection, economics (whether financial assistance or perceived return on investment) is hugely important in high-achieving students' decisions to attend HBCUs. An area that needs to be explored empirically is the role of leaders of HBCUs in influencing students to choose their institutions. For example, how and why are some leaders more successful than others in luring the top students to their institutions?

CHALLENGES FACING HBCUS ATTRACTING THE BEST AND BRIGHTEST AFRICAN AMERICAN STUDENTS

Building on the findings from college choice theorists, the findings in this chapter support the influence of mother, cultural affinity, and economic expectations, and the role of HBCU leaders, on the best and brightest choosing to attend HBCUs. It is revealing that the role that mothers play in the college choice process of high-achieving students shatters, in a way, the stereotype that researchers and policymakers apply to single-parent homes. This fact demonstrates that instead of writing off single mothers, there is much more to be examined about mothers who are successful in motivating their children not only to achieve but also to achieve at the highest level. This is an area that bears much greater understanding, particularly given the fact that there are many African American single-parent homes.

This research indicates that the profile of students choosing to attend HBCUs has been somewhat consistent over time. That is, it is difficult to determine by education and SES of parents alone the choice pattern of African American students. These findings would also tend to suggest that African American students' considerations of higher education institutions are influenced by the types of high schools attended and by cultural affinity. That is, based on the themes and patterns of more recent students' responses, students attending private/independent schools would consider attending HBCUs because of what they perceive as missing cultural connections. In contrast, students attending predominantly black high schools indicate a need to be in a mixed environment.

Just as in the 1970s and 1980s, financial aid is still a major consideration in determining the type of higher education institution (HBCU or PWI) African American students will choose to attend. Therefore, contrary to popular belief, high-achieving students will often choose to attend HBCUs if their financial aid awards are competitive.

For HBCUs to be competitive in the recruitment of students, particularly high-achieving students, the findings in this chapter tend to suggest a more strategic use of HBCU connections, more focus on a range of high school types (including private/independent schools), and the proactive involvement of the institution leadership (presidents) in the admissions process. The role of the leader in the college choice process has been seriously underexplored by college choice theorists.

For admissions officers at HBCUs, these findings hold importance. The research suggests that admissions officers at HBCUs could make better use of their alumni, teachers, and counselors at all high school types, especially those that have HBCU connections. In terms of HBCUs' use of admissions resources, these findings seem to suggest that recruitment at independent schools and other predominantly white high schools might provide a good return on investment. While the investment might not yield immediate results, it would appear that, over time, establishing a relationship at these schools, especially with counselors and teachers, would be beneficial in terms of HBCUs having access to some of the top students. It is important to remember that African American students who tend to express a disconnect from their culture and indicate a desire to become more culturally aware are potential recruits for HBCUs—at least based on the findings reported in this chapter.

These findings would tend to indicate that HBCUs are positioned to lure a wide variety of African American students—from a range of high school types, academic abilities, and socioeconomic backgrounds—and that has been consistent over time. Now is the time for these institutions to build on these opportunities.

REFERENCES

Allen, W. (1992). The color of success: African American college student outcomes at predominantly white and historically black colleges. *Harvard Educational Review, 62,* 26–44.

Anderson, J. (1988). *Education blacks in the South 1860–1935.* Chapel Hill: University of North Carolina Press.

Astin, H. S., & Cross, P. H. (1981). Black students in black and white institutions. In G. E. Thomas (Ed.), *Black students in higher education: Conditions and experiences in the 1970s* (pp. 11–17). Westport, CT: Greenwood Press.

Benavides, I. (1996, February 19). Historically black colleges buying muscle to up enrollment. *The Tennesseean,* p. 1A.

Bullock, H. (1967). *A history of Negro education in the South.* Cambridge, MA: Harvard University Press.

Davis, J. E. (1998). Cultural capital and the role of historically black colleges and universities in educational reproduction. In K. Freeman (Ed.), *African American culture and heritage in higher education research and practice* (pp. 143–154). Westport, CT: Praeger.

Fleming, J. (1984). *Blacks in college.* San Francisco: Jossey-Bass.

Freeman, K. (1999a). HBCUs or PWIs? African American high school students' consideration of higher education institution types. *Review of Higher Education, 23*(1), 91–106.

Freeman, K. (1999b). No services needed: The case for mentoring high achieving African American students. *Peabody Journal of Education, 74*(2), 15–27.

Gurin, P., & Epps, E. G. (1975). *Black consciousness, identity, and achievement: A study of students in historically black colleges.* New York: John Wiley & Sons.

Hanson, K. H., & Litten, L. H. (1989). Mapping the road to academe: A review of research on women, men, and the college-selection process. In P. J. Perun (Ed.), *The undergraduate woman: Issues in educational equity* (pp. 73–98). Lexington, MA: Lexington Books.

Hearn, J. C., Griswold, C. P., Marine, G. M., & McFarland, M. L. (1995). *Dreams realized and dreams deferred: A causal analysis of six years of educational expectations and attainment.* Paper presented at the annual meeting of the American Educational Research Association, New York.

Hossler, D., & Gallagher, K. (1987). A Study of student college choice: A three-phase model and the implications for policymakers. *College and University, 62*(3), 207–221.

McDonough, P., Antonio, A., & Trent, J. (1995). *Black students, Black colleges: An*

African American college choice model. Paper presented at the annual meeting
of the American Educational Research Association, San Francisco.

Murty, K. S., & Roebuck, J. B. (1993). *Historically Black colleges and universities: Their
place in American higher education.* Westport, CT: Praeger.

Nettles, M. (Ed.). (1988). *Toward Black undergraduate student equity in American
higher education.* Westport, CT: Greenwood Press.

Roach, R. (2000, October 26). Battling for the best: Black schools experience a re-
naissance in recruiting high-achieving students. *Black Issues in Higher Education, 17*(18), 36–41.

Willie, C., & Edmonds, R. (1978). *Black colleges in America: Challenges, development
and survival.* New York: Teachers College Press.

Wilson, R. (1994). The participation of African Americans in American higher education. In M. J. Justiz, R. Wilson, & L. G. Bjork (Eds.), *Minorities in higher
education* (pp. 195–211). Phoenix, AZ: Oryx Press.

CHAPTER 4

Other Things Being Equal: Federal Aid and the Politics of Equal Opportunity for Historically Black Colleges and Universities

Paul Green

... the Negro needs neither segregated schools nor mixed schools. What he needs is Education. What he must remember is that there is no magic, either in mixed schools or segregated schools. A mixed school with poor and un-sympathetic teachers, with hostile public opinion, and no teaching of truth concerning black folk, is bad. A segregated school with ignorant placehold-ers, inadequate equipment poor salaries, and wretched housing, is equally bad. Other things being equal, the mixed school is the broader, more natural basis for the education of all youth. It gives wider contacts; it inspires greater self-confidence; and suppresses the inferiority complex. But other things seldom are equal, and in that case, Sympathy, Knowledge, and the Truth, outweigh all that the mixed school can offer.

(W. E. B. Du Bois, 1935, p. 335)

INTRODUCTION

Without question, public historically black colleges and universities[1] have achieved the rare accomplishment of educating a significant portion or number of students, particularly African Americans, in spite of more than a century of inadequate funding by federal and state authorities. Despite changes in federal and state laws, the historic missions of publicly funded HBCUs are unchanged by law, statute, or administrative necessity. HBCUs remain dedicated to the successful matriculation of every student, regard-less of race, ethnicity, gender, religion, or socioeconomic status.

Historically, HBCUs have suffered from serious shortages of funds and underpaid administrators, faculty, and staff who devote disproportionate amounts of their time to teaching. In spite of these shortcomings, data suggest that 75 percent of all African Americans who hold Ph.Ds, 75 percent of all African American army officers, 80 percent of all African American federal judges, and 85 percent of all African American physicians received their undergraduate education at HBCUs. They are responsible for 28 percent of all African Americans who earn bachelor of arts degrees in the United States (Carter & Wilson, 1997). According to William Gray, president of the United Negro College Fund (UNCF),

HBCUs are a major source of African American college graduates and Black professionals in America . . . [yet] our schools have accomplished all this for a fraction of the cost compared to that of majority institutions. (Devarics, 1999, p. 8)

In addition, HBCUs are more affordable (Allen, 1986) and provide more supportive academic and social environments than historically white colleges and universities[2] (Walinksky, 1997; Ross, 1997). In so doing, they recruit, retain, and educate students who, in their absence, would select a two-year institution or elect not to pursue higher education (Constantine, 1995). The success that HBCUs have produced, with meager resources, is indisputable. It is precisely this record of success, and the inability of HWCUs to achieve similar results, which suggests that the preservation and support of these institutions is vital.

In spite of the accomplishments of HBCUs, legal and legislative strategies to increase institutional resources (e.g., physical facilities, instructional materials, programs, faculty salaries) have proven woefully inadequate. The results are decisions that endanger HBCUs and moreover threaten the scope of educational access and educational opportunity for poor nonwhite students in general and for African American students in particular. Further, this situation becomes extremely significant in light of the attack upon and dismantling of affirmative action[3] policies in employment and, more importantly, in admission and scholarship opportunities at HWCUs.

In an era of shrinking appropriations for public education, coupled with the rising costs of higher education, policy agendas for poor nonwhite students and for HBCUs—like those for students and institutions generally—focus heavily upon sources of funding. The current political climate is characterized by calls to eliminate and shrink programmatic budgets. Moreover, a conservative commitment to reduce the federal role in education and eliminate racial identifiability in public policy targets critical federal programs for HBCUs in general and students of color in particular.

With these circumstances in mind, the chapter will first situate the problem of federal student aid and higher educational opportunity within the context of principles of color blindness and race-neutral policies and their effect on subverting and undermining equal educational opportunity under the guise of equal access to institutions of higher education. Second, a brief history of the role of federal policy in higher education will be followed by an examination of the Higher Education Act of 1965 as an intervention strategy to reduce poverty and increase economic opportunity. Third, the chapter will discuss briefly the role of executive and legislative decision-making in dismantling educational opportunity in higher education for poor nonwhite students through the reauthorization of the Higher Education Act of 1986. Policy shifts away from adjusted funding of grants (i.e., Pell Grants) to reliance on student loans as a source of federal aid has been problematic for needy students. Fourth, the chapter will address the tenuous nature of federal support for higher education and the partisan politics that have placed federal dollars for student aid in opposition to funding for social welfare programs. In conclusion, the chapter will propose policy recommendations to address problems with student aid. While discussion of Title III and Title IIIB of the Higher Education Act are equally important to the survival of HBCUs as an essential financial resource, for the purposes of this chapter, Title IV will be examined in a later paper.

COLOR BLINDNESS, RACE NEUTRALITY, AND RACIAL POLITICS

The primary shortcoming in redressing and examining discriminatory policies and practices is an adherence to abstract principles in the face of structural and functional[4] inequalities. Supreme Court Justice John Harlan's lone dissent in the *Plessy* decision stated, "Our Constitution is color-blind, and neither knows nor tolerates classes among citizens" (*Plessy v. Ferguson*, 1896, p. 536). Unfortunately, the Constitution of the United States is not color-blind. For persons of color, women, and the poor, social justice is not a given, nor guaranteed. Asserting that difference does not matter simply perpetuates the conditions under which color, ethnicity, class, and gender matter even more.

The elimination of desegregationist strategies has refocused debate on the singular pursuit of color blindness, which insists neither on numerical balances nor on racial interaction but rather mandates that policy recognize differences only among individuals in the pursuit of "a true community" (Thernstrom & Thernstrom, 1997, p. 540). Color-blind liberalism (Glazer, 1975; Lind, 1995; Sleeper, 1997; Thernstrom & Thernstrom, 1997) with its myopic focus on individuals, fails to address adequately—and much less to dismantle—the group-based social, political, economic, cultural, and legal hierarchies that have historically privileged white Americans in varying degrees while marginalizing nonwhite groups to varying degrees. Neil Gotanda states that color blindness "not only offers a flawed behavioral model for private citizens, but its effectiveness in promoting social change is limited" (Gotanda, 1995, p. 269). In short, after the broad strokes of legal and legislative change, these color-blind and race-neutral policies and practices offer no strategy to redress and combat covert forms of discrimination and prejudice in public education let alone employment, housing, health care, or juvenile justice.

Concomitantly, the use of a color-blind standard locates social justice in the absence of racial awareness—a fictional state. Color blindness falsely conflates conscious recognition with prejudice and discrimination, failing to differentiate positive distinction from the promotion of group-based bias. Derrick Bell (1995) states that "we live in a time of racial rejection," which, whether undergirded by fear, guilt, greed, genuine commitment to principles of equality, or other rationales, has grave practical costs. Color blindness not only spares white citizens the responsibility of wrong-doing but robs them of the agency to be morally and socially just. Ignoring difference deprives people of both the harsh realities and the ultimate rewards of redressing problems associated with race. Both are losses for equity and social justice. Equity is the foundation of social justice.

To protect equity and promote social justice, differentiated or particularized policies are appropriate and necessary. For poor and nonwhite students, other things are not equal. Color-blind liberalism, followed by race-neutral policies, contributes to this negative condition. Hence equal opportunity and equal results must not be relinquished in favor of pursuing only the individualist goal of equal access. Fairness suggests that these three pillars undergird the foundations of social justice. The elimination or distortion of any of these pillars makes ineffectual the promises of equal opportunity—not to mention equal justice—under the law for all Americans.

The dismantling of civil rights policies and practices and the acceptance of color blindness as the basis for social, economic, and political opportunity blossomed under the executive leadership of presidents Ronald Reagan and George Herbert Walker Bush. Much of this was accomplished through conservative judicial appointments to the federal district courts, appellate courts, and most importantly, the Supreme Court.

Supreme Court justices appointed by Republican presidents Reagan and Bush have resulted in a conservative judiciary that opposes the federal role of courts in the battle against discrimination in employment, housing, criminal justice, and education. Jurists appointed and elected at the state level during this period further undermined important civil rights decisions in employment, education (lower-level and postsecondary), and housing discrimination but also helped to eliminate the social safety net for the most vulnerable in our society: the poor, children, and youth of color. In no uncertain terms, the courts have made discrimination suits more difficult to prove, and thus, where race and gender are concerned, they are subject to "strict scrutiny" and justified only by a "compelling interest of the state."[5] In addition, the courts have narrowed the focus of affirmative action in an attempt to eliminate it. This becomes all the more problematic when we consider the fact that courts do not operate independently of public opinion but often follow public opinion.

THE ROLE OF FEDERAL SUPPORT IN HIGHER EDUCATION

It is often observed that the government of the United States has no unified policy with respect to higher education. Instead, a multiplicity of federal policies, managed by different departments, initiatives, programs, agencies, offices, and associations under the supervision of committees of Congress, influence higher education in diverse ways. Congress, for example, designs tax laws in such a way as to be favorable to nonprofit educational institutions. The National Science Foundation and the Departments of Defense and Energy rely on universities to carry out basic and applied research. The G.I. Bill used higher education, at least in part, as a way to reward veterans while educating and preparing them to build a burgeoning industrial complex in the United States. In short, almost every agency of the government, as it carries out its tasks, develops some relationship to higher education (Keppel, 1987).

Yet, no department of the federal government, including the Department of Education, has been given direct responsibility for institutions of higher learning (Keppel, 1987). State governments are largely responsible for the public institutions that provide higher education for 80 percent of students; private institutions take much of the responsibility for the college education of the remaining 20 percent. Federal involvement in higher education policymaking historically reflects a reluctance to tread on state autonomy as established by the Tenth Amendment.[6] However, federal constraints may be mandated to expand access and opportunity to guarantee fairness. For example, the Morrill Act I of 1862 and Morrill Act II of 1890 extended educational opportunities in the form of financial funding to HBCUs. The Morrill Acts were necessary to ensure that land-grant colleges serving African Americans received at least minimal funding.

The Smith-Lever Act of 1914 made available the resources of academic research and teaching to nonstudent members of surrounding communities. The G.I. Bill rewarded World War II veterans for service and provided resources in the form of vocational, undergraduate, graduate, and professional education to ease the transition of servicemen from military to civilian life. However, through the decade of the 1950s, "one of the most distinctive attributes of America's political culture had been the tenacity with which the United States, unlike most nations, had resisted a national education policy" (Graham, 1984, p. xvii).

The National Defense Education Act (NDEA) of 1958[7] represented a turning point for federal involvement in lower-level and postsecondary education (Parsons, 1997). In brief, the NDEA authorized student loans for college;[8] fellowships for graduate school; grants for guidance, counseling, and testing; and grants for research centers and teacher training institutes to improve foreign language instruction; as well as matching grants to public schools or loans to private schools for equipment needed to teach science, mathematics, and foreign languages. The NDEA demonstrated a national interest "in the quality of education that states, communities and private institutions provided" (Sundquist, 1968, p. 168). However, like previous policies, the enactment of the NDEA proved the answer to a national need as much as to a need among citizens. In other words, the Morrill Acts I and II and the G.I. Bill were as much a means to invigorate the national economy as they were a means to help people.

In the midst of post–World War II, the Cold War, and industrial expansion, President Dwight Eisenhower, pressured by the Soviet Union's successful launch and orbit of the Sputnik rocket, faced increasing criticism of the country's education system. The belief was that curricula in public and private schools were not competitive, particularly in the sciences, engineering, and mathematics. Using the perceived weakness of programs in the aforementioned areas, the president advanced policies that overcame the obstacles of religion and race that had undermined prior attempts at major federal aid to education (Thomas, 1975). As a result, the most staunch states' rights opponents found it difficult to oppose education as a means of national defense.

As such, education again was a means to a larger national end rather than an end in itself. Further, the NDEA's success demonstrated that national education policy was negotiable. In fact, it assisted in widening the federal role in higher education and therein paving the way for the Higher Education Act of 1965 (HEA), which remains the defining piece of legislation relating to U.S. postsecondary education policy.

FEDERAL INTERVENTION AND THE WAR ON POVERTY

In 1965, President Lyndon Baines Johnson's administration and Congress were working together in harmony, as the executive branch, the House, and the Senate were all controlled by the Democratic Party. When it was passed in the fall of 1965, the Higher Education Act came closer to affecting all institutions of higher education than any federal legislation since the G.I. Bill in the years following World War II. On November 8,

1965, President Lyndon Baines Johnson signed the Higher Education Act of 1965 (Pub. L. No 89–329) at his alma mater, Southwestern Texas State College, stating:

This bill is only one more than two dozen education measures enacted by the first session of the 89th Congress. And history will forever record that this session— the first session of the 89th Congress—did more for the wonderful cause of education in America than all the previous 176 regular sessions of Congress put together . . . I consider the Higher Education Act—with its companion, the Elementary and Secondary Education Act of 1965, which we signed back in the spring of this year to be the keystones of this great fabulous 89th Congress. (*New York Times*, November 9, 1965, p. 28)

The HEA was considered by President Johnson an integral part of the Great Society programs of the mid-'60s. In fact, the HEA was intended, along with the Economic Opportunity Act, the Civil Rights Act of 1964, and the Elementary and Secondary Education Act, to eliminate poverty and discrimination. In tandem, the Elementary and Secondary Education Act (ESEA) and HEA secured education's place as a policy issue rather than a policy tool.

In President Johnson's administration, the War on Poverty guided many of the federal policy decisions (e.g., Head Start, Guaranteed Student Loans). Education developed a national mission: to give poor citizens educational access and opportunities as a means of social, economic, and political equality. Thus, HEA and ESEA were designed not so much to strengthen institutions themselves as to further a social cause through educational advancement. With its eight titles granting aid directly to institutions as well as to students, the HEA provided the first comprehensive federal assistance policy designed for higher education. Enacted initially for only two years, it has been subject to periodic reauthorization. Briefly, the titles are listed in Table 4.1.

With this in mind, the chapter will now focus on Title IV (student aid). Title IV provides funding to institutions serving students from low socioeconomic backgrounds. Historically Black Colleges and Universities continue to educate a disproportionate number of students from poor communities. Due to their low economic status, many of these students would not have the opportunity to attend a private or public college without federal support. In short, both student opportunity and HBCU enrollments depend upon financial aid packages.

REAUTHORIZATIONS OF TITLE IV

Title IV, written in 1965 to address the need for student financial aid, carried by far the largest authorizations and appropriations. In 1965, both the executive branch and Congress were particularly concerned about the inability of the poor to finance college education and about the resulting

Table 4.1
Higher Education Act of 1965: Titles I–VIII

Title I:	expanding the land-grant extension concept to urban universities;
Title II:	improving college and university libraries;
Title III:	assisting "developing institutions" directly;*
Title IV:	financing students directly through:
	1. Educational opportunity Grants to institutions (a scholarship fund);
	2. Expansion of the NDEA student loan program
	3. Guaranteed Student Loans (GSLs)
	4. College work study;
Title V:	establishing the National Teachers Corp;
Title VI:	improving undergraduate instruction;
Title VII:	amending the Higher Education Facilities Act;†
Title VIII:	outlining the general provisions for all of the above.

*This language was an expressly tailored veil for HBCUs, which are the primary recipients of this funding.

†The HEFA, creating a five-year program of matching grants and loans for construction projects, was part of the Kennedy administration's education policy package. After the assassination of President Kennedy, it was one of the only pieces of education legislation to carry over into the Johnson administration.

Source: Adapted from Higher Education Act of 1965, Pub. L. No. 89–329, 89th Cong., 1st sess., Nov. 8, 1965, pp. 1–34. Washington, DC: GPO.

loss of talent for society as a whole. The Senate Committee report noted:

The pressing requirement for fresh, vigorous congressional action in the general field of student assistance cannot be emphasized too strongly. . . . the aggravated plight of students who do not have the means to acquire education, demonstrates in clear terms the extent and depth of the problem. (Higher Education Act of 1965, p. 35)

Similarly, the House Committee report of July 1965 argued for student aid from the standpoint of developing talent for the good of the entire society:

. . . a recent study financed by the office of education, indicated all too clearly the appalling frequency with which a student is presently forced to forego the opportunity of postsecondary education because of inability to meet costs. (Higher Education Act of 1965, p. 21)

A key point of debate in the reauthorization of Title IV has been whether institutional or student assistance should be the culmination goal of federal involvement in postsecondary education. Negotiation in 1972 proved definitive on this question. Claiborne Pell (D-RI), then chair of the Subcommittee on Education, proposed a bill targeting individual equal opportunity. The key component was the creation of the Basic Educational Opportunity Grant (BEOG), which would guarantee a minimum amount of financial support for students, especially part-time and accredited vocational students. The BEOG, paid directly to students, could be used at any institution. The purpose was to assure students support and encourage greater interest in higher education. As BEOGs combined with existing Supplemental Educational Opportunity Grants (SEOGs) and NDEA loans, the federal government soon became the largest direct funding source for students.

The final amendment in 1972 reflected the congressional conclusion that "the Federal government has an obligation to people rather than institutions. . . . " Congress decided to place decisions "in the hands of the 'consumer' . . . rather than in the 'conduits' . . . " (Gladieux & Wolanin, 1976, p. 110). Important here is the fact that the defeat for institutions as the focus of policy would manifest their problem as a weak and arguably complacent collective lobby. Further, in 1972, education associations such as the American Council on Education and the National Association of State Universities and Land-Grant Colleges were positioned to take an active role in reauthorization.

While the organizations were included in the preliminary decision-making process (hearings and roundtables), their failure to lobby effectively made it easier for Senator Pell to push his student aid package through both the House and Senate. More precisely, their failure to provide a coherent presence consigned them to the fringes of the decision-making process. It was a Democratic Congress that garnered a stronger position. From 1958 to 1972 only the executive office had initiated and steered successful education policy proposals. Hereafter, Congress would play an even larger role.[9]

President Gerald Ford's administration was virtually silent in the 1976 reauthorizations. A few changes, however, were made. Among the most significant were: an increase in the maximum BEOG level, state incentives for the establishment of loan programs, and a restatement of the federal policy's basic goals of equal educational opportunity, access, and school choice. But issues were raised about grants and loans that would be revisited in 1980.

Middle-class discontent with a growing inability to meet the costs of higher education fueled the 1980 negotiation. Republicans pushed for tuition tax credits. Democrats expressed concern that this initiative would compromise the position of poorer families by breaking the informal but functional partnership between BEOGs and loans. Soon, tax credits began to replace loans as the building blocks of college finance; the least advantaged would suffer. Yet, without middle-class support, political backing for loan programs would disappear. In a compromise measure to prevent tax credits, President Jimmy Carter backed the Middle Income Assistance Act (MIAA) of 1978, which eliminated income requirements for Guaranteed Student Loans (GSLs).

The significance of the MIAA is that it forced Title IV student assistance beyond its original purpose of ensuring educational opportunity for the poor and students of color. Extending the student loan program to middle- and upper-income students diverted the focus of student financial aid from those who needed it most and, more importantly, from those whose collective voice is often unheard. With these changes, the BEOG was renamed the Pell Grant in honor of Senator Claiborne Pell and was no longer considered the foundation of college and university finance. Loans quickly took priority, and financial lenders became more visible players in the policymaking process.

Lenders were encouraged to become more involved through an increase in the special allowance paid to GSL lender institutions. This allowance comprised a 3.5 percent interest subsidy on top of the 90-day Treasury-Bill rate. Because the government guaranteed loans, lenders were assured a profit and were completely protected against losses. As a result, by 1985, the GSL program had grown to include 12,100 banks, 8,650 schools, 58 state and private guarantee agencies, 30 secondary markets, 22 loan servicers, and nine collection agencies, as well as the government's own Student Loan Marketing Association (Sallie Mae). With the inauguration of Ronald Reagan as president, cuts in spending for social and educational programs worsened the position of poor families of color.

RETRENCHMENT AND FEDERAL POLICY IN THE 1980s

The presidency of Ronald Reagan marked a dramatic repositioning of the executive office in negotiations. The economic, educational, and political atmosphere in which Congress considered amendments to the Higher Education Act in 1986 had changed markedly since 1965. Defense Department expenditures had risen substantially in recent years. Both Jimmy Carter and Ronald Reagan had, in effect, campaigned successfully on platforms opposed to big federal government, and it was no longer fashionable to turn to federal government for solutions to domestic problems; in 1986 it was not even suggested. The president and Congress in 1986 were seeking to blame each other for the mounting deficit, which had not been an issue in 1965.

Still, 21 years after the passage of the HEA, President Reagan signed the Higher Education Amendments of 1986 (Pub. L. No. 99–498; see Table 4.2), stating:

This administration has always supported, and will continue to support, programs properly designed to help our neediest young people acquire higher education. . . . I do have concerns about S. 1965 [Pub. L. No. 99–948], however. The bill does little to meet the Administration's major objectives for higher education: Restoring more appropriate and equitable student aid funding roles to states, schools, students and their families; targeting assistance on truly needy students; and eliminating excessive subsidies to interdisciplinary institutions such as banks, schools,

Table 4.2
Higher Education Amendments of 1986: Titles I–IV

Title I:	Postsecondary Programs for Nontraditional Students
	Part A: Program and Planning Grants
	Part B: National Programs
	Part C: The National Advisory Council on Continuing Education
Title II:	Libraries
Title III:	Institutional Aid
	Part A: Strengthening Institutions
	Part B: Strengthening Historically Black Colleges and Universities
	Part C: Challenge Grants for Institutions Eligible for Assistance Under Part A and Part B
	Part D: General Provisions
Title IV:	Student Assistance
	Part A: Grants to Students in Attendance at Institutions of Higher Education
	Subpart 1: Basic Educational Opportunity Grants
	Subpart 2: Supplemental Educational Opportunity Grants
	Subpart 3: Grants to States for State Student Incentives
	Subpart 4: Special Programs for Students from Disadvantaged Backgrounds
	Subpart 5: Special programs for Students Whose Families are Engaged in Migrant and Seasonal Farmwork
	Subpart 6: Robert C. Byrd Honors Scholarship Program
	Subpart 7: Assistance to Institutions of Higher Education
	Subpart 8: Special Childcare Services for Disadvantaged College Students
	Part B: Guaranteed Student Loan Program
	Part C: Work-Study Programs
	Part D: Income Contingent Direct Loan Demonstration Project
	Part E: Direct Loans to Students in Institutions of Higher Education
	Part F: Need Analysis
	Part G: General Provisions Relating to Student Assistance Programs

Source: Adapted from the United States Code Congressional and Administrative News, 99th Cong., 2nd sess. Member and Committees. No. 16, December 1986, pp. 1266–1273.

and loan-guarantee agencies. . . . I am signing this bill because the basic Higher Education Act authorities provide aid to deserving students and support important programs. However, the Administration remains committed to improving the higher education programs and to reducing their costs to the American taxpayer. We will continue to propose necessary changes and cost savings. (*Chronicle of Higher Education*, 1986, pp. 18–19)

According to Keppel (1989), congressional committees dealing with higher education, along with the higher education community itself, were caught up in the administration's policy triage. They had to choose between reducing defense expenditures and raising taxes. They could reduce social spending or take the blame for a federal deficit of unprecedented proportions. The congressional committees on education had direct influence only on the third option, social spending.

In the end, one result of the public policy decisions made during the Reagan administration was to force the education committees in the House and Senate to cut back on existing programs and to eliminate entirely some important ideas and proposals that involved major expenditures. The principal effect was to limit sharply the growth of Pell Grants, thereby discouraging the poor, especially nonwhites, from attempting higher education, and to restrict recruitment and special compensatory programs, such as TRIO.[10]

Included in President Reagan's first proposal to Congress were:

- limitation of Pell Grants to only the difference between actual academic costs and family and/or student contribution(s);
- limitation of GSLs to only remaining need, defined as academic costs minus all other aid and expected contributions;
- elimination of a provision that allowed GSLs to replace family contribution(s); and
- elimination of the GSL in-school interest subsidy and the post-school grace period.

While the package did not pass muster in the Democratically controlled Congress, its neoconservative agenda was apparent. These recommendations proved disastrous for poor and nonwhite students. These students could not count on levels of family support commensurate (either in amounts or percentages) with those of middle- and upper-income students. For example, African Americans, who are often the first generation to attend college, are required more frequently than others to cover their own tuition costs and school fees. With these limitations on the amounts covered by grants and loans, their chances for entrance, let alone matriculation, are seriously reduced.

Unshaken by congressional voting during reauthorization, the administration worked diligently toward its goals through a series of budget cuts—for instance, a $200 million reduction in the Pell Grant fund in 1981 and a 12 percent overall reduction of student aid funds in 1982. The president reinstated the need requirement for GSLs, which cut middle-class access. Ironically, this move allowed the administration to position itself as the voice of the disenfranchised while Democrats fought to preserve support for the middle class. Moreover, student Social Security benefits were eliminated and appropriation levels were capped as the purchasing power of federal aid declined in real terms.

Parsons (1997) describes the political climate surrounding higher education policy as openly hostile by 1986. Among other measures, the president promised to close the Department of Education, symbolizing his commitment to eliminating the federal role in education. The presence of this kind of overt threat galvanized the education lobby, which allied itself with more liberal coalitions in Congress. The White House, backed by the Republican Senate, made no formal policy recommendations (hoping to maintain the status quo) and focused on foiling aggressive recommendations from other camps. Though the battles were significant, the House managed to pass several reforms, including:

- increases in Pell Grants and GSLs;
- a three-year GSL deferment for students pursuing teaching careers;
- an extension of the loan grace period from six to nine months; and
- the elimination of excessive subsidies to intermediary lending institutions such as banks, schools, and loan-guarantee agencies.

While these gains were significant, student aid policy moved from a reliance on grants to a reliance on student loans as a means of financial support. The change in student aid policy was reflective both of market variables reshaping public elementary and secondary education (magnet and charter schools, vouchers, home schooling) and of egalitarian and meritocratic policies. More importantly, though, changes in student assistance served to further entrench the loss of access and opportunity for poor nonwhite students.

OPPORTUNITY DENIED: GRANTS VERSUS STUDENT LOANS IN THE 1990s

In spite of the aforementioned and other modest reprieves legislated during the presidency of George Bush, educational and social policy continued to drift in a direction that further disadvantaged poor and nonwhite students during the late 1980s and early 1990s. In higher education, the principal factor in this condition was and continues to be the shift from grants to loans as the bedrock of student financial aid. This policy focus has been pivotal in the relatively low college participation rates among low-income students, particularly African Americans.

The grant/loan imbalance represents a complete abandonment of the original equal opportunity mission for federal aid to poor nonwhite students enshrined in the Civil Rights Act of 1964, the Economic Opportunity Act, and the Higher Education Act of 1965.

In 1992, a liberal congressional coalition delivered a proposal to give Pell Grants entitlement status and guarantee automatic increases coordinated with overall inflation rates. The Bush administration objected strongly to expansion of the program, and congressional Republicans as well as bipartisan Budget Committee leadership (in both houses) backed the White House. The measure did not pass in either the Senate or the House. As a counterinitiative, Congress approved increases in maximum loan levels and increases in the Pell Grant authorization. However, Pell Grant authorization levels are not guaranteed, and there has been a growing gap between those levels and actual appropriations.

ROBBING PETER TO PAY PAUL

Through 1997, Pell Grants were authorized at $2,700 (see Table 4.3). Former House Speaker Newt Gingrich (R-GA) and Senate Majority Leader Trent Lott (R-MS) made a commitment to education tax cuts in writing. The Republican leaders planned to provide roughly $35 billion over five years for postsecondary education, including a deduction and tax credit:

We believe this package should be consistent with the objectives put forward in the Hope scholarship and tuition tax proposals contained in the administration's FY 1998 budget to assist middle-class parents. (Devarics, 1997b, p. 10)

The package shows that President William Jefferson Clinton and Republican leaders agreed to provide a $300 increase in the Pell Grant and to protect programs such Goals 2000, educational technology, Head Start, and bilingual education. However, federal funding for discretionary education, training, and social service programs not protected by the agreement was to remain frozen at $43.4 billion a year from 1998 to 2002. Programs that rely on this money include Chapter I education, college work/study, Title III funds (aid to HBCUs), and many job-training and social service programs.

In addition, Conservative Republicans pledged to eliminate unprotected programs such as AmeriCorps, President Clinton's national service program providing grant aid for higher education. Despite House and

Table 4.3
Federal Support for Higher Education Programs

Program Funds	1997 Plan	White House 1998 1998 Plan	House Plan 1998 Plan	Senate
HBCUs	$108. 90	$113.00	$120.00	$108.90
HBCU Graduate Institutions	$19.60	$19.60	$25.00	$525.00
TRIO	$500.00	$525.00	$532.00	$525.00
Pell Grants (max in dollars	$2,700.00	$3,000.00	$3,000.00	$3,000.00
College (Work-study	$830.00	$857.00	$860.00	$830.00

Source: Budget of the United States Government, Fiscal Year 2000, pp. 358–374. Washington, DC: GPO; National Center for Educational Statistics: Digest of Educational Statistics 1998, U.S. Department of Educational Research and Improvement, p. 342.

Senate passage, the agreement also faced opposition from many groups such as the Congressional Black Caucus (CBC), which criticized provisions such as capital-gains tax cuts and increases in defense spending. In response, the CBC developed its own alternative budget proposing funding for Head Start, Chapter I, and TRIO programs that recruit poor youth for college. "The Congressional Black Caucus makes no tax cuts until the federal budget is balanced," said Representative William Clay (D-MO), senior Democrat on the House Education Committee. "Unlike the so-called deal [between the White House and Republicans], the CBC budget does not seek a balanced budget on the backs of our nation's neediest families" (Devarics, 1997c, p. 9).

The bipartisan package also drew mixed reviews from some who noted that the package treated affluent households better than less affluent ones. Senator Paul Wellstone (D-MN), a staunch opponent of the package, which provided few or no tax credits for those with minimal or no income tax liability, noted, "With all the discussion about HOPE scholarships and tax credits, all families with incomes below $28,000 a year are not going to become eligible" (Devarics, 1997a, p. 27). Moreover, Windham (1984) found that "the very students and parents most likely to apply for assistance are the ones most likely, because of past extant educational and social disadvantage, to have difficulty in accommodating to the complex and arbitrary demands of the student assistance income reporting and documentation requirement" (p. 27).

Adding to the problem, relatively well-off families are receiving aid these days. The strategic use of merit aid to enroll students worries some supporters of traditional need-based scholarships. Many colleges provide merit aid—grants offered to students the schools wish to recruit, whether because of their high test scores and grades or record of community service. A student's chance of getting a break on tuition at a school depends heavily on how he or she ranks against the competition. Hence, instead of spending $20,000 on one needy student, private colleges may find it more financially advantageous to offer, for example, four affluent students $5,000 apiece in merit aid. Each of the four students enticed by the merit money often brings to the university thousands of extra dollars in tuition revenue through scholarships and student loans. Ben Wildalvsky (1999) asserts, "What you're basically doing is taking money away from the poor kids because you can get more for the buck for the middle-class and the merit kids" (p. 68).

The competition by students for the best merit aid packages was rivaled only by President Clinton's bipartisan agreement that shifted the focus of the spending debates. In brief, plans to increase education spending required equal offsetting cuts in social programs. Because proposals to boost education with cuts in defense are generally ruled out of order, lawmakers had two alternatives: use the tax code, or force domestic programs to compete against each other for limited funds—as in the case of Pell Grants versus social welfare programs. In effect, every increase in federal student aid would come with a concomitant cut in aid for social programs crucial to the social, emotional, and educational development of children and youth seeking educational opportunity.

Because the balanced budget agreement required correspondence between authorization and appropriations, students would actually receive the full increase. However, the current purchasing power of the Pell Grant is so limited that $3,000 promises too little for students in desperate need. Tuition costs have risen approximately 250 percent since 1980. The Pell Grant has increased only 75 percent. Today these grants cover less than 30 percent of college costs. Further, grants from the president's Helping Outstanding Pupils Educationally (HOPE) scholarship ($1,500) and AmeriCorps[11] programs only begin to scratch the surface of the aid needed to make higher education affordable. Furthermore, student loan costs have soared, with student debt rising from $21 million to well over $150 million from 1980 to 1999. For poor and nonwhite students, the financial burden of higher education has become excessive.

CONCLUSION AND POLICY RECOMMENDATIONS FOR HIGHER EDUCATION OPPORTUNITY

Federal support must return to its original mission of ensuring equal opportunity for poor students of color under the BEOG grant. To achieve this end, refocusing requires enhancement of the Pell Grant to reverse the grant/loan imbalance. Some possible suggestions:

- the Pell Grant must return to the center of the financial aid package;
- the Pell Grant must be separate from yet supplement other initiatives such as President Clinton's Hope Scholarship in the national needs assessment formula. Students must be eligible for both; and
- the Pell Grant must be guaranteed significant increases over time in order to restore balance to the grant/loan partnership. An example of a viable proposal is the College Access and Affordability Act, introduced by Rep. William Clay (D-MO), which would guarantee an annual $300 raise in the Pell Grant for the next five years.

Concurrently, federal loans must be made a more accessible and viable option for the poor and students of color. The Clinton administration offered several creative repayment options (e.g., Peace Corps, the National Health Service Corps) and special Internal Revenue Service plans for those who choose low-salaried service careers. Additionally, the following proposals may serve to restore grant/loan opportunities:

- eliminating loan origination fees for poorer students;
- reducing in-school interest rates; and
- restoring interest rate deductibility to the tax code, and removing scholarships and fellowships from taxable income status.

A student assistance plan that front-loads financial aid with grants in the first two years of study then back-loads with loans in the remaining two to three years of study appears more promising than financial aid packages structured primarily from fixed or subsidized loans. Many students leave school during their freshman or sophomore year. For African American students, financial aid comprises a major factor in recruitment as well as retention in higher education. Thus, if initial financial aid packages were composed of less than 20 percent loans, these students would have a better chance to matriculate through public and private undergraduate institutions. Moreover, default rates at HBCUs and HWCUs might decrease, as the federal government stands a far better chance of repayment from students who complete their degree programs. This last point is significant not only to students but to HBCUs.

The problem of default rates poses a threat not only to the future of student aid but also to the future of HBCUs with rates high enough to risk federal censure. The government requires institutional cooperation in encouraging students to repay their debts. In cases of excessive default, institutions are eliminated from federal program eligibility. Disqualification would threaten closure for most HBCUs, which would see enrollments drop critically without the ability to provide student aid packages. In 1993, nearly half of all HBCUs (public and private) suffered soaring default rates. However, a government intervention in the form a crackdown on institutions has mandated corrections. As a result, institutions are required to show due diligence in the collections process. This effort is achieved through mandatory exit interviews for students and enhanced procedures for alumni. However, for all HBCUs the balance is tenuous.

In 2000, Republican leaders signaled a willingness to provide additional funding for student aid for programs such as the Pell Grant. In fact, House GOP leaders endorsed a $400 increase in the maximum grant, the same amount requested by the UNCF and other organizations. However, the Clinton administration urged higher education organizations not to support the overall Republican budget plan, which it believed would result in cuts for education and social service programs.

When we consider that higher education institutions, especially HBCUs, continue to provide gateways to social, economic, and political opportunity and social justice for students, then particularized federal policy is needed. In the words of William Gray, "The nation's historically Black colleges and universities, Hispanic-serving institutions, and other minority institutions are best suited to enroll and educate tomorrow's workforce" (Devarics, 1999, p. 8). Changes in federal loan policy can help to make corrections more permanent. Other things remain unequal for poor nonwhite students, and therefore HBCUs need America's investment in its institutions and, more importantly, its students, rather than color-blind policies.

NOTES

1. Historically black colleges and universities (hereafter cited as HBCUs) refer to the more than 100 public and private institutions founded primarily for African Americans, although their institutional charters were not racially exclusionary. These institutions, serving or identified with service to African Americans, were established 50 to 150 years ago.

2. Historically white colleges and universities (hereafter referred to as HWCUs) refer to public institutions that were founded primarily for white citizens. Their institutional charters were in most instances racially exclusionary, not allowing for the admission of persons of color. These institutions served or were identified with service to white Americans.

3. Affirmative action has been defined as "steps taken to remedy the grossly disparate staffing and recruitment patterns that are present consequences of past

discrimination and to prevent the occurrence of employment discrimination in the future" (United States Civil Rights Commission).

4. Functional and structural analysis: Key questions draw attention to a fundamental epistemological question regarding how the terms of social and political analysis are to be defined. In essence, are social entities defined by what they do (operational definitions) or by what they are (nominal definitions)? Initially, political scientists adopted a structural view based upon nominal definitions. They assumed that the essential character of each social action or governmental body could be properly defined. Thus, we have the three branches of government—executive, legislative, and judicial. Functionalists, by contrast, insist that structure does not create governmental integrity; function does. Relying on operational definitions, functionalists define the basic elements of government by their results rather than their essential character. This debate has been examined in discussions of legal theory. In reviewing the role of the Supreme Court, strict constructionists hold a structural view of governance, believing that law is embodied entirely in its historic forms (constitution and statute). By contrast, judicial activists see law functionally, emphasizing the functional importance of producing just outcomes rather than preserving constitutional forms.

5. Strict scrutiny is applied when a policy or practice that discriminates based on race, national origin, or alienage is strictly scrutinized and can be justified only if compelling state interest can be proven. More importantly, strict scrutiny places the burden to prove a prima facie case of discrimination.

6. The Tenth Amendment to the Constitution reserves for the states those powers not delegated to the federal government in the Constitution. The provision of education is not mentioned in the Constitution; therefore, it has been left to state governments.

7. The National Defense Education Act provided assistance to state and local systems for strengthening instruction in science, math, modern foreign language, and other critical subjects, and improvement of state statistical services, guidance counseling, testing services, and training institutes. Most importantly, it provided funds for higher education student loans and fellowships.

8. These loans contained a provision for up to 50 percent forgiveness of the principal at a rate of 10 percent annually for every year the student taught public school.

9. Despite educational policy proposals, Richard Millhouse Nixon's proposals rallied little to no support from education associations such as the American Council on Education (ACE). The associations were suspicious of the president's political platform on education.

10. TRIO is a group of five federal support service programs designed for students who are economically disadvantaged or handicapped, and generally for members of groups who have been historically underrepresented in higher education. The programs, which include Talent Search, Upward Bound, Special Services for Disadvantaged Students, Equal Opportunity Centers, and Staff Development Activities, are funded under Title IV, subpart 4 of the Higher Education Act (Special Programs for Students from Disadvantaged Backgrounds).

11. The U.S. Corporation for National Service, created by Congress in 1993, offers Americans of all ages and backgrounds opportunities to strengthen their communities through service, as well as to earn money to pay for higher education. The organization's programs include Learn and Service America, a grants

program supporting teachers and community members who involve young people in service that relates to studies in school.

REFERENCES

Allen, W. (1986). *Gender and campus race differences in black student academic performance, racial attitudes and college satisfaction.* Atlanta: Southern Education Foundation.

Bell, D. (1995). Racial realism. In K. Crenshaw, N. Gotanda, G. Peller, & K. Thomas (Eds.), *Critical race theory.* New York: New Press.

Carter, D. J., & Wilson, R. (1997). *Minorities in higher education.* Washington: American Council on Higher Education.

Claibourne, P., Gladieux, L. E., & Thomas, R. (1976). *Congress and the colleges.* Lexington, MA: D.C. Heath.

Constantine, J. M. (1995). The effect of attending historically black colleges and universities on future wages of black students. *Industrial and Labor Relations Review, 48*(3), 538–539.

Devarics, C. (1997a). Despite criticism congress commits to educational tax cuts. *Black Issues in Higher Education.*

Devarics, C. (1997b). Robbing Peter to pay Paul: Reauthorizing the Higher Education Act amid the new political reality means some programs may lose so that others might gain. *Black Issues in Higher Education, 14*(16), 26–29.

Devarics, C. (1997c). Washington update. *Black Issues in Higher Education, 6.*

Devarics, C. (1999). UNCF urges more federal funding for black colleges in 2000. *Black Issues in Higher Education, 16*(6), 8–10.

Doyle, D. P., & Hartle, T. W. (1986). Student-aid muddle. *Atlantic, 257,* 32.

Du Bois, W. E. B. (1935). Does the Negro need separate schools? *Journal of Negro Education, 4.*

Elementary and Secondary Education Act of 1965.

Gladieux, L. E. (1980). What has congress wrought? *Change, 12,* 25–31.

Gladieux, L. E., Hauptman, A. E., & Green-Knapp, L. (1994). The federal government and higher education. In P. G. Altbach, R. O. Berdahl, & P. J. Gumport (Eds.), *Higher education in American society.* New York: Prometheus Books.

Gladieux, L. E. & Wolanin, T. R. (1976) Congress and the Colleges: The National Politics of Higher Education, Lexington, Mass.: Heath.

Glazer N. (1975). *Affirmative discrimination.* New York: Basic Books.

Gotanda, N. (1995). A critique of "Our constitution is color-blind." In K. Crenshaw, N. Gotanda, G. Peller, & K. Thomas (Eds.), *Critical race theory.* New York: New Press.

Graham, H. D. (1984). *The uncertain triumph.* Chapel Hill: University of North Carolina Press.

Greene, L. (1995). Race in the twenty-first century. In K. Crenshaw, N. Gotanda, G. Peller, & K. Thorne (Eds.), *Critical race theory.* New York: New Press.

Keppel, F. (1987). The Higher Education Acts Contrasted, 1965–1986: Has Federal Policy Come of Age. Harvard Educational Review, vol. 57, no. 1, pp. 49–67.

Lind, M. (1995). *The next American nation.* New York: Free Press.

Morrill Act, Statutes at large, vol. 12, ch. 130 1862 (Morrill Act I).

Morrill Act, Statutes at large, vol. 26, ch. 841 1890 (Morrill Act II).

National Defense and Education Act of 1958, Public Law 85–864, 72 Stat. 1580.

Nettles, M. T. (1991). Racial similarities and differences in the predictors of college student achievement. In W. Allen, E. G. Epps, & N. Z. Haniff (Eds.), *College in black and white.* Albany: State University of New York Press.

Norputh, H., & Segal, J. (1994). Popular influence on Supreme Court decisions. *American Political Science Review, 88*(3).

Parsons, M. D. (1997). *Power and politics.* Albany: State University of New York Press.

Roebuck, J. B., & Murty, K. S. (1993). *Historically black colleges and universities.* Westport, CT: Praeger.

Sleeper, J. (1997). *Liberal racism.* New York: Viking.

Smith-Levers Act of 1914, U.S. Code 1988 title 7, Stat. 372, May 8.

Stanfield, R. L. (1982). Student aid lobby learns new tricks to field Reagan's spending cutbacks. *National Journal, 14.*

Sundquist, J. L. (1968). *Politics and policy.* Washington, DC: Brookings Institution.

Thernstrom, S., & Thernstrom, A. (1997). *America in black and white.* New York: Simon and Schuster.

Thomas, N. (1975). *Education in national politics.* New York: David McKay.

United States Commission on Civil Rights. Statement of Affirmative Action for Equal Employment Opportunities. Washington, DC: author.

Walinsky, H. (1997). *Students at historically black colleges and universities.* Princeton, NJ: Policy Information Center.

Wildavsky, B. (1999). Is that the real price? *U.S. News & World Report, 127*(9), 64–70.

Windham, D. M. (1984). Federal financial aid policy: The case of the Pell Grant quality control study. *Review of Higher Education, 7*(4), 397–410.

CHAPTER 5

Interinstitutional Policies: Initiatives for Advancing African American Success in Higher Education

Wynetta Lee

INTRODUCTION

Barbara Jordan, an African American twentieth-century icon, once said, "Education remains the key to both economic and political empowerment" (Bell, 1995, p. 109). Research indicates that there is truth to her words since there is a relationship between education and earnings (Nettles & Perna, 1997). African Americans in the United States historically have been at a comparative disadvantage to whites in terms of both the end (economic and political power) and the means to the end (education). Historically black colleges and universities (HBCUs) have made a tremendous contribution to narrowing the education attainment gap between African Americans and whites, thereby enhancing economic and political power among African Americans. This success, however, has largely resulted from the aggregated performance of individual institutions working rather independently to establish appropriate curricular and extracurricular programs to foster success among traditional African American college students (18 to 24 years old, matriculation immediately following high school). Without question, this role must be continued well into the new millennium. Nonetheless, the emphasis on traditional African American students should be expanded to include a broader, more diverse undergraduate population seeking degree attainment. In higher education, adult African American students (25-plus years old), women (all races), and students from lower socioeconomic backgrounds are currently underserved and too often are unsuccessful (attrition prior to degree completion). HBCUs are equipped to promote the success of a broader, tremendously diverse underserved student population by build-ing on the lessons learned from educating traditional African American students.

This new role for HBCUs in the new millennium will require modi-fications in institutional policy that will redirect institutional practice, particularly those pertaining to student recruitment priorities and inter-institutional relationships. "Policy is the articulation of decisions made to systematically address a specific problem," states Lee (1998, p. 157), and it can have its genesis in either the private or public sector. Many public policies evolved to address the issue of parity in education—primarily from the stance of equity in access at all points along the educational pipeline, including higher education.

THE ROLE OF POLICY ON EDUCATIONAL PARITY IN HIGHER EDUCATION

The most known (and controversial) policy regarding African American access to postsecondary institutions was not initially developed specifi-cally for higher education. Affirmative action was created as an attempt to bring parity to all areas of federal government and entities receiving federal funding (Nettles, Perna, & Edelin, 1998). President Kennedy's Ex-ecutive Order 10925 established the policy in 1961 as a means of estab-lishing guidelines for salaries, career advancement, and hiring practices. The policy, originally directed toward federal entities, became a means of moving toward parity in higher education, as many colleges and univer-sities were the recipients of federal funding.

Society's drive for the end (economic and political power) is a major culprit in recent anti–affirmative action movements, which are gaining momentum in higher education (Davis, 1998; Garfield, 1996; Phillip, 1994). Access becomes an enabler and an empowerer because higher education is a rather secure pathway to a better quality of life through economic and political empowerment. Affirmative action is a way of reaching parity in higher education by ensuring that African Americans and other groups that were historically discriminated against gain access to the pathway that leads to a greater end. Although colleges and universities can serve large numbers of students, enrollments are finite, forcing students to ag-gressively pursue institutional admissions.

Affirmative action in higher education was not received unchallenged. Nettles, Perna, and Edelin, (1998) report that the *Regents of the University of California v. Bakke* case in 1978 resulted in the first formal Supreme Court decision, and Justice Lewis F. Powell's opinion was designated the judg-ment of the Court. Justice Powell's ruling prohibited setting quotas but found that considering race, together with other admission criteria, was a positive action for colleges and universities. The two legal theories that justify affirmative action in Justice Powell's opinion include taking race into account to compensate for institutions' prior discrimination against the student's minority group and the importance of diversity in generating a vigorous exchange of ideas as diverse as the country (Nettles et al., 1998). The *Bakke* case was the beginning of many similar challenges to higher education access via race-based policies and programs for underrepresented groups.

Although history indicates that African Americans were often denied opportunities to participate in the spoils of society, there are those who argue that there is no need for affirmative action programs because all is right in the world. In truth, this more confirms a backlash against affirmative action than a correction of historical discrimination (Gragg, 1995). Nationally we are still struggling with the effects of race in all areas of society—including higher education—with an intensity that makes the turbulent 1960s pale in comparison.

The Morrill Act of 1890 created black land-grant colleges and universities as a means of giving African Americans access to higher education via race-specific public colleges. These colleges, along with private HBCUs, have a demonstrated record of success in educating African Americans—thus providing a gateway to economic and political empowerment for those who otherwise would have been excluded. This is especially true at the undergraduate level, as evidenced by the proportion of degrees awarded to African Americans nationally by HBCUs compared to the number of degrees awarded to African Americans at predominantly white institutions (Nettles & Perna, 1997). Davis (1998) argues that the success of HBCUs extends beyond their ability to foster the cognitive and intellectual development of African Americans. These institutions are a tremendous resource for the development of cultural capital among African Americans through the noncognitive and personal (identity) development of their students.

Yet, past success does not justify future respites. There is still much that needs to be done in order to maintain past progress and to foster future gains. An HBCU effort to recruit, retain, and graduate traditional students (direct entry following secondary education) has indeed been successful, according to descriptive statistics (see following section), with a trend of improvement among that group. However, there is a large African American population that is underserved in higher education: nontraditional students who delay their education and enter higher education through two-year institutions. The erosion of affirmative action policies and programs, along with the high matriculation and attrition rates of African Americans in two-year institutions, gives added import to the role of HBCUs in educating African Americans in the new millennium.

AFRICAN AMERICAN PRESENCE IN HIGHER EDUCATION

Over the last two decades, educational researchers have produced voluminous research literature on college students and their educational experiences. Prolific reports on retaining students, the effects of college on students, students' academic performance, and other revelations regarding students in higher education (and minority students in higher education) inform us about the influence of many variables on student achievement in college (Astin, 1991; Astin, Tsui, & Avalos, 1996; Carreathers, Beckmann, Coatie, & Melson, 1996; Cochran-Smith, 1995; Ladson-Billings, 1995; Lang, 1992; Leon, Dougherty, & Maitland, 1997; Nettles, Thoney, Gosman, & Dandridge, 1985; Pascarella & Terenzini, 1991; Richardson & de los Santos, 1988; Wells-Lawson, 1994). Despite all that we know, however, progress for African Americans remains painfully slow (Astin, Tsui, & Avalos, 1996; Nettles & Perna, 1997).

African American undergraduate students lag behind whites in enrollment, and there is a similar pattern for degree attainment. African American undergraduate students who complete degrees are conspicuously underrepresented among degree recipients in science, engineering, and technology disciplines. This trend is alarming because science and technology fields are projected as the most lucrative economic fields in the next century (National Education Goals Panel, 1992). Thus, specific career fields are as important as is a college degree for attaining economic power in the future, and African Americans will be underrepresented in those fields.

DREAMS UNFULFILLED: THE INFLUENCE OF THE REVOLVING DOOR

National data indicate that there are more than 5 million students seeking degrees in the nation's two-year institutions, and nearly half of these students aspire to complete a baccalaureate degree (National Center for Education Statistics [NCES], 1997; Roche, 1997). Approximately 2.5 million students is a sizable pool of potential applicants for recruitment at four-year institutions—more than enough students to enhance enrollment at HBCUs. Although 50 percent of these students enter universities upon their first transfer experience, only 6.3 percent of the group earn a baccalaureate degree (Roche, 1997). A 93.7 percent attrition rate among any population merits attention.

COMMUNITY COLLEGE STUDENT PROFILE

The community college movement has made a substantial contribution to higher education access for the nation's citizens. There are more than

1,100 two-year institutions (public and private) across the country, and they serve a major role in providing affordable, geographically accessible postsecondary education, primarily to those who are either in the workforce or will be in a brief time. Since these institutions are predominantly open-door entities, issues of race, income, and academic preparation are not deterrents to learning. These institutions have large enrollments in continuing education programs that facilitate lifelong learning for noncredentialing purposes as well as numerous programs for certificates and associate degrees. The emphasis on training a skilled workforce is expanding beyond short-term technical vocational training to include academic preparation for transfer to a four-year institution for undergraduate degree completion. The community college student profile indicates that the community college population is predominantly female; lower-income adults (25-plus years old) and minorities are overrepresented in the population (American Association of Community Colleges [AACC], 1998). Liberal/general studies and humanities tend to be the most popular associate degree awards at community colleges, followed by business management and administrative services. Health professions and related sciences follow third, and engineering-related technologies rank fourth among associate degree awards nationally (AACC). While students in community colleges benefit from economic gains afforded by postsecondary education, as a group these students are missing the economic advancement associated with science and technology fields.

ACADEMIC PERFORMANCE AMONG TWO-YEAR COLLEGE STUDENTS

The attrition rate of community college transfer students is more alarming when considering minorities. An analysis of national longitudinal data on the cohort of students who entered higher education institutions in 1989 (Nettles & Perna, 1997) indicate that 45.2 percent of African Americans and 41.1 percent of Hispanic Americans in community colleges were seeking a baccalaureate degree. By the 1993 academic year, 1,145,527 baccalaureate degrees had been awarded to the cohort across all fields. Of this group, 6 percent of the degrees were awarded to African Americans and 4.8 percent were awarded to Hispanic Americans. When considering the degree awards in science, mathematics, engineering, and technology (SMET), only 5.4 percent were awarded to African Americans and 4.8 percent were awarded to Hispanic Americans. The effect of attrition among community college transfer students is even more drastic because the small number of bachelor's degrees awarded in SMET includes students who began their education in community colleges where 45.2 percent of African Americans and 41.1 percent of Hispanic Americans were seeking baccalaureate degrees. Although community college students take longer to complete degrees, the number of graduates will show small gains at best since only 4.5 percent of African Americans and 4 percent of Hispanic Americans were still enrolled in four-year institutions in 1994. Not only are there too few community college transfer students, including minorities, completing baccalaureate degrees, but too few are earning degrees in science, mathematics, engineering, and technology disciplines.

FOSTERING THE DREAM OF ECONOMIC EMPOWERMENT

Policies and programs that most strongly support African American presence in higher education will likely continue to shift away from affirmative action and will move toward interinstitutional partnerships, such as articulation agreements for college transfer (AACT). These agreements are becoming more visible around the country as uniformity in curricular standards evolves from public accountability demands. For example, English 101 should be the same across institutions (especially within mutual geographic regions), and should therefore transfer between institutions without question of its application toward degree completion. AACT allow students to pay for specific courses (usually core foundation courses) once and the time to degree completion is not extended due to course replication. AACT offer a smoother transition between institutions and reinforce the goal commitment that is so important for student persistence to degree completion (Tinto, 1975). These interinstitutional agreements are essential for the academic success of women and minority students, as so many begin and end their education in two-year institutions and so few attain a baccalaureate degree.

INTERINSTITUTIONAL POLICY IN THE NEW MILLENNIUM

AACT take on the function of interinstitutional contracts between a sending institution (two-year college) and a receiving institution (four-year college). They contribute to the seamless education of those who begin their undergraduate education at one institution and intend to complete their degree at a senior institution. The agreements can be between systems (e.g., two-year system and four-year system agreements) or between individual colleges (two-year college and four-year university). These agreements are not easily developed and can be rather political, given the autonomous nature of higher education. Nonetheless, AACT in higher education are gaining momentum that is likely to continue well into the new millennium. The following case examples present AACT models among HBCUs and two-year institutions.

AACT CASE EXAMPLES

The following examples were developed through an analysis of qualitative data. The main data source was institutional documents and an additional data source included interviews with essential staff. The cases are intended to be descriptive, illustrative reports that serve as a foundation for reflection among decision makers charged with the task of fostering African Americans' success in higher education. The case example AACT arrangements are not exhaustive, but they do represent a cross section of institutional characteristics (two-year/four-year institutions, public/private governance structures) and range in time from a few months to several years of implementation.

Case Example 1: Private Two-Year and Public Four-Year Institutions

Louisburg College (LC), founded in 1787, is a private, rural, coeducational, residential two-year institution affiliated with the Methodist Church. The college carries the honor of being the oldest postsecondary institution in North Carolina. The enrollment at LC is small (approximately 500 students), which allows for smaller class sizes and a stronger emphasis on the student-teacher relationship. LC still touts the mission of being a liberal arts college that focuses on the transfer function and has long-standing relationships with most of the four-year institutions in the state. Although the enrollment is small, the student body is approximately 30 percent African American—all of which are potential candidates for transfer into a four-year institution. LC students are 80 percent North Carolina residents, 75 percent residential, 60 percent first-generation, 60 percent male, and 81 percent eligible for need-based scholarships, and they average 18 to 19 years of age. It is important to note that 90 percent percent of LC students transfer to four-year institutions, which is considerably higher than the community college rate of transfer.

In May 1999 LC, under the presidential leadership of Dr. Rosemary Gillett-Karam, entered into an articulation agreement with North Carolina Central University (NCCU), which is a public HBCU. The agreements, known as the 2 + 2 Program, allows LC students to enter NCCU in the junior year for specific major areas of study.

North Carolina Central University originated in 1910 as the National Religious Training School, a private institution devoted to the academic and skill development of coeds for service to the nation. The institution became a public entity by legislative action in 1923. As a result of multiple legislative actions, name changes, and curricular expansions over the subsequent four decades, the institution became known as NCCU in 1969, a constituent institution of the University of North Carolina system. This transformation of governance made the institution the first public liberal arts institution for African Americans (North Carolina Central University, 1999). Teaching is a primary focus at NCCU, with scholarship and service viewed as strong contributors to learning. NCCU is a comprehensive university that awards degrees at the undergraduate and graduate levels, and its mission is to prepare its students academically and professionally and to raise the social conscience of its students regarding their responsibility to the state, the country, and the world. The university continues its tradition of serving African American students; however, it has expanded in order to serve a racially and socioeconomically diverse student body.

The articulation agreement between LC and NCCU is an unusual accomplishment and is the result of a combination of timing and leadership. Interinstitutional partnerships had a diminished priority prior to the installation of Rosemary Gillett-Karam as president of LC, even though the major mission of LC is to prepare students for degree completion at another institution. Within the first five months of her administration, Gillett-Karam reestablished historical linkages with four-year institutions in North Carolina. However, her vision as a newly appointed leader did not end there because these arrangements did not meet the needs of all students at LC, especially African American students. In an interview session in 1999, Gillett-Karam made it clear that the articulation agreement for the transfer of LC students to NCCU is essential for the academic success of African American students. Gillett-Karam indicated:

What is most important to me is that students have an identity. It is important to me that African American students at Louisburg College have an identity. Although our student enrollment is 30 percent African American, there currently are no administrators or faculty who are African American. The only role models African American students see [on campus] are in service positions. I want to do everything I can to change that. So I began to look at different kinds of ways that our [African American] students could be mentored and helped by positive role models. Because partnering [with four-year institutions] was a goal of mine, I looked to NCCU because of my old association with the NC University System and because I knew that Julius Chambers had just done wonders for that [institution]. I knew that they would have something to offer us in terms of reaching out to help us, and I was hoping that I would have something to offer them in return.

A major benefit (for African American students) of an articulation agreement with NCCU, which differs from benefits derived from predominantly white institutions, is that NCCU has an institutional culture that supports the cultural identity development of African American students. All students at LC are eligible for the 2+2 Program that would lead to degree completion at NCCU, just as all LC students can elect to transfer to a predominantly white institution. However, the majority of students who elect to transfer to NCCU are African American.

AACT between two-year and four-year institutions carry benefits for the institutions involved and most importantly for the people (students and staff) within those institutions. AACT serve as a means for addressing accountability issues in higher education by bringing consistency in curricular content across institutions. They benefit students by removing the uncertainty about which courses will transfer to which institution and to which academic programs within that institution. The specifics of AACT can grow exponentially and become rather prolific. Nonetheless, the benefits of these interinstitutional policies outweigh the inconveniences. The articulation agreement between LC and NCCU also benefits students and staff through shared resources and human relationship building. Gillett-Karam stated:

An articulation agreement has three major ingredients. One is to give students a transition from one level of education to another. It makes it very clear for students and institutions to know how their courses are exchanged and so on—it removes the mystery of [the interinstitutional] relationship, or the transition between one institution and another. The second purpose is to prove to the world that there are absolute standards about how curricula are determined, accepted, and understood and that these standards are shared between institutions. Most importantly, articulation agreements give the people the experience of knowing both institutions, partnering with both institutions, the exchange of students, the exchange of faculty, the exchange of curricula, the exchange of ideas. Those relationships are something that I am most interested in because I think that they are the most beneficial. In the final analysis it is usually people's relationships to other people that are remembered as much or more in higher education than the courses themselves.

The AACT between LC-NCCU is novel in that it will go beyond paper agreements regarding stringent rules for interinstitutional curricular content. This agreement will be a living entity in its implementation when NCCU faculty members start teaching on LC campus and vice versa. This exchange of faculty will allow LC students to establish relationships early with faculty at the receiving institution, and it will allow LC faculty to maintain contact with LC students postgraduation. The early relationship development between LC students and NCCU faculty is expected to provide sorely needed same-race mentors for African American students and to reinforce their goals for degree completion. Equally important, the faculty exchange and shared technology is expected to foster collegial, collaborative interinstitutional faculty relationships that will ultimately benefit all students at each institution.

Case Example 2A: AACT between Public Two-Year and Public Four-Year Institutions

The Virginia Community College System (VCCS) emphasizes the provision of high-quality, affordable, comprehensive postsecondary education, training, and services to Virginia residents. It is a public entity that has 23 colleges (single and multicampus sites) throughout the state. Tidewater Community College (TCC), part of the VCCS, is a public two-year commuter institution that serves the Chesapeake, Moss, Virginia Beach, and Portsmouth areas. In the fall of 1998, TCC had an enrollment of 19,084 students (10,000 full-time equivalents), which represented a 2 percent increase over the fall of 1997. Not only did the enrollments increase, there was a 7 percent increase in the number of full-time students. This trend of increased enrollments also extended to college transfer enrollments, which increased 6 percent over the fall of 1997.

College transfer student enrollments at TCC have nearly doubled over the last 10 years, and they now represent 48 percent of the student body. Improved articulation agreements between two-year and four-year institutions are credited for this increase. In addition to increasing the enrollment, the characteristics of transfer students depart from those of the usual TCC student. Transfer students tend to be full-time students, 18 to 21 years of age—fitting the profile of traditional students rather than nontraditional students that usually enroll in community colleges.

The transfer program, known as the University Parallel Program at TCC, offers both freshman- and sophomore-level courses in the arts and sciences. Preprofessional programs, which are congruent with standards for transfer into baccalaureate programs, are also included in the University Parallel Program. Tidewater Community College has articulation agreements with both Hampton University (a private HBCU) and with Norfolk State University (a public HBCU).

Case Example 2B: AACT between Public Two-Year and Private Four-Year Institutions

Hampton University (HU) was founded in 1868 as Hampton Normal and Agricultural Institute for the purpose of educating newly freed African Americans. It is currently a comprehensive institution that offers both undergraduate and graduate degree programs. HU is a private, coeducational, nonsectarian, residential institution situated on more than 200 acres in southeastern Virginia on the mid-Atlantic coast. The institution has a liberal arts core curriculum but has heavy emphasis on science and professional disciplines. HU has a diverse enrollment of approximately 5,000 students, the majority of whom are undergraduate students.

Norfolk State University (NSU) was founded in 1935 as a branch of Virginia Union University and became a freestanding institution in 1969 as the result of several legislative acts. NSU is an urban residential institution with an enrollment of approximately 6,500 students. The institution has a strong education mission, with emphasis on urban issues and social responsibility.

Longevity in Implementation

The AACT between TCC and HU and between TCC and NSU have several years of implementation experience. This experience serves as a foundation for revisions of curricular content and degree requirements. Although the AACT are guaranteed, they do carry specific course requirements for transfer by program area. Students in the University Parallel Program know which courses are required for transfer, by major, if they intend to continue their education at Norfolk State University or Hampton University. As Gillett-Karam indicated earlier, the mystery of moving between institutions is minimized because the sending and receiving institutions have agreed upon curricular standards. However, the guarantee is directed only toward the acceptance of specific community college courses that apply toward curricular requirements at the university—there is no guarantee of admission to the four-year institution. Students must maintain a minimum grade point average to remain eligible for the University Parallel Program, and they must successfully compete for admission to the four-year institution.

Rationale for AACT

AACT between HBCUs and two-year institutions arise from various circumstances. Some of the policies are initiated at the system level and are handed down to member institutions as mandates. Others emerge from the vision of institutional leaders. The cooperative arrangements are rather logical. HBCUs and two-year institutions share a mission of educating populations that would otherwise be excluded from higher education. Recent enrollment trends indicate that both types of institutions serve large African American populations, although those who enter two-year institutions are less likely to attain a baccalaureate degree than those attending HBCUs.

DISCUSSION

Providing equal opportunities for African Americans to attain economic and political power through higher education has a standing history as a political issue, resulting in both public and private policies for resolution. Issues of access continue to be topics of passionate debate at a time when African American progress in higher education is evident but slow. Anti-affirming acts coupled with high enrollment and attrition rates among students (especially women and minorities) at two-year institutions will likely result in a higher number of African Americans either being underserved in higher education or totally excluded from mainstream educational entities. HBCUs have a demonstrated track record of successful degree attainment among African Americans at these institutions and of graduating more African Americans than do predominantly white institutions (Astin et al., 1996; Nettles & Perna, 1997).

The role of HBCUs in advancing African American success in higher education will be even more vital in the new millennium. Future success in advancing African Americans in higher education in the new millennium will depend on the effectiveness of interinstitutional policies to aggressively expand the student population to include adult students who initiate their education at two-year institutions, to selectively expand degree offerings to include SMET disciplines (especially within AACT pacts), and to continuously seek empirical assessments to verify success.

REACHING UNDERSERVED AFRICAN AMERICANS

To meet these future challenges, HBCUs' visionary leaders must aggressively seek interinstitutional agreements that will substantially expand the traditional native undergraduate student population to include nontraditional adult students who initiate their education at two-year institutions. National goals of lifelong learning and the economic benefits associated with educational attainment will undoubtedly fuel growth in the student population, among all ages, particularly those who enter two-year institutions. An early linkage between institutions supports transfer students' educational goals and establishes commitment to the receiving institution, both of which support successful retention.

Empowerment through Degree Fields

Degree attainment enhances economic and political power. However, simply earning a degree will not be enough in the future. The strength of this power, especially economic power, will become discipline driven in the future. Income-earning power will increasingly be found in science, mathematics, engineering, and technology (SMET) disciplines, where African Americans historically have been underrepresented. Thus, it is essential that HBCUs build on past success with liberal education and aggressively work toward enhancing African Americans' level of degree attainment in SMET disciplines in the future.

Making the Case for Success

Public interest in higher education accountability is not likely to subside in the coming years; therefore, documented evidence of the success of these policies should be the focus of future assessments. Future research should determine the impact of the transfer policies on the sending and receiving institutions' culture and collaborative relationships. Particular attention should be directed toward the cost-effectiveness of developing and implementing the interinstitutional policies. College transfer policies are intended to benefit students and their successful cognitive, personal, and professional development along the pathway to degree completion. Future research should determine the impact of these policies on targeted students—emphasizing the extent to which the interinstitutional agreements have a differential effect on African Americans at HBCUs and at predominantly white institutions. Most importantly, future research should determine whether interinstitutional policies successfully increase the numbers of African Americans who attain economic and political power through the successful transition between institutions and the completion of undergraduate degrees.

CONCLUSION

Challenges to affirmative action and increasing tuition costs are powerful deterrents to higher education access for diverse populations (race, gender, age, income) nationally. These deterrents, if left unchecked, will cause higher education attainment to revert back to the narrowly defined population (elite whites) that was originally entitled to college access in the United States (Brubaker & Willis, 1997). Given the retrenchment of educational opportunity nationally, enhancing the success of African Americans is not the only role for HBCUs in the new millennium. Building on a historical record of success in educating those who are at a distinct disadvantage in American society, HBCUs will need to extend that success to those who are often excluded from higher education because of race/ethnicity, gender, and income. HBCUs, in the future, should demonstrate to the broader higher education community how to effectively develop, implement, and evaluate policies that will lead to interinstitutional relationships that benefit a more diverse body of students.

To this end, articulation agreements for college transfer between HBCUs and two-year institutions are essential. The development of these interinstitutional policies should not be taken lightly, as policy is the root of all programs—and programs define practice. Articulation agreements between HBCUs and two-year institutions benefit not only students (through degree attainment) but both institutions involved (through stabilized enrollments, maximum efficiency via shared resources, etc.). Obstacles to developing interinstitutional policies are quite manageable when visionary leaders are committed to developing student-centered institutions. Some operational models already exist. These arrangements will likely become a standard reality—rather than an infrequent occurrence—in the coming years.

REFERENCES

American Association of Community Colleges (AACC). (1998). *Pocket profile of community colleges: Trends and statistics, 1997–98.* Washington, DC: AACC.

Astin, A. W. (1991). *Assessment for excellence: The philosophy and practice of assessment and evaluation in higher education.* New York: Macmillan.

Astin, A. W., Tsui, L., & Avalos, J. (1996). *Degree attainment rates at American colleges and universities: Effects of race, gender and institutional type.* Los Angeles: Higher Education Research Institute, University of California.

Bell, J. C. (1995). *Famous black quotations.* New York: Warner Books.

Brubaker, J. S. & Willis, R. (1997). Higher Education in Transition: A History of American Colleges and Universities. 4th Edition. New Brunswick, NJ: Transaction Books.

Carreathers, K. R., Beckmann, L., Coatie, R. M., & Melson, W. L. (1996). Three exemplary retention programs. In I. H. Johnson & A. J. Ottens (Eds.), *Leveling the playing field: Promoting academic success for students of color* (pp. 35–54). San Francisco: Jossey-Bass.

Cochran-Smith, M. (1995). Color blindness and basket making are not the answers: Confronting the dilemmas of race, culture, and language diversity in teacher education. *American Educational Research Journal, 32*(3), 493–522.

Davis, J. E. (1998). Cultural capital and the role of historically black colleges and universities in educational reproduction. In K. Freeman (Ed.), *African American culture and heritage in higher education research and practice.* Westport, CT: Praeger.

Garfield, L. Y. (1996). Squaring affirmative action admissions policies with federal judicial guidelines: A model for the twenty-first century. *Journal of College and University Law, 22*(4), 895–934.

Gragg, D. (1995). Don't affirmative action critics watch old movies? *Black Issues in Higher Education, 12*(11), 60.

Ladson-Billings, G. (1995). Toward a theory of culturally relevant pedagogy. *American Educational Research Journal, 32*(3), 465–491.

Lang, M. (1992). Barriers to blacks' educational achievement in higher education: A statistical and conceptual review. *Journal of Black Studies, 22*(4), 510–522.

Lee, W. Y. (1998). Policy, practice, and performance: Strategies to foster the meaningful involvement of African Americans in higher education decision-making processes. In K. Freeman (Ed.), *African American culture and heritage in higher education research and practice.* Westport, CT: Praeger.

Leon, D. J., Dougherty, K. A., & Maitland, C. (1997). *Mentoring minorities in higher education: Passing the torch.* Washington, DC: National Education Association of the United States.

National Center for Education Statistics (NCES). (1997). *Digest of education statistics—1997.* Washington, DC: National Center for Education Statistics. Office of Educational Research and Improvement. U.S. Department of Education. (NCES 98–015)

National Education Goals Panel. (1992). *The national education goals report: Building a nation of learners.* Washington, DC: U.S. Government Printing Office.

Nettles, M. T., Perna, L. W., & Edelin, K. C. (1998). *The role of affirmative action in expanding student access at selective colleges and universities.* Fairfax, VA: Frederick D. Patterson Research Institute, United Negro College Fund.

Nettles, M. T., & Perna, L. W. (1997). *The African American education data book: Vol. I. Higher and adult education.* Fairfax, VA: Frederick D. Patterson Research Institute, United Negro College Fund.

Nettles, M. T., Thoney, A. R., Gosman, E. J., & Dandridge, B. A. (1985). *The causes and consequences of college students' performance: A focus on Black and White students' attrition rates, progression rates and grade point averages.* Nashville, TN: Tennessee Higher Education Commission.

North Carolina Central University. (1999). *North Carolina Central University: 1996–98 Course Catalog.* Retrieved Nov 29, 1999 from http://www.nccu.edu/catalog/toc.html

Pascarella, E. T., & Terenzini, P. (1991). *How college affects students: Findings and insights from twenty years of research.* San Francisco: Jossey-Bass.

Phillip, M. C. (1994). Affirmative action still saddled with negative image: Bad mouthing by beneficiaries baffles many. *Black Issues in Higher Education: The First Ten Years, 11*(2), 24–26.

Richardson, R. C., & de los Santos, F. G., Jr. (1988). *Helping minority students graduate from college: A comprehensive approach.* ERIC Digest. ED308795

Roche, J. (Ed.). (1997). *AACC annual, 1996–97.* Washington, DC: Community College Press.

Tinto, V. (1975). Dropout from higher education: A theoretical synthesis of recent research. *Review of Educational Research, 45*(1), 89–125.

Wells-Lawson, M. I. (1994). *The effects of race and type of institution on the college experiences of Black and White undergraduate students attending 30 predominately black and predominantly white colleges and universities.* Paper presented at the Annual Meeting of the American Educational Research Association, New Orleans, LA.

CHAPTER 6

HBCUs and the Digital Divide: Survival of the Fittest

Allison N. Clark

INTRODUCTION

The next decade of this digital age will prove to be a pivotal time for historically black colleges and universities (HBCUs). The Internet has changed the way society functions. It has improved our quality of life by impacting the way we work and play. However, this technological innovation threatens to further exacerbate the problems of the African American community by moving it toward a permanently disadvantaged caste status. It is crucial that digital equity is ensured for all citizens.

Schools use the Internet as a vast electronic library with untold possibilities. Doctors use the Internet to consult with colleagues half a world away. And even as the Internet offers a single global village, it threatens to create a second-class citizenship among those without access. As a new generation grows up as accustomed to communicating through a keyboard as in person, life on the Internet will become an increasingly important part of life on Earth. (PBS, 2000, website)

The digital divide has impacted HBCUs as well as individuals. Unfortunately, according to HBCU technology assessment studies commissioned by the National Association for Equal Opportunity in Higher Education (Myers, 2000) and the Thurgood Marshall Scholarship Fund (Booz Allen Hamilton et al., 2000), the majority of HBCUs lag behind in Internet access, computer equipment, technical training, and support. This affects the students who attend these schools. Faculty and staff believe that the more technologically equipped their campuses are, the better the education and opportunities available to their students (Booz Allen Hamilton et al., 2000; Myers, 2000).

Strategic planning and implementation must continue to keep open the doors of these African American institutions. This chapter examines the current state of technological affairs in the HBCU community. It gives a brief history of the Internet, defines the digital divide, and discusses existing programs and projects. The chapter concludes with a discussion of future implications and recommendations. Following the reference list is information on digital divide resources, funding opportunities, and educational technology resources.

THE INTERNET

In 1969 the Advanced Research Projects Agency (ARPA) of the U.S. government conceived a Cold War project that would later become the Internet. The original purpose of the Internet, then known as the Advanced Research Projects Agency Network, or ARPAnet, was to create a command structure that was centralized and controlled for the United States Armed Forces (Hardy, 1993). Research One universities participated in the development and deployment of the Internet.

The original ARPAnet design enabled decentralization from the mainframe computer concept to a peer-to-peer structure. This new network allowed research computers at one university to communicate with research computers at other universities (Leiner et al., 2000; Zakon, 2000). In 1972 Vinton Cerf was elected the first chairman of the InterNetworking Working Group (INWG). This organization was charged with setting the standards that would govern the growing network. Cerf later became known as the Father of the Internet (PBS, 2000).

Another Internet historical milestone occurred in 1976 with the creation of UNIX-to-UNIX copy protocol (UUCP) by Mike Lesk of AT&T Bell Labs. UUCP was later improved to enable users to log on remotely, transfer files, and send and receive electronic mail (Hardy, 1993; PBS, 2000).

Between 1982 and 1987 Vint Cerf and Bob Kahn were key members of the team that created Transmission Control Protocol/Internet Protocol (TCP/IP), which is the common language of all Internet computers. TCP/IP enables the computers to communicate with each other, thereby forming a network. This particular capability created the Internet as we know it today (PBS, 2000).

The innovation and further refinement of the Internet continued through government-funded programs such as the Defense Advanced Research Projects Agency (DARPA) and the National Science Foundation (NSF). The Computer Science Research Network (CSNET) was created so that major universities could connect to ARPAnet sites. These connections gave those universities advantages in recruiting students and conducting research (Hardy, 1993; PBS, 2000).

The most popular portion of the Internet is the World Wide Web (Leiner et al., 2000; PBS, 2000). Tim Berners-Lee saw the value in combining the concept of the Internet with hypertext to present information in a non-sequential manner (Leiner et al., 2000). Marc Andreesen was a member of the team at the National Center for Supercomputing Applications (NCSA) that built on hypertext technology to create NCSA Mosaic, the first graphical browser for the World Wide Web. Mosaic enabled users to access millions of pages of information. Thirty years after its earliest incarnation, the Internet is a public communications network available to hundreds of millions of people worldwide.

Digital Divide

The term "digital divide" refers to the gap between those Americans who have access to and effectively use information technologies and those who do not (NTIA, 2000). The Department of Commerce commissioned the surveys "Falling Through the Net 1–3" and "Falling Through the Net: Toward Digital Inclusion" to investigate the phenomenon of the digital divide (NTIA, 1995, 1998, 1999, 2000). These studies indicate that African Americans have increased their access to the Internet, but they still lag behind in Internet access when compared with white Americans (NTIA, 2000). From December 1998 to August 2000 the numbers of white non-Hispanic Americans with Internet access increased from 29.8 percent to 46.1 percent, an expansion rate of 58.5 percent. Asian Americans and Pacific Islanders, who have the highest percentage of access, gained from 36.0 percent to 56.8 percent. During this same time period, African American Internet access rose from 11.2 percent to 23.5 percent, an expansion rate of 109.8 percent.

The have-nots of the digital divide need more than access to the Internet. As a panelist at the National Telecommunications and Information Administration's Digital Divide Summit, Darien Dash, pioneer and activist in the new media community and founder of Digital Mafia Entertainment, stated, "There is a void in content, information, and services that would attach greater value to the interactive experience of minorities" (Dash, 1999).

Most Americans who have access to the Internet are college educated. While 53 percent of people with a college degree have Internet access, this demographic makes up only 23 percent of the total U.S. population. Access to the Internet cannot be equated with use of the Internet. White Americans lead in Internet use with 50.3 percent, followed by Asian Americans and Pacific Islanders with 49.4 percent, African American non-Hispanics with 29.3 percent, and Hispanics with 23.7 percent. Only African Americans and whites used the Internet at rates higher than their household online connections, at 23.5 percent and 46.1 percent, respectively (NTIA, 2000). People in urban areas were 50 percent more likely to have Internet access than their rural counterparts at some of the same income levels.

HBCU ASSESSMENT STUDIES

The National Association for Equal Opportunity in Higher Education (NAFEO) and the Thurgood Marshall Scholarship Fund surveyed their member institutions to gauge their technological usage and readiness. Both organizations published the results of the surveys along with recommendations to the HBCU community on what actions are needed to better equip their campuses.

HBCUs: An Assessment of Networking and Connectivity

In 2000 the National Telecommunications and Information Administration (NTIA) of the Department of Commerce released *Historically Black Colleges and Universities: An Assessment of Networking and Connectivity* (Myers, 2000). This HBCU Technology Assessment Study (TAS) was conducted by the NAFEO and was the first comprehensive assessment of the technology needs of HBCUs. The TAS assessed the networking, computing resources, and connectivity of HBCUs and other educational institutions that serve predominantly African American students. The researchers were encouraged to find that 98 percent of the respondents reported that they had basic access to campus networks, the Internet, and World Wide Web. Although these findings were better than expected, the research team remained only cautiously optimistic:

In our view, in light of the overall positive picture of networking and connectivity among HBCUs, it is possible for significant numbers of these institutions to make a *digital leap* into the 21st Century. However, such a leap will require focus of institutional resources to address several areas of weakness: (1) improvement of high-speed connectivity rates; (2) dramatic improvement of student-to-computer-ownership ratios; (3) improvement of the strategic planning process; and (4) willingness to incorporate innovative technologies into campus networks. (Myers, 2000, p. 7)

Other findings of the TAS were: Out of the 74 HBCUs that responded, 56 percent are located in urban or suburban centers and 43 percent in rural settings. This statistic is significant because the geographical location of a campus can impact its access to networking. None of the HBCUs required students to own computers, and fewer than 15 percent recommended it. Less than 25 percent of students own their own computers, while other institutions of higher learning report that 49 percent of their student populations own their computers. Only 3 percent of HBCUs surveyed reported providing financial assistance for students to purchase their own computer. Prior to the release of these findings, NAFEO and

Gateway Computers formed a partnership designed to promote computer ownership by HBCU students, faculty, and alumni through offers of discounts and rebates on computer equipment (Gateway Computers, 2000).

TMSF: An Assessment of Current Information Technology Usage

Booz Allen Hamilton, the Gallup Organization, and EVAXX Inc. conducted an information technology (IT) survey of the historically black public colleges and universities (HBPCUs) that are members of the Thurgood Marshall Scholarship Fund (TMSF) (2000). Survey results were released in *Historically Black Public Colleges and Universities: An Assessment of Current Information Technology Usage* (Booz Allen Hamilton et al., 2000).

The Booz Allen Hamilton technology usage model (Booz Allen & Hamilton, 1998) was used for this study. These metrics were designed specifically to compare best practices at top-tier institutions of higher learning with those of the TMSF HBPCUs. This study assessed levels of technological sophistication in the IT strategic planning of 45 HBPCUs. Three levels or stages were evaluated, with stage 1 the lowest or least sophisticated of the stages. The IT readiness categories were defined as follows: (a) strategy: IT strategic planning; (b) organization: strong IT organizational presence among staff; (c) finance: IT's percentage of annual budget; (d) technology: campus infrastructure and amount and availability of hardware; (e) teaching: support for faculty to use technology for teaching; and (f) training: computer literacy for students and staff.

The report did not identify the percentage of HBPCUs that achieved the three stages of the Booz Allen Hamilton model, making it problematic to delineate the level of technological readiness of the participants. The findings in the report do suggest that there is variability in the technological capacities of the various HBPCUs. For example, 42 of the 44 respondents reported having a campus network, yet 22 of the campuses are in stage 1 regarding PC-to-student ratio.

The goal of this survey was to help HBPCUs remain competitive and successful in their continuing efforts to attract top students, faculty, and staff (Booz Allen Hamilton et al., 2000). This report builds on the results of NAFEO's TAS and is designed to help HBPCUs compare their IT status to that of the top universities in the country and to "contribute to the development of persuasive arguments that support TMSF's national IT fund-raising initiatives" (Booz Allen Hamilton et al., 2000, p. 2).

The Power of the Internet for Learning: Moving from Promise to Practice

The Department of Education's commissioned bipartisan report, *The Power of the Internet for Learning: Moving from Promise to Practice* (Web-based

Education Commission [WBEC], 2000), is not limited to HBCUs or even to college or university levels. Still, the e-testimony from the United Negro College Fund (UNCF) regarding the technological readiness of its member institutions supports the aforementioned HBCU assessment reports. Two points listed in the WBEC report are particularly worth noting: (a) less than 50 percent of UNCF faculty have their own computer, compared to 74 percent of national faculty; and (b) there is a severe shortage of network servers, hubs, routers, and printers at UNCF campuses, and 75 percent of the existing equipment needs to be replaced (WBEC, 2000).

TECHNOLOGY PROGRAMS AND PROJECTS

Yahoo! has been publishing its *Yahoo! Internet Life Most Wired Campus* listing since 1997. Schools are judged on access and infrastructure, administrative services, general resources, and student support. In 2000, for the first time, three HBCUs made Yahoo!'s list—Morehouse College, Hampton University, and Tennessee State University (Bernstein, Caplan, & Glover, 2001). Fortunately, several technology programs and projects exist that are assisting HBCUs in their efforts to develop and sustain information technology on their campuses.

The Executive Leadership Council and Foundation's Technology Transfer Project

The Executive Leadership Council and Foundation (ELCF) was founded in 1986 and is comprised of senior-level African American executives. The council designs and implements charitable and educational activities to prepare future African American executives and entrepreneurs. One of the ELCF's projects is the Technology Transfer Project (TTP), which was created to enhance the digital equity at selected HBCUs. The project offers these HBCUs "networking capacity and infrastructure building, IT strategic planning, faculty development initiatives, and student development opportunities" (ELCF, 2001, Website). Many colleges and universities outside of the HBCU community also use the TTP Strategic Planning Model that was cocreated by TTP and Booz Allen Hamilton (Booz Allen Hamilton, 1998). Copies of the TTP Strategic Planning Model may be obtained from the ELCF (see resource listing for contact information).

Educause and EOT-PACI's AN-MSI Project

Educause is an organization of colleges, universities, and information technology corporations that serve higher education and related organizations and associations. The goal of Educause is to promote the use of information technology to advance higher education. Educause does this through a variety of programs, projects, and publications. One of these projects, the Advanced Networking with Minority Serving Institutions (AN-MSI), is targeted to minority-serving institutions (MSIs). The National Science Foundation's (NSF's) Computer and Information Science and Engineering (CISE) directorate began the funding for this project in 1999. AN-MSI works with Hispanic-serving institutions, tribal colleges and universities, and HBCUs to assist in the development of campus infrastructure.

The AN-MSI project includes a sub-award that was made to the Education, Outreach and Training Partnerships for Advanced Computational Infrastructure (EOT-PACI), a joint activity of the National Computational Science Alliance and the National Partnership for Advanced Computational Infrastructure. The EOT portion of the AN-MSI project assists MSIs that are engaged in the computational sciences, helping these schools develop the skills and infrastructure that are needed to utilize advanced computational tools and resources.

NASA's MU-SPIN

The National Aeronautics and Space Administration's Minority University-SPace Interdisciplinary Network (NASA's MU-SPIN) works with participating HBCUs to strengthen their science and technology programs (NASA, 2001). Toward this goal, MU-SPIN has partnered with various HBCUs to create Network Resources and Training Sites (NRTS). The NRTS work to improve infrastructure, technological expertise, and research to increase opportunities to participate in other federally funded programs as well as NASA-funded programs. In combination with MU-SPIN's educational programs, these technological enhancements impact students of color who are underrepresented in the areas of science, math, engineering, and technology.

Internet2

Internet2 (I2) is a partnership of the universities, government agencies, and industry sites that are supported by the nationwide advanced network called Abilene. The goal of this consortium is to hasten the creation of the next-generation Internet by working to "develop and deploy advanced network applications and technologies" (UCAD, 2001, website). Through Internet2 working groups, members of I2 can collaborate on: (a) advanced applications, (b) middleware, (c) new networking capabilities, (d) advanced network infrastructure, and (e) partnerships and alliances. At the time of this writing, two HBCUs are I2 members: Florida Agricultural and Mechanical University (FAMU) and Jackson State University (see www.internet2.org).

I2 recommends that members be prepared to spend a minimum of

$500,000 per year, depending on the state of the member's campus, on advanced networking readiness. Members must also commit to an annual membership fee of $25,000 per year. Institutions must be committed to "forming or joining local aggregation points called gigaPoPs," must establish broadband connectivity with other I2 institutions, and must "develop and demonstrate advanced network-based applications for the purposes of research and/or education and create a project team within the organization to support the development of such applications" (UCAD, 2001).

If more HBCUs are to participate in I2, there must be a willingness to move beyond the basic T-1 connection. NAFEO's TAS survey indicates that 88 percent of the HBCUs surveyed have access to T-1 lines from their local Internet service providers and that ISDN lines are the second most popular method of connectivity (Myers, 2000). Although 50 percent of the reporting institutions have T-3 connectivity available in their area, only 7.5 percent report using this broadband connectivity. The TAS could not assess why the HBCUs surveyed do not use the broadband connectivity available in their area; however, the study states that "lack of connectivity beyond T-1 level may be one of the key areas that hold back HBCUs from making the digital leap into the 21st Century!" (Myers, 2000, p. 36).

Nonmember institutions that are collaborating with I2 members may apply to be a sponsored participant, thus waiving the membership fee (UCAD, 2001). Schools that are interested in becoming members of I2 should first identify research and scientific interests that would be enabled through the establishment of advanced networking and infrastructure.

FUTURE IMPLICATIONS AND RECOMMENDATIONS

The social, economic, and political implications of a continuing technology gap are staggering given current demographic projections. President Clinton made digital equity an administrative priority. However, many of these initiatives are being reviewed by the Bush administration. Past reports of the Bush administration cutting the Technology Opportunities Program (TOP) budget have come to pass (Miller, 2001; PND, 2001; Trotter, 2001). Indeed the administration cut the TOP fiscal 2002 budget from $42.5 million to $15 million—a 65 percent decrease in funding. President Bush has also requested zero TOP future funding (Digital Empowerment, 2003) making the future of this program an uncertain one. Michael Powell, the new chairman of the Federal Communications Commission, has compared the digital divide "to a Mercedes divide—I'd like to have one, but can't afford one" (Miller, 2001, website; Philanthropy News Digest, 2001, website). It is clear that the dialogue begun between Republican leaders and HBCU presidents must continue and needs to include strategic technological planning to address last-mile issues. The "last mile" refers to the challenge to connect the customer to the nearest Internet exchange. More funding, programs, and polices are needed to narrow the digital divide. In his cover letter to the NAFEO TAS report, former secretary of commerce Norman Y. Mineta notes the progress that HBCUs have made, yet he is concerned that this is not enough:

Nonetheless, the report suggests that during this era of continuous innovation and change, continual upgrading of networking and connectivity is critical if these institutions are to take advantage of telecommunication opportunities such as Internet2 and third-generation wireless services. Presently, most HBCU campus networks rely on T-1 connectivity and over 75 percent of their students rely on campus computer labs to access the Internet and WWW. (Myers, 2000, p. 1)

Although the NAFEO and Thurgood Marshall report remains optimistic about the improvements HBCUs have made in their technological infrastructure, it is also cautious regarding the dilemma of the last mile. The NAFEO (Myers, 2000) report found that although broadband connectivity is available in some communities, the majority of HBCUs are not taking advantage of these high-speed connections.

HBCUs will need sufficient broadband capacity to participate in the future trends of information technology: ubiquitous grid computing, peer-to-peer computing, optical networks, and cutting-edge high-resolution visualization systems. Broadband enables the high-speed transmission of digital data. Learning is becoming more interactive and distant. Telemedicine allows continuing education, the teaching of medical concepts, and the possibility of virtual surgery. The remote use of scientific instruments allows access to remote social and scientific data. To fully participate in the digital age, HBCUs will need to move beyond T-1 connectivity to be able to collaborate in real time through systems that integrate audio, video, and interactive tools. Information technology will continue to evolve. Eventually there will be seamless worldwide wireless networking connectivity. This will allow persistent connection to the Internet, turning the PC into a personal digital assistant (PDA) that can fit into a pocket.

The report speculates that reasons for not implementing high-speed connections may be lack of training, funding, and strategic planning. I conducted an informal survey of black college chief information officers (CIOs) that yielded results that seem to support the findings of the NAFEO report and suggest other possible causes for the divide. One CIO commented that there is a shortage of skilled personnel at HBCUs and it is "hard to catch up and keep up."

HBCUs must demonstrate a compelling educational, scientific, or research collaborative initiative that requires connectivity on an end-to-end basis between and among institutions. Connectivity for the sake of connectivity will not generate assistance from funding agencies. Campuses must be willing to increase information sharing and to build collaborative relationships. HBCUs must take steps to educate, implement, and innovate. It cannot be emphasized enough that *funding agencies are no longer funding just connectivity.* Agencies are funding network-enabled science, education, and research. To garner funding, creative projects will be built on science, education, or research that requires connectivity.

HBCUs must assess the networking needs of their campuses so they are prepared to explore cost-effective means of connectivity. Pricing of local, regional, and national Internet service providers (ISP) may vary, so it is best to investigate available options. This same rule applies when exploring campus bandwidth needs. For example, some bandwidth options include burstable bandwidth and fractional bandwidth. A burstable T-3 or DS3 provides 45 megabits per second (Mbps) of bandwidth, yet the monthly bill calculates charges based on *use* of bandwidth. Thus the term "burstable"—a customer is only charged for the bursts of use and not a steady stream of connectivity. This method of connectivity has become popular with companies with sporadic data flow that are trying to limit their costs. The fractional DS3 provides a campus with 10 Mbps of bandwidth and ability to increase bandwidth to the full capacity of the DS3. The fractional DS3 option allows a campus to grow into the full use of a DS3. The burstable and fractional bandwidth options can be cost-effective ways for a campus to access high bandwidth. Investing in the proper technology will determine the contributions an HBCU institution can make in science, engineering, and education.

Proper funding is essential and strategic planning is necessary. Several reports and studies (Booz Allen Hamilton, 1998; Booz Allen Hamilton et al., 2000; Lord, 1998; Myers, 2000) indicate that many HBCUs lack a strategic technology plan, budget, staff, equipment, and training. Indeed, only 20 percent of the TAS-surveyed HBCUs are even networked with the U.S. government (Myers, 2000).

Strategic planning should involve members of senior-level administration—from the president to the CIO to faculty and staff. Various levels of the institution's staff must agree with the institution's strategic plan. Budgeting for training, hardware replacement, and software is critical in strategic planning. Capital campaigns directed to alumni, foundations, and corporations should be put in place. The participation of senior administrators may require educating them about the impact technology has on their recruitment of the students, faculty, and staff needed to keep their institutions open.

CONCLUSION

HBCUs must be willing to establish connectivity beyond their campus borders so that they are able to form *collaborative relationships* that can help decrease the costs of connectivity. HBCUs must become full participants in the digital era before they can have an opportunity to become technological innovators. With the establishment of collaborative relationships, HBCUs could have the opportunity to become technological innovators—not just participants in the digital era. They must make known that their institutions are determined to have the technological tools needed so that they can make an impact on science, education, and research.

There is something that is almost inexplicable about the determined spirit of the African American institutions that are known as HBCUs. For HBCUs to remain strong and competitive in higher education, they must continue to invest in the resources—whether human capital or hardware—that will bridge the digital divide. Only then will they be able to contribute to and benefit from the rapid advances in science and technology. IT is no longer an option—HBCUs must be technologically fit to survive the new millennium.

REFERENCES

Bernstein, R., Caplan, J., & Glover, E. (2001). *Yahoo! Internet Life: America's Most Wired Colleges 2000* [On-line]. Available: http://www.zdnet.com/yil/content/college. Retrieved September 25, 2001.

Booz Allen Hamilton. (1998). *Technology transfer project strategic planning.* New York: Executive Leadership Foundation.

Booz Allen Hamilton, The Gallup Organization, & EVAXX Inc. (2000). *Historically black public colleges and universities: An assessment of current information technology usage.* New York: Thurgood Marshall Scholarship Fund.

Dash, D. (1999, December 9). *Personal commentary.* Presented at the Digital Divide Summit, Department of Commerce, Washington DC.

DigitalEmpowerment.org. (2003). *Fiscal Year 2003 Federal Budget Snapshot: Administration Proposes the Elimination of Two Important Community Technology Programs* [On-Line]. Retrieved November, 06, 2003 from the World Wide Web: http://www.digitalemployment.org/background/budget.html/.

Executive Leadership Council and Foundation (ELCF). (2001). *Executive Leadership Council & Foundation* [On-line]. Available: http://www.elcinfo.com. Retrieved September 25, 2001.

Gateway Computers. (2000). *Higher education programs* [On-line]. Available: http://www.gateway.com/work/edu/hi-ed. Retrieved September 25, 2001.

Hardy, H. E. (1993). *The history of the net.* Unpublished master's thesis, Grand Valley State University, Allendale.

Leiner, B. M., Cerf, V. G., Clark, D. D., Kahn, R. E., Kleinrock, L., Lynch, D. C., Postel, J., Roberts, L. G., & Wolff, S. (2000, August 4). *A brief history of the Internet* [On-line]. Available: http://www.isoc.org/internet-history. Retrieved December 2000.

Lord, W. P. (1998). *Obstacles to the acquisition, implementation and utilization of technology at historically black colleges and universities.* ELCF TTP Faculty White Paper: Technology Enriched Education at Historically Black Colleges and Universities [On-line]. Available: http://www.elcinfo.com/tech_paper1.html. Retrieved September 25, 2001.

Miller, K. (2001, February 22). Digital divide now has 2 spans. *The Industry Standard*

[On-line]. Available: http://www.thestandard.com/article/0,1902,22407, 00.html. Retrieved July 19, 2001.

Myers, S. (2000). *Historically black colleges and universities: An assessment of networking and connectivity*. Washington, DC: National Association for Equal Opportunity in Higher Education for U.S. Department of Commerce, National Telecommunications and Information Administration Technologies Opportunities Program.

National Aeronautical Space Association. (2001). *Minority University-SPace Interdisciplinary Network (MU-SPIN)* [On-line]. Available: http://muspin. gsfc.nasa.gov/main/index.html. Retrieved September 25, 2001.

National Telecommunication and Information Administration. (1995). *Falling through the net. Full Report.* Washington DC: U.S. Department of Commerce.

National Telecommunication and Information Administration. (1998). *Falling through the net II: New data on the digital divide. Full report.* Washington DC: U.S. Department of Commerce.

National Telecommunication and Information Administration. (1999). *Falling through the net III: Defining the digital divide. Full report.* Washington DC: U.S. Department of Commerce.

National Telecommunication and Information Administration. (2000). *Falling through the net: Toward digital inclusion.* Washington DC: U.S. Department of Commerce.

Philanthropy News Digest. (2001, February 20). Bush administration may cut funding for digital divide programs. *Philanthropy News Digest, 7* [On-line], 8. Available: http://fdncenter.org/pnd/20010220/003981. Retrieved July 19, 2001.

Public Broadcasting System. (2000). Life on the Internet: Net timeline. *PBS Online* [On-line]. Available: http://www.pbs.org/internet/timeline/timeline-txt.html. Retrieved June 20, 2001.

Trotter, A. (2001, May 10). Closing the digital divide. *Education Week on the Web* [On-line]. Available: http://www.edweek.org/sreports/tc01/tc01article. cfm?slug=35Solutions.h20. Retrieved July 19, 2001.

University Corporation for Advanced Internet Development. (2001). Internet2 [On-line]. Available: http://www.internet2.org. Retrieved July 19, 2001.

Watts, J. C. (2000, June 15). *At historic summit, chairman Watts announces first GOP task force on black colleges* [News Release]. *GOP.gov.* Republican Conference, U.S. House of Representatives. Retrieved July 19, 2001 from the World Wide Web: http://www.gop.gov/00/item-news.asp?N=2000061516050.

Web-Based Education Commission (WBEC). (2000). The power of the Internet for learning: Moving from promise to practice. *U.S. Department of Education* [On-line]. Available: http://www.ed.gov/offices/AC/WBEC/FinalReport. Retrieved August 12, 2001.

Zakon, R. H. (2000). *Hobbes' Internet timeline* [On-line]. Available: http:// info.isoc.org/guest/zakon/Internet/History/HIT.html. Retrieved December 2000.

Digital Divide Resources

The Benton Foundation—http://www.benton.org
Digital Divide Network—http://www.digitaldividenetwork.org

Advanced Networking with Minority Serving Institutions (AN-MSI)—http://www.anmsi.org

Educational Technology Resources

Educause—http://www.educause.edu
EOT-PACI—http://www.eot.org
The Executive Leadership Council & Foundation—http://www.elcinfo.com
Internet2—http://www.internet2.edu
American Council on Education (ACENet)—http://www.acenet.edu/resources/

HBCU Resources

White House Initiative on HBCUs—http://www.ed.gov/about/inits/list/whhbcu/edlite-index.html
United Negro College Fund (UNCF)—http://www.uncf.org
National Association for Equal Opportunity (NAFEO)—http://www. nafeo.org

Federal Funding Opportunities

National Science Foundation—http://www.nsf.gov/home/programs/recent.htm
Department of Education—http://www.ed.gov/funding.html
Department of Commerce's National Telecommunications & Information Administration (NTIA) Technology Opportunity Program (TOP)—http://www.ntia.doc.gov/otiahome/top/
NASA's MU-SPIN—http://muspin.gsfc.nasa.gov/Home.html
Defense Advanced Research Agency (DARPA)—http://www.darpa.mil/

Other Funding Resources

Andrew W. Mellon Foundation—http://www.mellon.org/
AOL Time Warner Foundation—http://www.aoltimewarnerfoundation. org/
AT&T Foundation—http://www.att.com/foundation/
Bill & Melinda Gates Foundation—http://www.gatesfoundation.org
Carnegie Foundation—http://www.carnegiefoundation.org/
Ford Foundation—http://www.fordfound.org/
The Foundation Center—http://fdncenter.org/
General Electric Foundation—http://www.ge.com/community/fund/index.html
Knowledge Works Foundation—http://www.kwfdn.org/
Lucent Technologies Foundation—http://www.lucent.com/news/foundation/home.html
The Pew Charitable Trusts—http://www.pewtrusts.com/
W. K. Kellogg Foundation—http://www.wkkf.org/

Digital Divide Reports

Research Foundations on Successful Participation of Underrepresented Minorities in Information Technology: A Cyber Conference—http://www.cise.nsf.gov/itminorities.html

Department of Commerce Reports—http://www.ntia.doc.gov/ntiahome/digitaldivide/

Pew Internet and American Life Project: African-Americans and the Internet—http://www.pewinternet.org/reports/toc.asp?Report = 25

PART II

Issues of Praxis

CHAPTER 7

College in Black and White: White Faculty at Black Colleges

Lenoar Foster and Janet A. Guyden

INTRODUCTION

Historically black colleges and universities (HBCUs) have always navigated the "balance between identity and participation" (Parsons, 1969, p. 71) in educating African American students for participation in the wider context of American society. According to Parsons, this "identity in some sense always involves an aspect of separateness, but not absolute separation, while participation, by contrast, requires by definition access to and experience with the rest of the society" (p. 76). Within this context of dualism, Pettigrew (1971) has observed that "the missions of the black college over the past century, then, have ranged from producing an articulate black middle class and concerted protest for change to serving as cultural repositories and links to Africa" (p. 816). Thompson (1978) further observes that "the central challenging mission of black colleges has always been that of transforming socioeconomically and academically handicapped black youth into productive citizens, competent professionals, businessmen, and leaders" (p. 188). Indeed, the cultivation and attainment of academic achievement within a concerned, caring, focused, and success-oriented academic community remains a defining mark for HBCUs in the arena of contemporary higher education in America (Brazzell, 1996; Jordon-Cox, 1987; Wagener & Nettles, 1998).

Central and crucial to the attainment of these missions and tasks have been the faculty of HBCUs. In describing the quality and motivations of faculty at black colleges and universities, Thompson (1978) has noted that "the overall quality of black college faculties varied greatly from one institution to the other and from time to time in the history of any in-dividual school. Hardly any black college has ever been without a small, stable core of good-to-great teachers. Teaching is for them a calling in which they find both deep personal and professional satisfaction. Inci-dentally, many excellent white teachers are in black colleges for this same reason" (pp. 188–189).

Since the earliest foundations of higher education for African Americans in the United States, white missionary societies (an early source of faculty for emerging black institutions of higher education) and African American leaders and religious organizations that came to own and control HBCUs have shared a mutual and evolving conception of the appropriate education for African American youth in higher education institutions. Indeed, prior to and during the drive to integrate America's institutions of higher edu-cation, there has remained a cadre of white faculty who have deliberately chosen to pursue and live out their academic and social lives within the environment of institutions that are dedicated to the education and em-powerment of African American youth. It is this incidental group of fac-ulty at black colleges and universities that this chapter will focus upon. Specifically, it will be our purpose to explore the presence and role, past and present, of white faculty at black colleges and universities.

An exploration of the presence and role of white faculty in HBCUs is not without its cautions. These cautions pertain to black and white faculty and to the institutions in which they carry out their academic and atten-dant roles. These cautions find particular relevancy in the observations made by Smith and Borgstedt (1985):

The black college campus is an interesting laboratory for the study of interracial interaction. White faculty who have been socialized in the majority role are abruptly assuming a minority role within the black institution. Inherent within this new role is ambiguity related to role patterns and their current situation. Both white and black faculty and black students and administrators bring with them to their interaction their racial orientation and experiences from the dominant society. Their interaction is also influenced by the social context of the black col-lege, which is the reverse of the dominant society. In this environment, the social climate is one of black-in-charge, white as subordinate. Because racial issues are very salient in the black colleges, white faculty who have dealt with race at a distance or only on an intellectual level are required to confront the whole issue of race and to explore their own reactions, personal prejudices, and other internal and external barriers to effective interracial relationships. (p. 149)

Challenging in this context too is the behavior, both overt and covert, of black faculty, administrators, and students who view white faculty mem-bers as "other," "minority," and "representative of the dominant external culture" within the majority environment of the black institution.

We explore the presence and role of white faculty in HBCU institutions from a broad historical span and from an analysis of that presence to contemporary times. In this task we take an interpretive approach similar to that employed by Tobe Johnson (1971) in his "The Black College as System." Namely, our analysis is a reflective effort to unfold the typology of the white faculty member, past and present, at HBCU institutions from multiple sources, formal and informal. We seek to articulate what is known from the perspectives of black and white faculty members in HBCU institutions, and what is often unspoken by both groups and by the institutions in which they serve together. Within this interpretive framework, we also seek to challenge HBCU institutions in their assessment of the presence of white faculty on their campuses, and what their presence says about the commitment of these institutions to a wider diversity of input and expression as a "balance between identity and participation" in the education of African American students in this millennium.

HISTORY AND NECESSITY AS CONTEXT

The racial patterns of faculty composition in historically black colleges are, in part, a holdover from the earlier days when white-dominated religious and philanthropic societies took on the task of staffing segregated schools established for the freedmen shortly after the Civil War. Historically, the greatest growth in colleges and universities for African Americans occurred in the South during the 30 years following the Civil War, although earlier denominational efforts in the North had resulted in the establishment of Ashmun Institute (later Lincoln University) by the Presbyterian Church in 1854 and in the founding of Wilberforce University by the African Methodist Episcopal Church in Ohio in 1856. In the South the establishment of higher education institutions was led by "northern white benevolent societies and denominational bodies (missionary philanthropy) and black religious organizations (Negro philanthropy)" (Anderson, 1988, p. 239). Such organizations included the American Missionary Association, the American Baptist Home Mission Society, the Presbyterian Board of Missions for Freedmen, the African Methodist Episcopal Church, the African Methodist Episcopal Zion Church, and the Freedmen's Aid Society of the Methodist Episcopal Church. Of these white missionary groups, Browning and Williams (1978) observe:

... the missionaries tended to mix social, economic, and religious ideas in their dedication to the task of uplifting the freed men and women. They were moved not only by their religious convictions but also by the social and economic values that had produced the Yankee Protestant society of the North—particularly in New England. They were in agreement that someone needed to demonstrate that former slaves could be remade into the ideal of a Yankee, Calvinist, American citizen. Their common goals were to save souls, educate the minds, care for the bodies, and prepare the freed men and women for their responsibilities as new citizens of the South. (p. 69)

With the exception of those institutions founded by black religious organizations, northern white mission societies were primarily responsible for administering and maintaining the majority of the early collegiate institutions established for African Americans in the South. For almost a quarter century after the establishment of these institutions, the majority of administrators and faculty were white idealistic missionaries who were assisted in their educational endeavors by a nominal group of blacks that had been educated in the North (Browning & Williams, 1978; Brubacher & Rudy, 1997; Harris, 1971). Slater (1993) notes, "Even well into the twentieth century, most black colleges were still controlled and dependent on whites for operating funds. For the most part, these institutions were ruled by white administrations and staffed by white faculty" (p. 67). So predominant was the presence of white faculty and administrators in these institutions that "it was not until 1926 that Mordecai Johnson became the first black president of Howard University—60 years after the institution was founded" (Slater, p. 67).

Johnson (1971) observed that "faculty recruitment at all but a few black colleges is based on two elemental desiderata: (1) the need for faculty to teach the courses offered, and (2) the need for a sufficient number of persons with advanced degrees to meet the accreditation requirements of the regional accrediting agencies" (p. 804). By 1895, black colleges had produced 1,150 college graduates (Brazzell, 1996), and many of that number took positions as faculty in black colleges supported by religious organizations and in the 12 public black institutions established in the South under the Second Morrill Act of 1890.

From 1916 to 1942, a series of reports by the federal government and individual surveys by W. E. B. Du Bois and the Phelps-Stokes Fund provided public information on the curricula and quality of education in black colleges. These reports were credited, in large part, with providing the stimulus for black colleges to seek approval by regional accrediting agencies, a process that would mark black colleges as legitimate enterprises of higher education. Anderson (1988) noted that "no formal accrediting agency took black colleges seriously until 1928, when the Southern Association of Colleges and Secondary Schools decided to rate black institutions separately" (p. 250). As the stamp of accreditation increasingly marked the status and quality of higher education institutions in America from 1900 onward, an important goal of black colleges was to be accredited by their respective regional accrediting associations. As accrediting requirements called for certain percentages of faculty to hold terminal and advanced degrees, black colleges experienced varying degrees of difficulty in complying with this provision. Institutions such as the Atlanta University Center (now Clark Atlanta University), Fisk, Howard, and Tuskegee had little difficulty in attracting blacks with Ph.D. degrees. Johnson (1971) noted that "Because these schools graduated most of the students who subsequently took doctor's degrees, they were in a somewhat privileged competitive position in securing the young graduate's services. . . . and . . . they provided the best employment opportunities" (p. 805). Private and religiously affiliated black colleges continued to depend upon the services of white faculty, who had aligned themselves with these institutions for various religious, social, and political reasons, to meet the accrediting standards.

During the 1940s and 1950s, an increasingly valuable and available faculty pool for many black colleges was comprised of European immigrants, many of them Jewish scholars fleeing Europe to escape the tyranny of oppressive regimes and restrictions. As the Civil Rights Movement of the late 1950s, 1960s, and 1970s pervaded the national landscape, eliminating de jure segregation laws, faculty diversity at both private and public black colleges was enhanced by the presence of young, liberal, and idealistic white faculty seeking to carry forth the hard-won promises of the new American society grounded in equal rights and opportunities for all. Johnson (1971) noted, "These young people brought with them some strange and exciting new ideas from such places as Berkeley, MIT, and the Peace Corps. They also brought a not inconsiderable capacity for work, which leavened the impact of their ideas" (p. 806). In more contemporary times white faculty have been increasingly attracted to HBCUs because these institutions remain among the few higher education institutions where opportunities for academic employment remain open and viable, amid shrinking full-time and tenure-track professorial ranks in academe at predominantly white institutions.

THROUGH BIFOCAL LENSES: FRAMES OF REFERENCE

Because of the historical circumstances that surround the founding and administration of many of the early HBCU institutions and the varied roles (from egalitarian to paternalistic, from controlling to pacifying, from a work of service/mission to career opportunism) that whites have played in the life and development of these institutions, public and internal dialogue about faculty diversity on black campuses has been pointed and excoriating (Foster, 2001). Critically, Johnson (1971)—similar to voices on black campuses where Afrocentric scholarly perspectives are increasingly playing an important role in educational direction and pedagogy—has called into question whether the multiracial composition of the faculty at many black colleges and universities is necessarily synonymous with cosmopolitanism, and he observes that "it is not patent that the nonblack presence on these campuses has always been in the best interests of black educational development" (p. 805).

Several views about the motivations and reasons why white faculty teach at HBCU institutions are contained in the limited literature on the topic, and these views, at least among some black faculty, continue to persist in the informal underground of thinking about the role and place of white faculty members at black colleges and universities. Warnat (1976) states that it has been a general assumption by the dominant white culture that "white members of faculties at black institutions of higher learning, most often, are those individuals who are unable to obtain faculty positions at white institutions of higher learning, primarily due to a low level of competence in the particular academic discipline" (p. 335). Smith and Borgstedt (1985), for example, in their study of factors influencing the adjustment of white faculty in six predominantly black public and private colleges in the South and North, found that negative attitudes and comments from significant others, family members, and friends "attached some stigma to their position" (p. 159). While maintaining that the quality of white faculty is variable at black higher education institutions, Johnson (1971) has asserted that on many black campuses "these teachers are all too often political refugees who neither understand the culture nor speak the language intelligibly; retired professors whose energy level does not always measure up to their awesome responsibilities; and wives of professors who are comfortably employed at neighboring white schools" (p. 806).

The historical causality underlying faculty diversity at black colleges and universities and the continuing public and internal debate occasioned by it has prompted several black scholars to propose archetypes to define and assess the role, purposes, and outcomes of the presence of white faculty in black higher education institutions. Thompson (1978) has suggested that white faculty at black institutions fall into four distinct types: the missionary zealot (including the guilt-ridden zealot), the dedicated professional, the young and idealistic white scholar, and the academic reject.

A taxonomy of four classifications, which provide a perspective on some of the various roles played by white faculty, has been proposed by Warnat (1976). These classifications include white faculty as: (1) the Moron, (2) the Martyr, (3) the Messiah, and (4) the Marginal Man. According to Warnat, limited academic ability and limited or no access to white higher education institutions impel white faculty characterized as *Moron* to remain in the black institution. For white faculty members working in black institutions under this characterization, "all personal incompetencies can then be blamed on the institutional setting, thereby absolving personal feelings of frustration and inadequacy" (p. 335). The work of white faculty typed as *Martyr* is compared to that of "the zealous missionary who will do virtually anything in his power to relieve his guilt, including being punished for the errors committed by society" (pp. 335–336). Such faculty take on the drudge work of the institution and elicit the sympathy and condolence of black faculty for their willingness to tackle such responsibilities with a high measure of dedication. The major role of faculty typed as *Messiah* is "to attempt to provide the direction which they feel has been lacking" in the black institution in which they serve (p. 336). Lastly, *Marginal Man* white faculty live in two worlds and struggle to find their place and meaning in each. According to Warnat, this type of white faculty member "joins the black college faculty, but continues to remain an alien because of his affiliation with the white social structure" (p. 337). While this faculty member is motivated by the academic contribution that can be made to the advancement of the institution and its students, the task of "effectively combining conflicting cultures is unending" (p. 338).

The professional relationships and work of white faculty who are characterized by the archetypes proposed by Warnat (1976) and Thompson (1978), the perceptions they engender, the socialization and acculturation they undergo, the difficulties they may encounter in both academic and interpersonal encounters, and the acceptance and successes they experience vary widely (Anderson & Lancaster, in press; Foster & Guyden, 1998; Levy, 1967; Redinger, in press; Slater, 1993; Smith, 1982; Smith & Borgstedt, 1985). White faculty who are viewed as enhancing their own status through their unwarranted and unsubstantiated criticisms of black institutions can run the risk of being easily identified with "those ills inflicted by the white population and directly related to the black segment of the population" (Warnat, 1976, p. 335). Faculty who are perceived as well-intentioned yet deprecating in their assessment of their own status and worth to the black institution may enjoy good relations with students and other black colleagues, but may not realize that conscious acceptance of this status may, in the end, lessen the power of their contributions to the institution and serve as a barrier to their advancement of the vision of the institution. Faculty who consciously or unconsciously portray themselves as saviors, behavior indicative of a lack of respect for the history, customs, traditions, and successes of the institution, may encounter the most negative feelings on the part of their black colleagues and students. According to Warnat, "More than any other element of the white faculty, this one tends to foster mistrust and feelings of alienation and hostility among his colleagues towards him. Being a constant source of irritation, this individual is one whom colleagues would most like to eliminate" (p. 336).

New and young white faculty in black institutions may be the most clearly at risk because many of them come to higher education and to black institutions with new understandings of diversity and inclusion but continue to have to balance conflicting cultural perspectives and stereotypes that are the residue of a continuing "lack of social acceptance on the part of both whites and blacks in the imposition of social distance between them, and a real or perceived value conflict between blacks and whites" (Smith, 1982, p. 2) that continues in American society. For both black and white faculty at black colleges and universities it is instructive to review how the archetypes suggested by Warnat (1976) and Thompson (1978) give credence, through historical reality and through feelings and perceptions based on that history, to the continuing social distance between groups and to each group's perceptions of the other.

SOCIALIZATION AND ACCULTURATION: A CASE STUDY

An understanding of socialization and acculturation requires an analysis of a newcomer's experience in a new culture. Ostensibly, according to Reynolds (1992), "this means making sense of the individual's views in three of the world view categories: self, other, and relationship to other" (p. 638). For white faculty members in black colleges, the dynamics at work in the environment of a black majority provide a context of challenge and response. Chief among these challenges is the need for those participating in the process, white faculty member and the black majority constituency, to constantly reexamine realities—or, more accurately, their personal and institutional perspectives on the realities—of race, class, and gender. The opportunity the black college presents to white faculty and to its majority black constituency (both students and faculty) is the chance to broaden and challenge perceptions and perspectives within an atmosphere of mutual respect, civility, intellectual reciprocity, and equality. The response to this opportunity involves a validation of superficial differences, a recognition of deeper similarities, an acknowledgment of historical and contemporary inequities, and a commitment to eradicating structures and practices in a democratic society that hinder and negate the full potentialities of all citizens.

The case study that follows illustrates the complexities of this task in the context of the black college and points to the need for intellectual vigilance, understanding, and patience in the realization of personal and institutional goals. The case also outlines the consequences and benefits that accrue to white faculty and to the majority constituency of the black college who engage in mutually respectful dialogue and exchange. This case study represents the actual experiences of a white faculty member at two black institutions of higher education. Pseudonyms are used to protect the identity of the white faculty member and of the institutions.

GETTING TO KNOW YOU AND ME

Craig Bickenson was one of 13 freshly minted history Ph.D.s from a major university in the western part of the United States, and he, like his classmates, envisioned a tenure-track job right after graduation. The odds of snatching such a position were long, to say the least—few of the previous year's graduates had been successful in landing tenure-track positions. He began filling out applications for various positions in the fall of 1992, and after a few interviews at history conferences and a campus visit, his prospects for immediate employment in his field did not appear to be good. Craig's first experience with life on an HBCU campus came about as a result of his response to Stanfield College's job announcement for a position in history in the *Chronicle of Higher Education* in the last week of May 1993. The ad, while making no mention of tenure, did note that the school was a "small residential private liberal arts college [that] focuses on producing scholars." To achieve this goal, the school sought applicants who understood the nature and purpose of a liberal arts education. The position seemed to fit Craig well.

In the course of his job search, Craig had been careful to research all of the positions for which he had applied, but when he went to seek out Stanfield College, he could find little information. With a feeling of shooting in an unknown space, Craig applied for the position. In the days following the submission of his application and placement file, Stanfield College remained an enigma. It was not until a telephone interview three weeks later that Craig actually discovered that Stanfield was a black college. He learned of the school's identity when he was queried by the school's academic dean as to how the school's mission of educating African American students would affect the way he performed his job. After the question sunk in for a few seconds, Craig replied that he would, of course, need to adjust the traditional "Great White Man" way of teaching history to make his courses more meaningful to the students of Stanfield College. The rest of the telephone interview went well, and Craig was invited to visit the campus for a face-to-face interview in late July.

As Craig prepared to journey to Stanfield College for the campus visit, he had to do some hasty consideration of where his life was taking him. He had not completely come to grips with the very real possibility that he might get a job at a predominantly black college. He approached the on-campus interview with considerable trepidation, although he was excited about the challenges inherent in teaching at a school that reflected a reality so radically different from the one he lived in the West.

The campus visit to Stanfield was a cordial affair. The people with whom Craig would eventually work expressed great interest in him and in his perspectives for restructuring a World Civilizations course to emphasize Afrocentric themes. Craig made it clear during the interview that this would be a position into which he would need to grow, since his whole experience in education centered on Western themes of civilization. At the end of the two-day interview, Craig noticed that none of the members of the search committee had addressed the issue which at the time seemed most obvious, that of his race. During the last scheduled meeting with the school's academic dean, Craig broached the subject. He remarked, "Frankly, I was curious why a black college would want to hire me, a kid from the West." The dean replied by noting the perceived need of the institution to broaden the perspectives of its students to prepare them for the world. The response seemed reasonable and appropriate. Craig accepted the position at Stanfield College.

From his first stroll across Stanfield's campus as a faculty member, Craig sensed a strange, unspoken aura about the place. Craig reflected:

It is still unclear to me today whether or not this feeling was one that arose from me, or rather from those who saw me as an outsider. I am, however, sure of the sense of profound loneliness which I felt walking across the campus to the student union building. I think it odd now, and thought it odd then, that this sense that I was intruding on unfamiliar ground did not dissipate as the months passed. A feeling of pressure settled on me when I drove onto the campus. In spite of my efforts to know the place and integrate into the life of the campus, it remained *terra incognita*.

Craig's faculty colleagues, particularly those in his own academic department, greeted his arrival on campus with genuine hospitality. Most of the people on the search committee were his departmental faculty members, and for them he was more of a known quantity than was the case for most of the college's other faculty. In assessing the hospitality of his home department, Craig remembered: "This may have been because our department, comprising the disciplines of history, political science, and psychology, was the only one on campus with more than a single white faculty member (the racial breakdown of our department was five African Americans, three white faculty, and one Middle Eastern faculty member)." For a school that prided itself on its smallness, friendliness, and accessibility, however, Craig noticed that the faculty as a whole seemed little interested in getting to know him. Indeed, few went out of their way to welcome him and to make him feel at ease within the campus community.

From the perspective of the student body, Craig merited the politeness any faculty member deserved. Most of his students seemed to take his presence on campus in stride. As he learned in informal conversations with some of the students, they were simply used to white teachers. Many of his students had had white teachers from their earliest years in school. What Craig came to realize from talks with other students was

that he represented the only white person many of the students at Stanfield saw on a day-to-day basis. Actually, as he came to realize, he was
the only white person with whom many of them had any daily contact.
He was told that they went to the black malls, the black grocery stores,
and the black dance clubs, and they watched the black channel on
television.

The deferential veneer of respect and tolerance that Craig came to expect from students, he soon learned, masked many of the attitudes em-
braced by a more Afrocentrically oriented faction of the student body. This
veneer was finally ripped away near the end of the second semester at
Stanfield. A heated exchange in one of his classes made it clear that there
was a significant percentage of the student body for which Craig's race
was a problem. One student stood up, with the encouragement of others,
and raised the issue that students were paying a relatively high tuition to
go to a historically black college only to have to take classes from a white
professor. Sensing that he had stumbled upon a "teachable moment,"
Craig turned the issue around on the student to help her and others see
the problem from a new perspective. He asked, "Suppose you were a
professor at a predominantly white school, and I complained that I had
to pay to take a class from a black woman. Would that not be a racist
comment?" She agreed that, of course, it would be, but insisted that the
situation at Stanfield was different. Craig was not clear on the finer points
of the distinctions she was willing to draw. He was, however, clear on the
fact that this day affected the rest of his classes at Stanfield. Whenever
Craig spoke, he was aware of the fact that there were students who could
not look beyond the color of his skin. He remembered that his department
chair remained steadfastly supportive of him—even welcoming a representative of the student faction to confer with him and the department
chair in his office. With sadness Craig remembered that the school's administration avoided openly defending him against the prejudicial atti-
tude in the student body, even when these very students met with the
president of the institution.

Craig remained at Stanfield College for two years and left that institution when his term of appointment was completed. While still searching
for jobs in a tight educational market, he accepted an adjunct position in
history at Rosa Parks State University, a state-supported historically black
institution that was situated in the same state as his previous place of
employment. Craig found that the more globally representative and
broad-based student body at the state university provided him with a
more congenial welcome than that which he had received at Stanfield
College. He soon discovered that within a context of welcome and mutual
respect, the work he had begun at Stanfield College to adjust his historical
field of vision continued and began to bear results. Commenting upon his
experience at the two institutions, Craig reflected:

I found that the awareness that arose out of my experiences at Stanfield College served me well at my new institution. Clearly, the classroom dynamic at Parks University was different from what it had been at Stanfield. At Stanfield, students were, on the whole, extraordinarily passive recipients of knowledge. But at Parks State University students were more aggressive in their pursuit of ideas. They challenged me more. As I was drawing them into deeper understandings of the relationships between African and Asian civilizations, they were demanding more of me. Perhaps most rewarding for me was the opportunity to help reeducate my students, whose high school history experiences reflected the same sort of older assumptions about history that I had been spending time undoing in myself.

During his time at Rosa Parks State University, Craig faced a unique opportunity to test his new perspectives on the place of underrepresented groups in history when he got an opportunity to teach a Western Civilizations course at a predominantly white branch of the state university system. He recounted:

This was a wonderful opportunity for me to see how many of these themes would fly when presented to an audience that resembled the institutions that I had attended as a student, i.e., the institutions at which I learned a more Eurocentric view of history. Unfortunately, the experience failed to be as full a comparison as I had hoped. The curriculum of Western Civilization history left less room for consideration of other civilization centers such as Africa, India, Asia, and pre-Columbian Latin America. I was able, however, to transfer many of the newer understandings of the position of women and minority groups in Western society. This effort reflected favorably in my students' reactions to the course, which many considered to be the first "real history" course they had taken.

When an opportunity presented itself for Craig to teach in a college near his home in the West, after two years of teaching at Stanfield College and one year at Rosa Parks State University, he joyously welcomed the chance to be near family relations and accepted the position. In remembering his departure, he commented:

In packing up my offices I boxed up more than simply books, pens, and class notes. It was clear to me that I was also packing up a whole gamut of new experiences and perspectives. I was a different person than I had been three years before. It was not yet clear to me how these new insights and awarenesses would translate to what was essentially my old world. It was clear, however, that they would change forever the ways I pursued my career.

In his new teaching position at a moderate-sized state university in the western part of the United States, Craig has responsibility for teaching a series of three upper-division courses in U.S. history. His classes do not come close to resembling the diversity of students he encountered at Stanfield College and at Parks State University. In teaching his new courses to what amounts to a homogenous group of students who come to the university from similar communities, Craig has found opportunities and challenges. With regard to a course titled *Birth of Modern America, 1877–1914,* Craig reports:

In keeping with the newer perspectives that I gained teaching U.S. history at Stanfield College and at Parks State University, I spend a great deal of time examining the histories of African American sharecroppers and tenant farmers in the post-Reconstruction period and the rise of the Black Farmer's Alliance in the 1890s in the course I teach. I also help my students to examine the conditions that made the establishment of the NAACP necessary in 1909 and the roles played by African Americans in World War I.

In one class session, after several such inclusive lectures as Craig recounted above, one of his white students spoke up and said, "What is this? A black history class?" While he was initially shocked by the comment, Craig was able to turn the comment into a jumping-off point for discussion of what, after all, is American society. "What I was trying to emphasize," he says, "was that, in the words of a former colleague at Stanfield College, *they're us.*" Craig was attempting to communicate to his students that an understanding of the histories of all people who make up the fabric of the nation was essential to a whole history of who we are as Americans and as a nation. "Clearly," he said, "I had changed what I believed about history."

Craig's case offers insight into the dynamics of challenge and response that await new—and even seasoned—white faculty in black colleges whose prior training may not be congruent with spoken or unspoken institutional expectations. In particular, this case provides insightful evidence of what can happen to the individual white faculty member, to students, and to the institution when there is incongruence between what is expected and what actually transpires in both academic and social venues. It is clear that in Craig's situation at Stanfield College, the type of mentoring that might have allowed him to be accepted more fully within the campus community was missing. Whether this deficit of support is attributable to the facade of academic freedom, with its consequences that institutions shroud themselves in to build cases for support or nonsupport, is not totally clear in Craig's case. What is disconcerting is that in practice Stanfield College did not measure up to the traditional legacy of providing guidance and support for one member of its academic community, a tradition prized by HBCU institutions and condemned by critics of predominantly white institutions where minority faculty are summarily dismissed on many levels.

Can the residual effects of Craig's personal transformation and the inclusive disciplinary growth he experienced at Stanfield College and Parks

State University be said to have had an effect on his career, and by association, on the learning environment that students who come under his tutelage later will experience? From what he says, the answer is yes. But should HBCU institutions frame themselves as training grounds for creating these individuals who will leave their campuses and spread the good news of that transformation? The answer is unequivocally no. The eventual conflicts over ideology and academic grounding, as in Afrocentric perspectives to disciplinary content and discovery, and the subsequent transformations that can occur among and between white faculty, black faculty, and students in black colleges, do not make the institutions microcosms for experimenting with plausible solutions to race relations in the nation. Such interaction does make HBCU institutions models of the kinds of frank and honest discourse, based on mutual respect and support, that should be taking place within the wider society. To this end, faculty diversity facilitates and champions liberation from all sorts of myths, stereotypes, and presumed superiorities and inferiorities. The effect becomes empowering through mutual interactions involving authentic exchange and becomes efficacious for the living out of authentic truth in the wider society. In this journey HBCU institutions bear the same responsibilities as other institutions of higher education, while remaining true and faithful to their traditional missions of service to students through access and service to the community through the contributions of educated citizens.

Increasingly, as HBCU institutions attempt to attract more students of diverse backgrounds to their student bodies, they will have to answer the same questions that continue to plague majority institutions: How does what we do serve to welcome diversity in kind and in fact, and how do our institutional culture and history both inform and support inclusive practices? The response to these questions will not only provide insight into the need to support diverse faculty, but will also provide a framework for valuing the very diversity within color that characterizes the best in black higher education.

REFERENCES

Anderson, J. D. (1988). *The education of blacks in the South, 1860–1935.* Chapel Hill: University of North Carolina Press.

Anderson, T. P., & Lancaster, J. S. (1999). Building conversations of respect: The voice of white faculty at black colleges. In L. Foster, J. A. Guyden, & A. L. Miller (Eds.), *Affirmed action: Essays on the academic and social lives of white faculty members at historically black colleges and universities.* Lanham, MD: Rowman & Littlefield.

Brazzell, J. C. (1996). Diversification of postsecondary institutions. In S. R. Komives & D. W. Woodard (Eds.), *Student services: A handbook for the profession* (pp. 43–63). San Francisco: Jossey-Bass.

Browning, J. E., & Williams, J. B. (1978). History and goals of black institutions of higher learning. In C. V. Willie & R. R. Edmonds (Eds.), *Black colleges in America* (pp. 68–93). New York: Teachers College Press.

Brubacher, J. S., & Rudy, W. (1997). *Higher education in transition: A history of American colleges and universities.* New Brunswick, NJ: Transaction Publishers.

Foster, L., & Guyden, J. A. (1998). *Content analysis of the viewpoints of selected white faculty members at HBCUs.* Symposium presented at the Fifth National HBCU Faculty Development Network Conference, Miami, FL.

Foster, L. (2001). The not-so-invisible professors: White faculty at The black College. *Urban Education, 36*(5), 611–629.

Harris, P. R. (1971). The Negro college and its community. *Daedalus, 100*(3), 720–731.

Holmes, D. O. W. (1972). *The evolution of the Negro College.* New York: AMS Press.

Johnson, T. (1971). The black colleges as system. *Daedalus, 100*(3), 798–812.

Jordan-Cox, C. A. (1987). Psychosocial development of students in traditionally black institutions. *Journal of College Student Personnel, 28*(6), 504–512.

Levy, C. (1967). *The process of integrating white faculty into a predominantly Negro college.* Washington, DC: Department of Health, Education and Welfare. (ERIC Document Reproduction Service No. ED 052 744)

Pettigrew, T. F. (1971). The role of whites in the black college of the future. *Daedalus, 100*(3), 813–832.

Redinger, M. A. (1999). You just wouldn't understand. In L. Foster, J. A. Guyden, & A. L. Miller (Eds.), *Affirmed action: Essays on the academic and social lives of white faculty members at historically black colleges and universities.* Lanham, MD: Rowman & Littlefield.

Reynolds, A. (1992). Charting the changes in junior faculty: Relationships among socialization, acculturation, and gender. *Journal of Higher Education, 63*(6), 637–652.

Slater, R. B. (1993). White professors at black colleges. *Journal of Blacks in Higher Education, 1*(1), 67–70.

Smith, S. L. (1982). *Dynamics of interracial relationships involving white faculty in black colleges: Review, systematization, and directives.* Paper presented at the annual meeting of the Council for Social Work Education, New York.

Smith, S. L., & Borgstedt, K. W. (1985). Factors influencing adjustment of white faculty in predominantly black colleges. *Journal of Negro Education, 54*(2), 148–163.

Thompson, C. H. (1978). Control and administration of the Negro college. *Journal of Educational Sociology, 19*(5), 162–201.

Wagener, U., & Nettles, M. T. (1998). It takes a community to educate students. *Change, 30*(2), 18–25.

Warnat, W. I. (1976). The role of white faculty on the black college campus. *Journal of Negro Education, 45*(3), 334–338.

CHAPTER 8

Orientation and Colleagues: Making a Difference in the Socialization of Black College Faculty

Barbara J. Johnson

INTRODUCTION

A function of socialization is to provide individuals with the formal and informal knowledge necessary to be successful within an organization. In essence, new faculty cannot be expected to learn what is necessary to be successful at their new place of employment through osmosis. Another purpose of socialization is to build loyalty and commitment to the institution (Schein, 1968). However, a sense of allegiance to an organization does not occur by virtue of an individual's employment. Hence, historically black colleges and universities (HBCUs) must take steps to provide a positive socialization experience for faculty or risk faculty entering and leaving the institution through a revolving door.

AFRICAN AMERICAN FACULTY AT HBCUS

HBCUs employ faculty from a variety of racial and ethnic backgrounds. Roebuck and Murty (1993) report that 55 percent of full-time African American faculty are concentrated at HBCUs, which comprise only 3 percent of the United States' educational institutions. Caucasians and other minorities and foreigners account for 40 percent and 5 percent, respectively, of the faculty at HBCUs (Roebuck & Murty, 1993). Given the diversity of faculty at HBCUs versus that of traditionally white institutions, the reader may anticipate an abundance of research on HBCU faculty, but few studies in any form have focused on faculty at HBCUs.

Relatedly, there is limited research on minority faculty, who are disproportionately underrepresented in higher education. In the academic year

1993–1994, there were 533,770 full-time faculty, of which 25,269 (4.7 percent) were Asian; 25,658 (4.8 percent) were African American; 12,076 (2.3 percent) were Hispanic; and 1,997 (0.4 percent) were American Indian (Carter & Wilson, 1996). As indicated by these figures, minority faculty comprise only 12 percent of all U.S. faculty while minorities make up approximately 25 percent of the total U.S. population. For example, in 1991 the U.S. Bureau of the Census reported that African Americans comprised 12.1 percent of the U.S. population, in contrast to their representation in academe of 4.5 percent.

The National Center for Education Statistics reports that 7,777 (58 percent) of the 13,406 full-time faculty at HBCUs are African American, with women accounting for 45 percent of African American faculty (cited in Fields, 1997). Even though African Americans comprise more than half of the faculty at HBCUs, the National Advisory Committee reported that Caucasians and Asian Americans were more likely than African Americans to hold the rank of professor and associate professor at HBCUs (cited in Billingsley, 1982). Another study found that only one in five full-time African American faculty at HBCUs holds the rank of professor (Fields, 1997). African American faculty were also found to be underrepresented at the rank of assistant professor at HBCUs (Billingsley, 1982).

Roebuck and Murty (1993) reported that many African American faculty members prefer to teach at HBCUs to avoid the status ambiguities and racial conflict they may encounter at traditionally white institutions. African American faculty viewed themselves as belonging to an "extended-family academic group" which resulted in feelings of belonging, psychological comfort, and success, with all faculty perceiving their work as a career not a job. Faculty at HBCUs indicate dissatisfaction with a perceived lack of professional recognition, levels of bureaucracy, low wages, heavy teaching loads, and inadequate or poor facilities (Diener, 1985), which is similar to what studies of white faculty at traditionally white institutions have found. Billingsley (1982) concluded that one reason African American faculty remain at HBCUs is because of the large African American student population and their desire to educate African American students as well as to build "strong black faculties."

SOCIALIZATION DEFINED

Socialization, as defined by Merton (1957), is a process through which individuals acquire the values, attitudes, norms, knowledge, and skills needed to exist in a given society. Socialization generally occurs when a new faculty member enters the organization. Additionally, socialization takes place continuously and may happen implicitly or explicitly. It is difficult to observe and analyze implicit socialization because it is spontaneous and unobtrusive, whereas explicit socialization involves clearly defined cultural structures (Tierney & Rhoads, 1994). Tierney and Bensimon (1996) characterize socialization as the rite of passage that begins with probationary membership in the department and concludes, if one is successful, with the granting of lifetime tenure or, if unsuccessful, with immediate termination.

Faculty socialization involves two stages: anticipatory socialization and the organizational stage. Anticipatory socialization occurs prior to employment, generally during graduate school, and involves taking on the norms of the profession. Wanous defines anticipatory socialization as how nonmembers take on the attitudes, actions, and values of the group to which they aspire (cited in Tierney & Rhoads, 1994). The organizational stage involves two phases: initial entry and role continuance. Initial entry involves interactions that might occur during the recruitment and selection process, as well as the early period of organizational learning that occurs when the new faculty member begins employment. The phase of role continuance begins after the individual is situated in the organization (Tierney & Rhoads, 1994).

IMPORTANCE OF SOCIALIZATION

Faculty members who have a positive socialization experience tend to be more satisfied, less stressed, and in general more productive and successful, resulting in their retention at the institution (Tierney & Rhoads, 1994). When a faculty member leaves an institution because of poor socialization, the institution suffers because it has invested time, energy, and resources in the faculty member. A faculty member's departure results in the institution engaging in another search process, which costs the institution in terms of relocation and interviewing expenses, time and energy of faculty and staff, and possible low morale among faculty and students relative to the loss of a valued colleague. Conversely, some faculty who experience a poor socialization may stay at the institution, which could result in a lack of productivity and bitter feelings toward the institution (Boice, 1992a).

One may wonder if faculty socialization at HBCUs is of concern, since Roebuck and Murty (1993) report that the majority (55 percent) of full-time African American faculty work at HBCUs. Roebuck and Murty found African American faculty at HBCUs "adjusted well in a familiar milieu that met their personal, social and career needs" (p. 118). Furthermore, Johnson (1999) concluded that the overall experience of African American faculty at HBCUs was positive. However, this does not mean HBCUs can rest on their laurels and do nothing. HBCUs must take steps now to implement policy and procedures to ensure that the socialization experience is positive and effective. For example, even though Johnson concluded that the overall experience of African American faculty at HBCUs was positive, an overwhelming majority of the faculty in the study stated that senior faculty were not showing them the ropes. Showing faculty the ropes involves not just being informed of the promotion and tenure expectations but encompasses the shortcuts, advising and registration procedures, and so on, which are an integral part of the socialization experience.

It is anticipated that there will be a mass exodus of faculty retiring in the early twenty-first century and that institutions will scurry for faculty members. This expected exodus would create employment opportunities at institutions with great resources, support, and opportunities for research, which many HBCUs may be unable to offer. Herein lies the significance of a positive socialization experience at HBCUs. If HBCUs are effective in providing new faculty with a positive socialization experience, perhaps new faculty will decide to stay at HBCUs when opportunities offering perceived greater benefits arise. By providing a positive socialization experience, HBCUs build commitment and loyalty to the institution while also informing faculty of what is necessary to be successful, which could reduce the number of faculty who choose to leave. It is up to administrators and faculty at HBCUs to identify and understand how faculty are currently socialized and to take steps to enhance the socialization experience instead of remaining passive and hoping that the environment will be enough to not only retain quality faculty but attract new faculty as well.

Accordingly, this chapter explores the positive influences of the socialization process for African American faculty. It is recognized that institutional leadership, type, and discipline influence the organizational culture, which in turn affects all aspects of the socialization process; however, this chapter focuses on the positive influences in the socialization process at HBCUs.

Orientation and colleague support are two methods that can be utilized to enhance the socialization experience of faculty at HBCUs. Orientation is a systematic method of building loyalty and commitment to the institution while also informing faculty of the formal and informal information necessary to be successful. Fink (1992) asserts that orientation provides new faculty with a head start by affording them the opportunity to meet faculty and administrators and informing them of institutional norms, values, expectations, and policies. Colleagues are instrumental in communicating the informal and formal norms and guidelines while simultaneously strengthening a new faculty member's commitment and loyalty to the institution. Furthermore, research confirms that colleague support is influential in the performance of new faculty (Austin, 1992; Boice, 1992b; Jarvis, 1992).

HBCUs can have a direct impact on orientation as well as influence the type and amount of support colleagues provide to new faculty. The following are suggested methods relative to colleagues and orientation that HBCUs can implement to have a positive impact on faculty socialization.

ORIENTATION

As stated previously, an orientation is a way for HBCUs to begin the process of building faculty loyalty and commitment to the institution. The primary purpose of an orientation should be to introduce new faculty to the institution's culture by way of the institution's formal rules, guidelines, and procedures as well as through interactions with senior faculty and other new faculty across disciplines and departments (Fink, 1992). An initial orientation to the institution can alleviate some of the anxieties new faculty experience as they enter a new environment. Orientations can bring about a sense of collegiality through a common experience that could enhance and improve working relationships (Alexander-Snow & Johnson, 1999). Moreover, orientation programs can provide faculty with a head start, letting them know where they are, with whom they are working, and the preferred norms, values, and policies (Fink, 1992).

Institutionwide orientations organized by the human resources office are critical to ensuring that faculty are able to complete all human resources related tasks (i.e., payroll, benefits, 401(k), parking, identification cards, etc.) in a central location. New faculty could be required to attend institutionwide orientation sessions, as more general aspects of employee orientation are covered. However, HBCUs should not fool themselves into thinking that an institutionwide orientation is sufficient to meet the needs of new faculty. Orientations designed specifically for new faculty would provide a deeper level of insight into the institution, an understanding of institutional values and expectations, and the opportunity to meet other faculty with related research interests. A new faculty orientation, organized by academic affairs, designed specifically for new faculty, might include the following:

- a review of policies and procedures relative to office hours, course syllabi, class content, meeting schedules, exam schedules, contact hours, advisement, committee assignments, and departmental meetings;
- introductions to pertinent offices—benefits, grants, travel, computing, payroll;
- a faculty handbook that can be revised or updated as needed. The handbook should include promotion and tenure rules and regulations as well as what to expect at different points in the academic process. Additionally, a timeline of where faculty should be at different points in their career will help faculty gauge their progress;
- an overview of the library system;
- a sense of what the institution values and emphasizes;
- a review of standard operating policies and procedures;
- a campus tour; and
- introductions to the primary players on campus.

Institutions should ensure, if at all possible, that faculty are hired at least one month prior to the beginning of the semester. This will give new faculty more time to become acclimated not only to the institution but to the locality as well. When new faculty are notified of job offers close to the beginning of the semester, they are put at a disadvantage. For example, new faculty may miss the orientation sessions that provide an official introduction to the institution as well as to other newcomers. Unfortunately, this type of introduction to the institution is stressful and induces the elements of a negative socialization experience, which is why the institution must take action.

Institutions could make the transition easier if new faculty were hired earlier (midsummer at the latest) to alleviate some of the stress related to accepting a new position when starting within a few weeks of the semester. However, if circumstances do not allow for the optimal hiring situation, then a designated individual could assist new faculty with the transition by helping with academic and personal issues. This would indicate that the institution is committed to the individual's success while also building the foundation for the individual's allegiance to the institution.

Given all of the demands on faculty, particularly new faculty, at the beginning of the semester, it would be prudent to provide faculty with a general introduction to the institution prior to the start of the semester and have monthly orientation seminars throughout the first year, or first semester at a minimum. It seems rather odd that new students are not expected to learn what is necessary for success in one day but new faculty are. Many institutions offer freshman orientation seminars throughout the first semester to help new students with the transition to college. Likewise, institutions should institute monthly orientation sessions for new faculty to allow them to obtain information about relevant topics in a reasonable and unhurried manner without everything being crammed into one day. The initial new faculty orientation could focus on immediate issues which may be of concern to faculty—parking, benefits, library, identification cards, payroll, banks, cleaners, a campus tour, copy center, computing center. This will assist faculty in become acclimated to the institution and city more quickly.

Monthly new faculty orientation sessions would provide a way for the institution to touch base with new faculty—to see how they are doing and to provide assistance in solving problems while allowing new faculty to bond and discuss common issues. Another important function of the monthly orientation sessions would entail focusing on aspects of significance to new faculty in a comprehensive manner. For example, promotion and tenure, internal and external grants, travel funds, policies and procedures, and registration and advising are typical areas of which new faculty need to have an in-depth understanding. However, the initial new faculty orientation, usually held in August, is not the optimal time to discuss these issues as new faculty are still acclimating to the institution and community and are likely to remember only key details regarding immediate concerns.

The monthly orientation sessions would allow new faculty to learn about aspects critical to their success and transition to the institution. Faculty should be required to attend at least half of the monthly orientation sessions, which should be scheduled at various times and days to allow the maximum number of faculty to attend. Planning and coordinating the monthly orientation sessions may be additional work for the office of academic affairs; however, the benefits of a positive faculty socialization experience will not be for naught as faculty retention increases. Additionally, HBCUs should continually evaluate whether each session is effectively providing new faculty with information necessary to be successful and make changes as needed. Accordingly, a new faculty orientation experience must be strategically planned, or the loss of faculty to other institutions and/or industry will have profound effects on faculty retention.

COLLEAGUES

Even though a comprehensive new faculty orientation program would provide critical information to new faculty, it is still not enough to ensure the success of new faculty members. Everything a new faculty member needs to know cannot be covered in an orientation session, nor can new faculty be expected to learn all the idiosyncrasies of academic life through trial and error or by observation. Hence, colleagues need to serve as guides or role models for new faculty members throughout the first year, at a minimum. The literature has found that new faculty members view senior faculty as role models who provide nurturing (Boice, 1992a; Creswell, 1985; Tierney & Bensimon, 1996). Accordingly, Boice (1992b) found that colleagues enhance the research productivity and teaching performance of new faculty. Johnson's (1999) study of African American faculty at HBCUs confirmed that new faculty perceived that senior colleagues were crucial for communicating the explicit rules and implicit values of the institution via formal and informal means.

A possible reason that colleagues are supportive of new faculty members and share information about the values and expectations of the institution could be attributed to the environment of HBCUs. The supportive and nurturing environment of HBCUs promotes both collegiality and solidarity, so colleagues want new faculty to succeed. As experienced faculty informally communicate the values and expectations of the institution to new faculty, the meaning of information obtained from formal sources, such as faculty handbooks and meetings with department chairs, is enhanced and new faculty members in turn receive informal mentoring from their colleagues.

If new faculty do not have senior faculty members serving as guides or mentors, new faculty could use their time inefficiently as they attempt to locate information and individuals who may be of assistance. New faculty not only need colleagues to inform them about the values and expectations of the institution as it relates to promotion and tenure, but also to explain the culture, disclose shortcuts, and inform them about policies and procedures as well as recent changes in the advising and registration process that a newcomer would be unaware of. To minimize the stress, inefficient utilization of time, frustration, and ignorance of new faculty, it is imperative that experienced colleagues take a more active role in helping new faculty make a smooth transition to the institution.

For example, colleagues can assist in alleviating additional stress on new faculty by providing training or ensuring that new faculty do not have advising responsibilities immediately, specifically the first semester. Colleagues should be sensitive to the fact that new faculty members are learning and internalizing institutional guidelines and requirements for students while also adjusting to the new academic environment. Accordingly, new faculty members should be paired with experienced colleagues to observe the advising process over a minimum of three days before they begin to advise students. Thus, new faculty will have the opportunity to observe and ask questions about the advising and registration process as well as to gain a greater understanding of the requirements, acceptable course substitutes, or course name changes. Yes, this training process may be time consuming, but new faculty will be grateful for the training, better prepared, and more confident in advising students. Once again, this process lays the foundation for building the new faculty member's commitment to the institution and indicates to new faculty that the institution is concerned with their success.

It is the responsibility of *all* faculty within the department to ensure that new faculty members have a positive socialization experience. Each new faculty member should be matched with a compatible colleague to ensure that there is an experienced faculty member designated to assist the new arrival with the idiosyncrasies (registration, textbook orders, reserve materials, etc.) of academic life. All faculty should view their role in assisting new faculty as one of utmost importance to the department and institution.

Institutions need to recognize that the best policies and procedures for an effective socialization experience cannot be implemented if faculty members do not understand the concept of socialization and why it is important to both the department and the institution. Accordingly, seminars could be conducted in the spring to familiarize colleagues with socialization theory and to suggest how experienced faculty can positively impact a new faculty member's socialization experience. This speaks to the institution's commitment to providing a positive and effective socialization experience as a mechanism to increase faculty retention.

Once the significance of socialization is understood, institutions could implement policies to make the department accountable if there is continuous high turnover among tenure-track faculty. Given that sometimes a good match between the institution and individual will cause separation, it could also very well indicate that the department, otherwise known as the faculty, is not providing a positive or effective socialization experience. Faculty members who depart from the institution should participate in exit interviews with the human resources office as well as the office of academic affairs to assess the overall socialization experience. Consequently, if a departing faculty member raises valid concerns relative to the socialization experience, then appropriate steps should be taken to improve the program's effectiveness. Furthermore, departments could be asked to complete annual evaluations of what they are doing to assist new faculty in a successful transition to the institution. This information could be shared throughout the institution to assist departments that may not be doing a satisfactory job of socializing newcomers and may be uncertain of what to do.

DEPARTMENT CHAIR

As a member of both the administration and the faculty, the department chair is placed in a unique role of providing formal information for new faculty relative to institutional values and role expectations and responsibilities. Sorcinelli (1992) confirmed the importance of the department chair in clarifying expectations and providing guidance for new faculty. Additionally, department chairs can ensure that new faculty understand the criteria under which they will be evaluated and how the assessment of these criteria will occur.

Annual reviews by the department chair help faculty members formally acquire the values, knowledge, and skills needed to be successful in the organization and to ultimately succeed in their quest for promotion and tenure. The information obtained from the department chair in the annual review enhances what faculty find in written publications and are told by colleagues. The reviews provide faculty with official knowledge of what the institution expects of new faculty and informs them of their progress, weaknesses, and strengths to assist them in successfully obtaining promotion and tenure. During annual reviews, department chairs should offer suggestions as to how faculty can satisfy promotion and tenure criteria—good committees to serve on to fulfill service obligations, prospective journals to submit work to, or teaching tips. It is evident that formal colleague support, along with informal colleague support, is necessary if new faculty are to be effectively socialized.

INITIATING CHANGE: ENHANCING FACULTY SOCIALIZATION

The adage "You must know where you've been before you know where you are going" applies in the case of faculty socialization as well. Prior to an institution establishing an effective socialization program, an objective evaluation must be conducted of the current environment new faculty encounter. An external reviewer would conduct interviews and utilize surveys to assess the environment and discern how new faculty acquire the knowledge, skills, values, and so on necessary to be successful at the institution. Given the particular institutional context, the reviewer would suggest appropriate strategies to enhance faculty socialization and retention. Hence, a model is provided for HBCUs to establish the infrastructure for a positive and effective faculty socialization program for new faculty in year one. Because colleague support usually occurs informally and is continuous, it is not included as a structured part of the model. However, institutions must encourage and provide incentives for colleagues to provide implicit and explicit knowledge to newcomers, as research indicates that collegiality positively impacts the teaching and research performance of new faculty (Boire 1992a).

The reader is cautioned that this framework focuses only on year one for new faculty and that additional socialization activities are necessary after year one if the institution is indeed serious about ensuring that faculty have a positive socialization experience and increasing faculty retention. Furthermore, complementary evaluation methods (qualitative and quantitative) should be utilized to continually assess the socialization experience of new faculty while the model is refined to meet the needs of each year in the initial entry phase of organizational socialization. Additionally, institutions may need to address other issues of relevance (salary, course load, release time, professional development, etc.) to ensure that the program is able to operate in an optimal manner.

CONCLUSION

Now is the time for HBCUs to implement programs that will ultimately increase faculty retention. Formal and informal methods are necessary for faculty to be positively and effectively socialized. Orientation and department chairs are two formal methods by which new faculty learn the institutional values and expectations, while colleagues provide informal knowledge of the implicit and explicit norms governing academic life.

Table 8.1
Initiating Change: Enhancing Faculty Socialization (Year 1)

Time Period	Proposed Activities
Pre-Planning	
Mid-Fall-Early Spring	External assessment of current socialization experience
Mid-Spring	Orientation of current faculty/staff on socialization basics (concept, significance); Plan for Year 1
Spring Semester-Early Summer	Contracts for new faculty signed; current departmental faculty assist with housing, acclimation to city, etc.; discuss anticipated courses and provide course text and recent syllabi
Year 1	
Early August	Human resource orientation (benefits, payroll, parking, identification cards, tour, etc.); new faculty opening orientation (values and expectations, policies and procedures, handbook, library overview); departmental meeting (teaching load, syllabi, office hours, meetings, committees, advising, informal guidelines, meeting current faculty)
September	Promotion and tenure policies and procedures; outline annual review packet requirements
October	Advising/registration process
November	Developing and implementing research agenda
December	Networking among colleagues
January	Professional development
February	Grants (internal and external)
March	Preparation of annual review packet
April	Feedback on year 1; suggestions for year 2 socialization
April	Evaluation of year 1 activities; refine and plan for year 1 (newly hired faculty); plan socialization activities for year 2 (current 1st year)

Colleagues and a comprehensive orientation program, in collaboration, will provide new faculty with the elements of a positive socialization experience. Accordingly, HBCUs must systematically approach faculty socialization as a method to increase faculty retention. A comprehensive socialization program must be developed for each year of the initial entry phase of organizational socialization until role continuance is achieved. Institutions that do not build upon the model outlined beyond year one are making a conscious decision to neglect faculty after their first year. By developing a comprehensive program for faculty socialization, HBCUs will build faculty commitment and loyalty to the institution while informing faculty of what is necessary for success through each year until promotion and/or tenure is obtained.

HBCUs that take steps to enhance the socialization experience of faculty now will lose few faculty members when the expected mass exodus of faculty occurs nationally. Accordingly, adequate time and resources must be dedicated to ensuring the success of an effective socialization program on a consistent basis. An institutional program without ample resources and commitment from key individuals throughout the organization is doomed to fail, as are HBCUs that do nothing to enhance the socialization of faculty. HBCUs that do nothing to enhance faculty socialization run the risk of African American faculty choosing employment at other institutions, for a myriad of reasons.

HBCUs must recognize that a positive socialization experience significantly enhances both new and current faculty morale, efficiency, effectiveness, productivity, and retention. Proactive institutions taking the necessary steps to prepare for the new millennium and the expected mass exodus of faculty will attract and retain quality faculty. Other institutions will be haphazardly creating programs to enhance the socialization of new faculty, but it may very well be too late. The faculty enhancement program for year one is just the beginning but it is a step in the right direction for HBCUs ready to make the commitment to ensure the success of new faculty.

REFERENCES

Alexander-Snow, M., & Johnson, B. J. (1999). Perspectives on faculty of color. In R. J. Menges & Associates (Eds.), *Faculty in new jobs: A guide to settling in, becoming established and building institutional support.* San Francisco: Jossey-Bass.

Austin, A. E. (1992). Supporting junior faculty through a teaching fellow program. In M. D. Sorcinelli & A. E. Austin (Eds.), *New directions for teaching and learning: No. 50. Developing new and junior faculty.* San Francisco: Jossey-Bass.

Billingsley, A. (1982). Building strong faculties in black colleges. *Journal of Negro Education, 51,* 4–15.

Boice, R. (1992a). *The new faculty member: Supporting and fostering professional development.* San Francisco: Jossey-Bass.

Boice, R. (1992b). Lessons learned about mentoring. In M. D. Sorcinelli & A. E. Austin (Eds.), *New directions for teaching and learning: No. 50. Developing new and junior faculty.* San Francisco: Jossey-Bass.

Carter, D. J., & Wilson, R. (1996). *Fourteenth annual status report on minorities in higher education.* Washington, DC: American Council on Education.

Creswell, (1985). *Faculty research performance.* Washington, DC: Association for the Study of Higher Education. (ASHE-ERIC Higher Education Report No. 4)

Diener, T. (1985). Job satisfaction and college faculty in two predominantly black institutions. *The Journal of Negro Education, 54,* 558–565.

Fields, C. D. (1997). Tenure at HBCUs. *Black Issues in Higher Education, 14*(17), 30.

Fink, L. D. (1992). Orientation programs for new faculty. In M. D. Sorcinelli & A. E. Austin (Eds.), *New directions for teaching and learning: No. 50. Developing new and junior faculty.* San Francisco: Jossey-Bass.

Jarvis, D. K. (1992). Improving new faculty scholarship. In M. D. Sorcinelli & A. E. Austin (Eds.), *New directions for teaching and learning: No. 50. Developing new and junior faculty.* San Francisco: Jossey-Bass.

Johnson, B. J. (1999). *Nurtured or neglected: An analysis of African-American faculty socialization at historically black colleges and universities.* Unpublished doctoral dissertation, Vanderbilt University, Nashville, TN.

Merton, R. K. (1957). *Social theory and social structure.* Glencoe, IL: Free Press.

Roebuck, J. B., & Murty, K. S. (1993). *Historically black colleges and universities: Their place in American higher education.* Westport, CT: Praeger.

Schein, E. H. (1968). Organizational socialization. *Industrial Management Review* 9(2), 1–16.

Sorcinelli, M. D. (1992). New and junior faculty stress: Research and responses. In M. D. Sorcinelli & A. E. Austin (Eds.), *New directions for teaching and learning: No. 50. Developing new and junior faculty.* San Francisco: Jossey-Bass.

Tierney, W. G., & Bensimon, E. M. (1996). *Promotion and tenure: Community and socialization in academe.* Albany: State University of New York Press.

Tierney, W. G., & Rhoads, R. A. (1994). *Faculty socialization as a cultural process: A mirror of institutional commitment.* Washington, DC: George Washington University, School of Education and Human Development. (ASHE-ERIC Higher Education Report No. 93–6)

U.S. Bureau of the Census (1991). *Statistical abstract of the U.S. 1991.* Washington, DC: U.S. Department of Commerce/U.S. Government Printing Office.

CHAPTER 9

Toward Strategic Planning: Issues and Status of Black Colleges

Bruce Anthony Jones

INTRODUCTION

Over the past two decades there have been vociferous calls for institutions of higher education to undergo fundamental change. In particular, beginning in the 1980s, institutions of higher education entered an unprecedented *age of accountability.* The traditional cozy and comfortable relationships between government and institutions of higher education began to collapse in an environment of federal devolution and dwindling resources at the federal and state levels of government. Fierce competition emerged between higher education interests and an array of political groups (e.g., human and social services, corporate, transportation, elementary and secondary education advocate and lobby groups, etc.) vying for these dwindling resources. This competition was also intensified by widespread public dissatisfaction with tax-supported education and public institutions overall. For example, a public outcry emerged during this period based on the perception that universities were hoarding resources, as university endowments skyrocketed coupled with exponential rises in student tuition costs. Matters were not helped during this period when it was discovered that several of the top-ranking institutions of higher education were involved in leadership and research-related scandals and cover-ups.

Black colleges have not escaped the environment described above. On top of this environment, black institutions of higher education have had to endure threats of merger with predominantly white institutions of higher education or threats of outright closure. In this regard, there are numerous distinctions between the experiences of predominantly white institutions of higher education and black colleges in this age of accountability. According to Johnson (1993), through all of this period of shrinking budgets, mismanagement, and scandal, "most predominantly white institutions were not faced with the burden of justifying their existence as educational institutions [as will black colleges]." Moreover, according to Jones (1997) black colleges were assaulted by an insidious political twist in the *desegregation agenda*. This twist entailed changing the focus on desegregating predominantly white institutions of higher education to a focus on desegregating black colleges. This *change in focus* came with the view that black colleges are relics of a segregated past—and these relics violate the goal to desegregate society. With this change in focus a political smoke screen was created, as predominantly white institutions of higher education escaped scrutiny from desegregation advocates and black colleges were further placed on the defensive about their relevance to society.

A number of institutions of higher education have employed strategic planning as a method of addressing the public demands for change in the way higher education operates and of bringing about organizational change that is intrinsically valuable to the institution. In some circles, such planning is referred to as *niche planning* or *priority setting* (Jones, 1998). Strategic planning in general is described as a process of repositioning an institution to meet short- and long-term organizational needs relative to the political, social, and economic realities of the external environment and the established internal mission of the organization. In the broadest sense, three organizational approaches to strategic planning may be employed:

- a *linear approach* to planning that places emphasis on establishing organizational goals and objectives and assessing how the institution meets and achieves these goals and objectives;
- an *adaptive approach* that is more fluid than the linear approach and that emphasizes the development of plans geared toward changing the institution relative to demands from the external environment and the internal needs of the organization; or
- an *interpretive approach* that emphasizes the need to understand the values, traditions, norms, and culture of the organization as a way to achieve the ends of strategic planning (Chaffe, 1984).

Given these definitions, what are the context and challenges for historically black colleges as they engage in strategic planning and broad policy development? How are the causes and challenges for historically black colleges that engage in strategic planning similar to and different from those of other institutions of higher education? How important is it for historically black colleges to engage in this type of planning—is such planning appropriate?

CONTEXT AND CHALLENGE

More often than not, the catalyst for engaging in strategic planning is crisis related. Some event occurs in the external environment that causes institutions to engage in some form of self-assessment or planning. The focus on such planning is aimed frequently at improving the *internal development* of the organization (i.e., student enrollment patterns, faculty morale, curriculum change, changes in governance structures, etc.) and *external relations* (i.e., relations with alumni, the business community, tax-payers, the state legislature, etc.).

The issues that surround strategic planning for historically black colleges and other institutions of higher education are at the same time both similar and dissimilar. For example, problems that are *financial* in nature and related to a need to restore *public confidence* and *student enrollment* concerns were cited in a national survey conducted by the State Higher Education Executive Officers as three of the most critical issues faced by all institutions of higher education (McGuinness, 1994). However, these issues tend to be more acute among historically black colleges when compared with predominantly white institutions of higher education because of the unique history, original purpose, and mission of these colleges. Historically black colleges also have had to deal with the desegregationist political agenda in a way that predominantly white institutions have not experienced. With this agenda, historically black colleges have been faced with threats of mergers with predominantly white institutions of higher education or closure.

FINANCE CONCERNS

Under the rubric of the need for internal institutional development, several causes for engagement in strategic planning are cited in the literature. The most frequently cited causes are financial in nature (McGuinness, 1994). Throughout the 1980s, federal and state government cutbacks in support of research, student aid, and capital improvements forced many institutions of higher education to think more strategically about securing financial resources to remain viable. According to Verstegen (1990), the federal government stance toward education was actively hostile throughout the 1980s:

[The policy direction of the federal government was clear and] included dismantling the Department of Education; deregulation of education programs; decentralization of programs and services to the states; deemphasis of the position of education on the federal agenda; and diminution of the federal budget in education altogether. (Vestegen, 1990)

Historically black colleges were already faced with infrastructure-related crises prior to the 1980s. Many of these institutions suffered from poor physical plants, libraries, and research laboratory facilities as well as deteriorating student housing and classroom buildings. Unlike their predominantly white institution counterparts, historically black colleges did not have well-developed alumni giving programs to help counter campus physical deterioration. Historically black colleges traditionally have not benefited from large institutional endowments (Wagener & Smith, 1993; Townsend, Newell, & Wiese, 1992; DuBois, 1990). This factor means that on average almost double the amount of per capita expenditures are available to students at predominantly white institutions compared to what is available to students who attend historically black colleges. For example, for every federal dollar that goes to black public colleges, states pay only 50 cents. Predominantly white public institutions receive $5–7 for every dollar from the federal government (Glanton, 2002).

Table 9.1 provides listings of the market value of the endowments of the 39 private historically black colleges in comparison to the endowments of the top 8 predominantly white institutions of higher education. The combined value of all the endowments of the private historically black colleges does not surpass or approach the value of even one institutional endowment of any of the top predominantly white institutions of higher education, with the exception of the College of William and Mary.

The *Carnegie category status,* according to Wagner and Smith (1993), has had a negative impact on the ability of historically black colleges to secure federal research dollar support. Under the Carnegie category system, universities that are designated *Research I* receive the bulk of federal research support in higher education. Research I universities are the institutions with advanced graduate-level programming. However, most historically black colleges are undergraduate institutions with little or no emphasis on graduate education (Willie & MacLeish, 1978). According to Wagner & Smith (1993), 37 universities in the United States received 50 percent of all of the foundation (or philanthropic) dollars given to higher education and 40 received 50 percent of all corporate dollars. Not one historically black college made either list.

An earlier study by The National Science Foundation revealed that in 1988 the federal government disbursed over $6.3 billion to the top 50 institutions of higher education in the United States. Johns Hopkins University topped the list with a $592 million appropriation. In other words, according to Fort, "$592 million went to one institution, which is more than one half of the $900 million that was appropriated to all 114 Historically Black Colleges" (p. 43). Stanford, University of Michigan, MIT, Cornell, University of California–Los Angeles, Columbia University, and University of California–San Francisco were in the top 10 along with Johns Hopkins. Only one historically black college made this list: Howard University (Fort, 1991).

Table 9.1

Endowment Figures: Sample of Private Colleges

Historically Black Private Colleges	1993-94	1995-96	1996-97
Barber-Scotia College	$3,039	$3,488	$3,700
Benedict College	14,942	16,432	17,424
Bennett College	9,507	11,391	12,482
Bethune-Cookman College	15,033	18,557	21,461
Claflin College	7,301	9,405	10,087
Clark Atlanta University	23,571	21,808	31,338
Dillard University	27,333	37,831	43,680
Edward Waters College	948	1,073	1,057
Fisk University	7,926	11,215	11,575
Florida Memorial College	3,317	4,687	3,991
Huston-Tillotson College	5,196	7,007	7,803
Interdenom Theological Center	7,452	8,636	8,604
Jarvis Christian College	13,643	15,009	13,051
Johnson C. Smith University	14,954	20,798	25,570
Lane College	1,680	1,727	1,974
Lemoyne-Owen College	8,250	9,000	10,154
Livingstone College	2,228	2,922	2,872
Miles College	1,500	3,907	4,109
Morehouse College	59,060	80,000	99,319
Morris Brown College	6,744	8,367	9,293
Morris College	2,846	3,208	3,515
Oakwood College	4,936	5,775	6,900
Paine College	7,044	8,073	7,394
Paul Quinn College	1,540	2,816	3,717
Philander Smith College	3,860	4,248	4,212
Rust College	15,614	16,700	15,700
St. Augustine's College	18,063	18,634	18,755
St. Paul's College	3,452	4,443	5,878
Shaw University	6,715	9,047	12,000
Spelman College	110,050	142,178	156,376
Stillman College	17,387	19,060	20,400
Talladega College	7,698	8,008	6,679
Tougaloo College	8,060	10,610	12,702
Tuskegee University	40,337	43,389	43,021
Virginia Union University	8,072	9,107	11,049
Voorhees College	4,463	4,499	4,558
Wilberforce University	7,259	7,963	1,813
Wiley College	3,629	2,763	2,167
Xavier University of Louisiana	19,690	22,606	27,713
TOTAL	**$524,339**	**$636,387**	**$704,093**
AVERAGE	**$13,445**	**$16,318**	**$18,054**

(*continued*)

Table 9.1
(Continued)

Predominantly White Institutions			
Private Colleges	As of 6/30/97	As of 6/30/98	1 Year Change
Columbia University	3,038,907	3,425,992	12.7%
Cornell University	2,125,070	2,527,871	19.0%
University of Pennsylvania	2,535,312	3,059,401	20.7%
Yale University	5,742,000	6,624,449	13.0%
Brown University	949,574	1,111,760	17.1%
Harvard University	10,919,670	13,019,736	19.2%
College of William & Mary	295,621	354,472	19.9%
Princeton University	4,940,900	5,582,800	13.0%
TOTAL	**$31,824,807**	**$37,226,189**	

Source: Patterson Institute, 1998.

STUDENT ENROLLMENT

Across the higher education spectrum, declines in student enrollment have been a serious concern. A significant portion of the fiscal resources of universities is derived from student tuition. For example, at the private liberal arts colleges, tuition revenue accounts for approximately 55 percent of the revenue needed to run the institutions. At the privately run historically black colleges this figure is approximately 33 percent (Wagener & Smith, 1993). Therefore, universities constantly struggle with ways to grow student enrollment while increasingly competing for students from the same student pools.

Despite the general student enrollment trend described above, between 1988 and 1993 the enrollment of students at historically black colleges actually grew at a faster rate than the total U.S. college enrollment (17 percent and 11 percent, respectively). Overall there has been a steady resurgence and growth in the enrollment of African Americans at historically black colleges. In 1980 185,780 African Americans enrolled in historically black colleges. This figure rose to 213,904 in 1991 and 260,000 in 1994 (Ware, 1994). The student enrollment at the public historically black colleges is approximately 187,735 and approximately 72,262 at the private historically black colleges (National Center for Education Statistics [NCES], 1996). Moreover, between 1982 (n = 23,040) and 1992 (n = 36,203) historically black colleges experienced a 16 percent increase in the number of white student enrollees (Mercer, 1995).

For historically black colleges, issues of strategic planning and student enrollment center more on preparation and retention issues. Once students get into college, how can they be kept there and prepared to graduate? According to the American Council on Education (2002) the rate of

African American student transition to college continues to trail other ethnic groups.

College preparation issues are likely to emerge along race and class lines when comparing African American to European American high school students. According to Nettles (1991), "Nearly 50 percent of all African Americans below the age of 18 live in poverty compared with 15 percent of their European American peers . . . African Americans attend relatively poor schools, are more frequently enrolled in the non-academic tracks of their high schools, have lower levels of academic achievement and often drop out altogether" (p. 8).

PUBLIC CONFIDENCE CONCERNS

A factor that is associated with both the internal development and external relations of institutions of higher education is public confidence. There is a critical need to use strategic planning as one vehicle to restore and constantly renew public confidence in higher education. This is supported in the survey research by McGuinness (1994), who reported that institutions of higher education must demonstrate that they are effective at their missions and are willing to embrace the role of being accountable to the public and the university community.

Institutions of higher education have suffered severe losses in public confidence as mismanagement, political scandal, and corruption crises have overtaken a number of university communities across the country. These crises also served to diminish internal faculty and student morale. According to the *Chronicle of Higher Education,* during the decade of the 1980s there were more than 25 reported incidents of higher education scandal or corruption.

Historically black colleges experienced a share of this scandal or corruption, which inhibited program efforts to garner alumni support as well as other kinds of resource contributions that could have advanced these institutions (Wagener & Smith, 1993; Wilson, 1994). According to Healey (1997):

State officials in Texas, Ohio, Missouri, Louisiana, and North Carolina have increased accountability requirements at the higher education level and questioned management practices at Historically Black Colleges. There has been an across the board call for a reduction in the autonomy of these institutions.

The impact of claims of mismanagement on historically black colleges has resulted in some instances in the total disruption of campus life. In the aftermath of such claims, several historically black colleges have been faced with the real threat of closure. On one campus, following such a threat, the students engaged in widespread protests, shutting down buildings and classrooms. In anger, one administrator reported that a dual standard of treatment existed. The threat of closure did not apply in the same way to predominantly white institutions engaged in scandal: " . . . if you have a scandal at Tennessee State University you don't close it, you fix the problem" (Jaschik & Mercer, 1992, p. 22).

THE DESEGREGATION AGENDA

One of the biggest threats faced by historically black colleges is the threat of closure or merger. With regard to the latter, since the 1960s four public historically black colleges have changed into predominantly white institutions as a result of merger activity. These institutions are Bluefield State College, West Virginia State College, Kentucky State College, and Lincoln University (Missouri) (Joint Center for Political and Economic Studies, 1997). Mercer (1992) reports that there are five possible types of mergers that may serve as an alternative to the outright closing of an institution:

- *pure merger*—involves one college being dissolved into another, leaving the second as the sole surviving institution. Because one college will lose its identity, this is essentially an acquisition;
- *consolidation*—creates an entirely new college or university through the dissolving of two or more institutions. This could provide the ultimate in synergy within the context of a win-win situation. However, because of racial prejudice this option is unlikely to be selected by those considering a merger between a historically black college and a predominantly white institution;
- *asset transfer*—occurs when an institution assigns the rights, title, and interest of some or all of its assets to a second institution which agrees to operate some or all of the first institution's programs. An example of this occurred in 1979 when Peabody College transferred its assets to Vanderbilt University. This is problematic within the historically black college merger debate because it will be assumed that the historically black college will do the transferring;
- *collaboration*—involves consortia, federations, and associations of the institutions in a series of mutual obligations among participating colleges and universities that have the common objective of sharing resources. The aims of collaboration may include elimination of duplicate course offerings and expanding and sharing library facilities; and
- *joint venture*—happens with the establishment of educational affiliations. Arrangements are made to preserve the respective identities and governance structures of participating institutions. This option pursues the ultimate idea of preserving the identities of both institutions. (Mercer, 1992, p. 23)

According to Jones (1997) the pure merger option or outright closing option is what has been frequently leveled at historically black colleges. Under the guise of desegregation, policymakers throughout the South have begun to question the relevance of historically black colleges. The U.S. Supreme Court ruling in *United States v. Fordice* (Mississippi) has not been used to force predominantly white institutions to integrate but rather has been used as a weapon to justify the closure or merger of historically black colleges. This is ironic considering that historically black colleges (see Table 9.2) are more integrated along faculty, administrator, and student ranks than are predominantly white institutions of higher education.

CONCLUSION: A DUALISM PHENOMENON

A dualism phenomenon exists with respect to the purposes of the need for historically black colleges to engage in strategic planning for the future. On the one hand, historically black colleges face similar issues to those confronted by other institutions of higher education with regard to the need to engage in strategic planning. On the other hand, black colleges have been treated differently when faced with the challenge of implementing strategic planning. For example, predominantly white institutions of higher education are seldom faced with the threat of closure when they do not meet public expectations. Moreover, predominantly white institutions have not been challenged by the need to overcome decades of racism and inequity that have been structurally embedded in a segregated society.

Wagner and Smith (1993) provided brief studies of the strategic planning efforts that occurred at three historically black colleges: Fisk University, Tougaloo College, and Howard University. The key issue tackled by each institution was financial crisis. Closely tied to financial crisis was a crisis in public confidence in these institutions and a negative history of racism. Elements of Chaffe's (1984) strategic planning typology appeared to be adopted at all three institutions. The greatest amount of emphasis appeared to be placed on the linear approach (establish clear goals and

Table 9.2
Integration Percentages

	African American	Non-African American
Historically Black Institutions		
Faculty	61%	39%
Administration	84%	16%
Student Body	89%	11%
Predominantly White Institutions		
Faculty	4.0%	96.0%
Administration	1.5%	98.5%
Student Body	6.0%	94.0%

Source: Jones, 1997.

objectives with a plan that adheres closely to these goals and objectives) and the least emphasis on the interpretive approach (work on consensus-building activities to develop a shared institutional vision) to strategic planning. Adaptive approaches (planning that is guided by how the institution will adapt and respond to the external environment) appeared to play an important secondary role. At each of these institutions, strategic planning goals were aimed at reducing and eliminating the budget deficits coupled with the effort to build institutional endowments and corporate and alumni contributions. At one college (Tougaloo), a history of racism negatively affected external relations between the college and the white business community. During the 1960s, Tougaloo served as the central meeting place for establishing a civil rights agenda, sit-ins, and protests. The white business community shunned the college as a result. Also during this time, the state legislature attempted to punish the college with attempts to revoke the ability of the college to award degrees (Wagener & Smith, 1993). In this context, strategic planning had to include ways to overcome the history of negative relations in order to move forward.

As strategic planning becomes more of a critical tool enabling historically black colleges to survive and move more strategically into the future, more systematic research will be required that examines the actual impact of such planning. The three institutions mentioned above (Fisk, Tougaloo, and Howard) have experienced some success using such planning. However, the planning was limited mostly to a goals-based or linear approach. Additionally, the strategic planning centered primarily on the administration aspects of these institutions. Very little attention was given to the need for strategic planning at the academic-unit level. It is probably at the academic-unit level that interpretive approaches to strategic planning are necessary, given the focus on curriculum issues and the numerous viewpoints with traditions that arise around these issues. Thus, more research will be required that helps to explain the effectiveness of multiple approaches (not just the goals-based or linear approaches) to strategic planning at historically black colleges.

REFERENCES

American Council on Education (2002). *Minorities in Higher Education 2001–2002*. Washington, DC: American Council on Education.

Chaffe, E. E. (1984). Successful strategic management in small private colleges. *Journal of Higher Education, 55*, 212–241.

DuBois, P. M. (1990). The nation's black colleges: A noble past, a troubled present, a questionable future. In S. Barnes (Ed.), *Points of view on American higher education: Vol. 2. Institutions and issues.* Lewiston: Edwin Mellen Press.

Fort, E. B. (1991). *Oversight hearing before the subcommittee on post secondary education.* New Orleans, LA: Committee on Education and Labor, House of Representatives. (ERIC Document Reproduction Service No. ED 342297)

Glanton, D. (2002). Black colleges fight to survive. *Chicago Tribune*. October 21, p. 1.

Healey, P. (1997). A public black college faces state pressure to improve management or lose autonomy. *The Chronicle of Higher Education, 43*(46), 33–34.

Jaschik, K. S., & Mercer, J. (1992). Public black colleges face new pressures. *The Chronicle of Higher Education, 38*(45), 21–23.

Johnson, A. M. (1993). Bid whisk, task and United States v. Fordice: Why integrationism fails African Americans again. *California Law Review, 81,* 1408.

Joint Center for Political and Economic Studies (1997). *Do the white thing: Black Colleges try to promote diversity while maintaining character.* Washington, DC: Joint Center for Political and Economic Studies.

Jones, B. A. (1997). Desegregation: Education, politics and policy legacies. *Journal of Negro Education Review, 48,* 3–4, 109–119.

Jones, B. A. (1998). The relationship between evaluation effort and institutional culture: Mixing oil and water. In K. Freeman (Ed.), *African American culture and heritage in higher education research and practice,* pp. 173–179. Westport: CT, Praeger.

McGuinness, (1994). State policy and faculty workload: Trends across the United States. *Higher Education Policy, 7*(2), 47–49.

Mercer, J. (1995). Black colleges reach out to white alumni. *The Chronicle of Higher Education, 41*(21), 29–30.

National Center for Education Statistics (1996). *Minorities in higher education.* Washington, DC: U.S. Department of Education. (No. 9, OERI, NCES, 97–372)

Nettles, M. (1991). *Assessing progress in minority access and achievement in American higher education.* Denver, CO: State Policy and Assessment in Higher Education, Education Commission of the States.

Patterson Institute. (1998). *Market value of endowment funds.* Fairfax, VA: author.

Townsend, B. K., Newell, J. L., & Wiese, M. D. (1992). *Creating distinctiveness: Lessons from uncommon colleges and universities (Report No. 6).* Washington DC: George Washington University. (ERIC Document Reproduction Service No. ED 356702)

Vestegen, D. A. (1990). Educational fiscal policy in the Reagan Administration. *Educational Evaluation and Policy Analysis, 12*(4), 355–373.

Wagner, U., & Smith, E. (1993, January/February). Maintaining a competitive edge: Strategic planning for historically black institutions. *Change, 25*(1), 40–49.

Ware, L. (1994). The most visible vestige: Black colleges after Fordice. *Boston College Law Review, 35,* 676.

Willie, C. V., & MacLeish, M. Y. (1978). The priorities of presidents of black colleges. In C. V. Willie & R. R. Edmonds (Eds.), *Black colleges in America: Challenge, development, survival,* pp. 132–148. New York: Teachers College Press.

Wilson, R. C. (1994). Crisis at Morehouse: President resigns after audit finds he spent college money lavishly. *The Chronicle of Higher Education, 41*(6), 19.

CHAPTER 10

The Challenges and Needs of High-Achieving Black College Students

Sharon Fries-Britt

INTRODUCTION

Prior to 1960 a significant majority of black students were educated at historically black colleges and universities (HBCUs) (Roebuck & Murty, 1997). The social fabric and legal structure of our nation more than 40 years ago made it nearly impossible for black students to consider alternative educational environments. Today black students have a range of institutional types to consider, resulting in increased competition for HBCUs in attracting the best and the brightest black collegians.

The community of black collegians is diverse and multifaceted. Although there has been an escalation in research on black students (Allen, 1992; Allen, Epps, & Haniff, 1991; Fleming, 1984; Gurin & Epps, 1975; Mow & Nettles, 1990; Willie, 1981; Willie & McCord, 1972) we know far less about the experiences of high-achieving black collegians (Freeman, 1999; Fries-Britt, 1998; Fries-Britt & Turner, 2001; Noldon & Sedlacek, 1998). In addition to being understudied, this segment of the black student population is often presumed nonexistent. The image and portrait of black students in the literature suggest that they are largely underachievers with associated risk factors such as poverty, low family involvement, and low motivation.

The purpose of this chapter is to examine factors that shape the experiences of high-achieving black collegians and to outline the challenges and opportunities that HBCUs have in continuing to meet the needs of this segment of the black student population. The chapter sets the context by examining issues of achievement and the complexity involved in defining intelligence. It then explores several themes that challenge high-achieving blacks and concludes with implications for HBCUs.

In addition to the literature on black college students, qualitative data from three studies on high achievers were used to inform the themes in this chapter. The participants were enrolled in both HBCUs and tradition-ally white institutions (TWIs) and in some cases transferred from one type of institution to another. Combining the data from the three studies pro-vides a unique opportunity to learn from students who have a diverse range of collegiate experiences. Students who attended both types of in-stitutions offer a distinct perspective and insight. All of the students were defined as successful based on one of several factors: their enrollment in an honors program and/or other academic scholarship programs at their respective institutions, or because they maintained a GPA of at least 3.0.

In all three studies a combination of individual interviews and/or focus group techniques was used to learn about students' peer and faculty re-lationships, academic experiences on campus, and the factors that shape students' intellectual and racial sense of self. Of the 65 students, 40 stu-dents participated in individual interviews and 25 participated in three focus group sessions. Fifteen of the students attended a public HBCU and, of the 15, four indicated that they were previously enrolled at a TWI. Similarly, in another sample, six of the 15 students who were enrolled at a TWI had transferred from a public and/or private HBCU, resulting in approximately one-third of the students having direct experiences at an HBCU.

UNDERSTANDING ACHIEVEMENT AND INTELLECTUAL ABILITY

The disproportionate focus in the literature on the underachievement of black students is explainable, in part, because of the achievement gap on standardized test scores between blacks and their white and Asian peers. Understanding what has caused the achievement gap between whites and non-Asian minorities is increasingly gaining attention in edu-cation (Bell-Rose, 1998; College Board, 1999; Jencks & Phillips, 1998; Miller, 1995). Recently, Stephanie Bell-Rose (1998) identified that less than 2 per-cent of black students could be counted among the highest scorers on standardized tests. Miller (1995) found that even within the same socio-economic cohorts the achievement gap continues to exist between blacks and their white and Asian peers. According to Miller, "Variations among social classes do not fully account for racial/ethnic differences in academic achievement; there are also large within-social-class differences in aca-demic achievement patterns among groups. At each social class level, whites and Asians tend to do much better academically than blacks, His-panics and American Indians" (p. 338).

The National Task Force on Minority High Achievement, sponsored by the College Board (1999), found that a complex array of factors—including social inequities, educational policy, economics, racism, and school environment, as well as cultural factors and family practices—contributed to the achievement gap. The complexity of the topic suggests that understanding patterns of achievement requires a number of frameworks that consider a diverse set of factors, including structural inequities, societal forces, and cultural indicators. The Task Force sought to understand and evaluate achievement from two distinct but interrelated viewpoints. Achievement was evaluated based on educational attainment as demonstrated by degree completion (bachelor's and graduate degrees), and academic achievement as measured by "superior academic skills and subject mastery at each level of education" (p. 4). In exploring the differences in the two types of achievement, the Task Force reported:

It is fairly easy to define and recognize the importance of high educational attainment. Credentials play a gate-keeping role for entry into most professions. In many fields, from engineering to school teaching, a bachelor's degree is the minimum credential. Advanced degrees are required for entry into many desirable professions, such as law and medicine. In some areas of scientific research, postdoctoral study is increasingly essential. On the other hand, defining high academic achievement and gauging its importance is less clear-cut. (p. 4)

Academic excellence can be gauged in a number of ways, such as assessing whether students achieve superior grades and performance in highly competitive and academically ranked schools, or whether students rank in the top 10–25 percent of their class, or whether they are the recipients of distinguished academic awards (College Board, 1999). Although some may dispute what constitutes high achievement, we know for sure that the cultivation of strong academic skills is essential for advanced educational opportunities and highly skilled careers.

Juxtaposed to the complexity of achievement is the difficulty of defining and understanding measures of intelligence. Categorizing students by intellectual ability has always caused controversy because of the assumption that intelligence tests are racially and/or culturally biased (Jencks, 1998). Although the numbers of black students among the top performers on standardized tests is small (Bell-Rose, 1998; Miller, 1995), black collegians, like other students, demonstrate academic potential and intelligence in ways that are not captured by conventional achievement tests. Jencks asserts that:

... it seems fair to say that the invention of standardized tests has harmed blacks as a group, both because of labeling bias and because of selection system bias. This does not mean the tests themselves are flawed. The skill differences that the tests measure are real, and these skills have real consequences both at school and at work. But inability to measure the other predictors of performance, on which blacks seem to be far less disadvantaged, poses a huge social problem. (p. 84)

Fortunately, how we define and understand intelligence has expanded over time to include other predictors of performance and intelligence (e.g., artistic ability, originality, divergent thinking, leadership, visual and performing arts) (Ford, 1996). Ford, in her review of the changing definition of giftedness, identified a significant evolution in the 1978 definition by the federal government, which allowed for the inclusion of the "potentially gifted." This expansion recognizes that there are students who have academic ability but who for various reasons have not fully developed their potential. Ford explains, "Potentially gifted students include underachievers, minority students, economically disadvantaged students, students with learning and behavioral disorders, and physically disabled or challenged students" (p. 13). Even with expanded definitions of intelligence, however, society tends to value cognitive measures of ability over other forms of intellectual expression. Consequently, it is important that black students develop superior academic skills.

Tests that assign low academic classification early in students' careers can be damaging and can severely impede a student's ability to successfully move up the academic ladder. Institutions that rely primarily on conventional measures impede the opportunities of students whose academic potential has yet to manifest itself. Historically black institutions have consistently provided educational opportunities for the gifted as well as for the potentially gifted. In every way, these institutions serve as the safety net for black students who endeavor to go to college but who have limited options because of their academic performance. HBCUs' unwavering mission to invest in and educate black students at varied intellectual levels (Anderson, 1988) places an enormous challenge on their ability to be competitive with TWIs that are more restrictive in their admissions process.

The misuse of testing has contributed to harmful stereotypes about the intellectual ability of blacks. Black students, particularly those who attend TWIs, are more likely to encounter negative stereotypes about their academic ability (Smedley, Myers, & Harrell, 1993) and may experience greater difficulty in gaining individual recognition for their accomplishments. However, because high-achieving students are described as the best and the brightest (Solano, 1987) they are often assumed to have little to no difficulty in their college transition. We know from the literature, however, that high-achieving blacks experience many of the same issues as other students, yet they have their own unique and distinct challenges.

DEALING WITH STEREOTYPES AND THE PROVING PROCESS

The stereotypes that high-achieving blacks encounter are generally no different from those encountered by other black students. Blacks who attend TWIs encounter a number of stereotypes based on race (Smedley et al., 1993; Hummel & Steele, 1996; Steele, 1992). Several students who were interviewed shared their perceptions of how they believe whites perceive blacks. A male student at a TWI commented that "stereotypes about African American students included [sic] that they are always late for class, that they have gotten into the university because of affirmative action, that they are not really as qualified as other students, and that they are lazy." Similarly, a female student at a TWI shared that "people thought of black students as not being as smart as other students and that they were a dumber ethnicity overall." Consistently, the students at the TWI talked about the perceptions that people had of blacks as lazy, ignorant, and involved in crime.

Although black students at HBCUs find a more welcoming racial climate, faculty support, and peer connections (Allen, 1992; Fleming, 1984; Fries-Britt & Turner, 2002), they face stereotypes outside of the campus environment and encounter racial tensions on campus. Many of the students attending the HBCU confronted stereotypes about the quality of their educational experience. A female student observed:

I think with society and the way they put down blacks anyway, they have it in their minds that they can get a better education at a white school. . . . they have that mind-set and they really don't have anything to stand on. I have challenged a lot of people on it because I have been on both sides. I started at a black school, transferred, and then came back . . . to me, people always say that you get a better education [at a white school], but I don't agree.

Several of the students who attended the HBCU echoed these same comments and felt that there was a pervasive stereotype that HBCUs were considered less rigorous. Some have argued that HBCUs offer less academically rigorous experiences relative to predominately white colleges and universities (Sowell, 1972).

The evidence is clear that the differences in academic programs and resources between HBCUs and majority white campuses is entrenched in a history of economic, legal, and political oppression which limited the success of HBCUs in educating blacks and providing competitive curricula (Anderson, 1988; Hope, 1996). Despite significant financial, social, and political barriers, HBCUs continue to demonstrate success in educating the largest share of black undergraduates (Davis, 1998; Hope, 1996) and awarding first professional degrees for fields such as medicine, law, pharmacy, and dentistry (Hope).

Black students at HBCUs also encounter the stereotype that black colleges do not represent the real world. In a focus group session, several students gave accounts of how people assumed that HBCUs were not the real world, in part because they provide too much nurturing and in part because they are majority black environments in a majority white nation. Representative of these comments were those offered by a female student who stated that:

... some people think it is better that you don't have that nurturing environment. I have a friend who chose to go to a predominately white institution because she said that is how the real world is going to be and we don't need to be babied and all that stuff. But it's not that it's babying; I just look at it as, "I am a black student, you are a black professor, and you know what I feel and can relate to me better than a white person." That's the way I look at it.

For some students it is important to be in an environment where they feel connected to the culture, the traditions, and the people. In the above case the student wanted to be on a campus where that connection was based on racial affiliation. Some students seek this connection based on other referent group affiliations, such as those represented by women's colleges or religious affiliated schools. Students who attend HBCUs are likely to have white professors as well as black ones; however, the difference is that many black students who attend TWIs never have a black professor.

A male student weighing in on the "real world" conversation explained that he had been in several black environments in which there were mostly black students being taught by white teachers, and they had good relationships. He explained that he then transferred to a white school and realized that he was unhappy and that he took a number of things for granted. He consoled himself by saying that his experience at the TWI was the real world. As time passed he realized that in fact the white teachers at the black schools were also the real world.

Some might argue that no college or university represents the real world; nevertheless, one thing we know for sure is that HBCUs represent racially mixed environments that offer important advantages. Fleming (1984) observed:

Black colleges provide the closest approximation to racially balanced educational institutions that can be found. Indeed, research findings in both Georgia and Texas uncovered tension-fraught dealings with whites on black campuses; these findings remind us that the faculty and staff of many black schools are well integrated. However, at black colleges, race related tensions occur in the context of (and may actually be related to) positive developmental outcomes. Because black schools offer something closer to racially balanced teaching environments, they may allow students to adjust more gradually to the realities of integrated settings. (p. 153)

Although high-achieving blacks encounter similar stereotypes as other black students, they face specific stereotypes because of their interest in academics. Many talented black students are accused of "acting white"

(Fordham & Ogbu, 1986), a charge leveled against them by other blacks. Even those students who attended HBCUs reported that throughout their academic career they faced charges by some blacks that they were "trying to be white" or "acting white" because they were excelling in school.

The accusation that one is acting white impacts a black student's sense of racial and academic identity. It also challenges the nature of the relationships that high-achieving blacks have with their peers and the perceptions that their peers have of them. Fries-Britt (2000) found that high-ability students tend to conceal their ability for different reasons. One male student shared that he kept quiet about his grades because he didn't want to be accused of being a nerd and risk losing his position in the in crowd. Being perceived as a nerd or being excluded from the in crowd is a central motivation for many talented students to camouflage their academic ability.

This notion of acting white is complex and is shaped by a variety of factors that impact the behaviors and beliefs of blacks. Although the purposes of this chapter prevent a detailed exploration of the origins of this theme, the observations of two scholars who have attempted to unravel the evidence are worth noting. Ogbu (1993), an anthropologist, has argued that the academic status and performance of blacks in the United States is directly related to their relationship as involuntary minorities forced to incorporate the values of the dominant (white) society. Over time, blacks developed coping mechanisms to survive in a society in which there is little trust for the dominant system. One survival technique is to develop an oppositional identity and oppositional cultural frame of reference from the majority culture. According to Ogbu:

One of the devices in the oppositional cultural frame of reference is "cultural inversion." In a broad sense, cultural inversion refers to the various ways in which the minorities express their opposition to the dominant group. In a narrow sense it refers to specific forms of behavior, specific events, symbols, and meanings which involuntary minorities regard as not appropriate for them because they are characteristic of Euro-Americans. At the same time the minorities approve of and emphasize other forms of behaviors, events, symbols, and meanings as more appropriate for themselves because these are not a part of Euro-Americans [sic] way of life. (p. 491)

If studying and demonstrating an interest in academics is considered something that whites (and increasingly Asians) do, then black students who demonstrate an interest in academics and who participate in programs that are majority white would be displaying characteristics and values that would associate them with Euro-Americans. Although Ogbu's work has been controversial, this notion of cultural inversion is evidenced in other work.

Using a psychological framework of stereotype threat, Claude Steele (1992, 1997) and Steele and Aronson (1995, 1998) found that black students can experience "disidentification" with the educational process if they are constantly challenged with stereotypes that erode their confidence in the academic domain. The disidentification with the educational process, while different from cultural inversion, results in the same behavior: black students step away from activities and interests that are associated with academics. The essence of Steele and Aronson's work is that black students encounter a wide range of stereotypes and experience a number of incidents over the course of their lives that begin to diminish their self-confidence. The stereotypes about the academic abilities of blacks transfer over into the collegiate environment and can create significant stress for all students, especially high-achieving blacks who identify with the academic environment. Students begin to feel that their academic abilities are constantly being judged and that they are on trial in the classroom. As these pressures add up over time, students can begin to feel that it is not worth the investment of their time to remain involved in academics, so they begin to disidentify.

Because of the stereotypes about blacks and their academic potential, high-achieving black students at TWIs reported pressure to prove that they are academically capable. They provided examples of how they felt pressure in the classroom with white peers and faculty to not only represent themselves well, but to represent excellence in the black community. Many of the students commented that they wanted to do well in classes to prove that they belonged and that they had earned their admission to the university. Some of the students spent an enormous amount of time dealing with their own and others' perceptions of their abilities. A female student offered a vivid example:

Well, when I find that I'm the only black person in a class, I feel that I have to prove myself just as intelligent, just as smart, just as worthy, of the same grade as somebody else who's not my race. I'm not extremely competitive, but I feel competitive in that instance where I have to prove myself to be a strong student, to compete with those in my classroom. It's been that way since high school because I was going up against a mostly Asian and white, student population, so I've always felt that I had to prove myself when I've always been the one black person in that class.

Similarly, another female student shared:

As far as my major, I am one of a few African American students and it's hard for me to see what people think or whatever. But when I first got here I had to prove myself, prove myself, and prove myself. It was not like I would go up to them and say, "Now you see?" But it's like they kept doubting me, and doubting me, and doubting me.

Both of these accounts are powerful reminders of the constant pressure that some black students at TWIs feel to do well and to prove that they are capable. Their persistence and productivity despite others' doubts demonstrates the determination they have to face the stresses of their environment. While their success and graduation from college may signal academic achievement on one level, it could also mean that they have sustained more damage because of the stress over time (Smedley et al., 1993).

Unlike their peers at TWIs, blacks students at HBCUs did not feel like they had to prove themselves in the classroom. Rather, they described strong support from faculty and peers and felt comfortable asking for help. These students talked about a community of support at the HBCU that provided them a strong foundation to protect them from negative images about blacks and to instill a sense of pride in the black culture. A male student's comments reflect the general nature of this theme. He commented:

There's nothing like a strong foundation. I come from a community where you don't have a lot of black cohesiveness; it's not together. So you come to a foundation where everybody is working together. Here everybody is working and trying to do something and you have that foundation; you know who you are and you know where you come from, and you can do more.

Prior to entering the HBCU environment this student had not been in a majority black community to experience an atmosphere of black cohesiveness in which blacks worked together to support one another. The difference for this student was a sense of belonging and a feeling that he had the support to accomplish more. While black students at HBCUs did not experience the same pressure to prove themselves in the classroom, they did encounter pressure to prove that they were as capable as students who attended TWIs. This seemed to be directly connected to the stereotypes that HBCUs are less rigorous.

DEALING WITH ISOLATION AND CONNECTING WITH A COMMUNITY OF PEERS

In light of the stereotypes and proving process that blacks encounter, it is not surprising that black students report a degree of isolation in college (Allen, 1992; Fleming, 1984; Mow & Nettles, 1990). We know from the literature that black students who attend HBCUs are less likely to experience isolation relative to their black peers at TWIs (Allen, 1988, 1992; Fleming, 1984). High-achieving black students, particularly those at TWIs, describe a sense of isolation (Fries-Britt, 1998; Smedley et al., 1993) that is somewhat distinct and could be considered a double threat. They are likely to experience isolation from white peers as well as from less talented black peers on campus. The nature of the isolation tends to manifest itself in two ways. First there is a structural isolation that occurs because many academically talented blacks enrolled in honors classes or gifted and talented programs describe low numbers of other black peers in their classrooms. All of the study participants enrolled at TWIs noticed that African American students were underrepresented in honors classes and nearly all commented that they had been the only minority in a class and/or the only black. They tended to experience this more in high school but acknowledged that even in college they had this experience several times.

I talk about the nature of the isolation in an earlier study in which I found that, "even in cases where students attended a predominately Black high school, they still had less than satisfactory experiences in their interactions and relationships with other high achieving Blacks. Although the high school was overwhelmingly Black, the majority of the students in the honors or college accelerated classes were White. Consequently, fewer opportunities existed to establish relationships with other Black students who were interested in academics" (Fries-Britt, 1998, p. 563). Not all black students who attend predominately black high schools experience isolation; however, black students in predominately white educational settings are likely to feel isolated.

A male student who was reflecting on his high-school honors classes observed that "there were minorities in the class, but there weren't too many African Americans in the class. ... It was Asian American and white, Jewish, only a couple, or a few black kids. ... I thought of it every time; on the first day of school every time I was looking around ... any new faces here?" Similarly, a female student commented that when most people think of the honors program they think it is all white. She shared, "I'm still usually the only black person in my class or the only minority in my class."

The second type of isolation occurred when students were accused of acting white. Essentially, when high-achieving blacks have fewer peers interested in academics, they have less of a support system available to make it cool to study. A male student who was a member of a merit scholarship program said it well:

Programs like this are very important because it puts an emphasis on doing well and showing that it is positive. We hear about stars like Michael Jordan, Michael Jackson, Janet Jackson, but how often do we hear about Dr. Ben Carson, who is a star? We don't put a lot of emphasis on that in the black community. You are considered cool if you are smart, although this is the first place I ever found where it was cool to be smart.

Even though high-achieving black students have the support of parents and extended family members, it is still important for them to connect with a like-type community of peers. The need to connect with a community of like-type peers is central to the sense of belonging for high achievers. Like all college students they seek ways to connect with peers who share similar goals and aspirations. For high-achieving students the connections must begin early in their academic careers if they are to be successful in finding the support systems they need to deal with the inevitable peer pressure to not study.

At the collegiate level the connections are no more automatic than they are pre-college. The students interviewed for this study report significantly different experiences. One student talked about how a program he belonged to in college with other high-achieving blacks changed his perspective on his black peers. He expressed the fact that in high school he really didn't associate with other African Americans because of their lack of interest in academics. His perception was that blacks were not as smart and interested in academics. However, after he gained membership in a merit-based program for high-achieving blacks, he credited the program with changing his perspective. He shared that because of the program he learned how to study and get along with other blacks. This late connection and identity with other blacks raises concerns for issues of self-esteem, self-concept, and racial identity.

Not all students found it difficult connecting with peers. Several students expressed that it was very easy for them to connect with a variety of students. In fact, some of these students emphasized that they sought more friendships outside of the community of high achievers because they wanted to expand their circle of friends and they did not want to be limited in their interactions. One of the ways that students stayed connected to the larger community of black peers was through their involvement in black organizations (e.g., black student union, Greek organizations, black engineers). These organizations served as their primary source of support and connection to the campus. As students talked about their connection to the black community, it became apparent that the role of parents and other mentors was important in the transmission of cultural knowledge and the development of the students' commitment to the black community.

The students in all three studies indicated that it was important to have financial support and access to programs and institutions that have advanced facilities, technological resources, and committed faculty who are willing to work with students on research projects. Those who attended TWIs were attracted to institutions that demonstrated a commitment to diversity and offered a range of social and cultural outlets.

IMPLICATIONS FOR BLACK COLLEGES

The issues raised in this chapter suggest continued opportunities and challenges for black colleges. The experiences of high-achieving blacks suggest that these students may encounter different social experiences prior to and during college. While the overall HBCU environment is more supportive, this segment of the black student population may need strategic opportunities to connect with black peers who are equally interested in academics, particularly if they have had minimal contact prior to college with other achieving blacks. Even in a majority black environment, students who demonstrate a greater interest in academics may still encounter some isolation from peers who perceive their interests as acting white.

Because HBCUs serve a wide range of students with differing academic abilities, they are challenged, often with fewer resources than TWIs, with providing services to meet the needs of all students—from those who demonstrate advanced skill abilities to those who need remedial work. Academically talented students are attracted to state-of-the art facilities with faculty doing cutting-edge research. HBCUs must continue to seek parity in academic programs and facilities so that they can remain competitive and provide viable academic experiences for all students, especially high-achieving students who are likely to apply to graduate school and pursue terminal degrees.

HBCUs have a sustained record of building black intellectual capital and successfully graduating more blacks than any other type of institution. HBCUs must emphasize this fact to benefactors who seek ways to invest in black education. Black colleges are in a position to build on a strong historical legacy of providing socially supportive and intellectually enhancing environments for students.

HBCUs should continue to promote at every opportunity their distinguished alumni, students, and faculty and premium programs. It is important that they continue to highlight their unique mission and demonstrate their service in the educational process relative to other types of institutions. Bowen and Bok (1998), in *The Shape of the River,* write about the important role of 28 highly selective TWIs in shaping the experiences of students during and after college. In explaining the purpose of their study, they stated that they were "concerned with the flow of talent—particularly of talented black men and women—through the country's system of higher education and on into the marketplace and the larger society" (p. xxi). Bowen and Bok continue:

We often hear of the importance of keeping young people moving through the "pipeline" from elementary school to high school to college, on through graduate and professional schools, and into jobs, family responsibilities, and civic life. But this image is misleading, with its connotation of a smooth, well-defined, and well understood passage. It is moving down a winding river, with rock-strewn rapids and slow channels, muddy at times and clear at others. Particularly when race is involved, there is nothing simple, smooth, or highly predictable about the education of young people. (p. xxi)

HBCUs understand the challenge in getting black students, at all levels of talent, through the pipeline of education. They know that it is not always easy, and they accept that there will be numerous obstacles given the wide range and diversity of students they serve. While HBCUs may not have the resources or academic reputation that highly selective TWIs have, they nevertheless have a significant story that has been chronicled over the years. HBCUs must continue to present the complexities and richness of their environments for faculty and students so that others can understand the distinct role these institutions play in American education. Just as Bowen and Bok chronicle the success of black graduates from selective TWIs, HBCUs must continue to demonstrate how the graduates of their programs go on to contribute to significant civic responsibilities and leadership positions nationally and internationally. HBCUs have been the primary educational pipeline for undergraduate and professional degree attainment in the black community. It is imperative that they continue to show, in a broader context, their contribution over time to higher education.

Finally, black campuses must highlight the fact that they offer a faculty that more closely reflects the diversity of the real world than do the faculty at TWIs. Given the important role and relationship of faculty contact to student success (Pascarella & Terenzini, 1991), this characteristic of the HBCU environment is essential to meeting the needs of a changing student body. Although black students have more options available to them in the twenty-first century, it is important that they understand the ways in which they are likely to be enriched by the HBCU experience.

REFERENCES

Allen, W. (1988). The education of black students on white college campuses: What quality the experience? In M. T. Nettles (Ed.), *Toward black undergraduate student equality in American higher education* (pp. 57–85). New York: Greenwood Press.

Allen, W. (1992). The color of success: African-American college student outcomes at predominantly white and historically black public colleges and universities. *Harvard Educational Review, 62*(1), 26–44.

Allen, W. R., Epps, E. G., & Haniff, N. Z. (1991). *College in black and white.* Albany: State University of New York Press.

Anderson, J. (1988). *The education of blacks in the South, 1860–1935.* Chapel Hill: University of North Carolina Press.

Bell-Rose, S. (1998). What it takes: A look at black achievers. *The College Board Review, 187,* 8–19.

Bowen, W. G., & Bok, D. (1998). *The shape of the river: Long-term consequences of considering race in college and university admissions.* Princeton, NJ: Princeton University Press.

College Board National Task Force on Minority High Achievement. (1999). *Reach-

ing the top: A report of the national task force on minority high achievement. New York: College Entrance Examination Board.

Davis, J. (1998). Cultural capital and the role of historically black colleges and universities in educational reproduction. In K. Freeman (Ed.), *African American culture and heritage in higher education research and practice* (pp. 143–153). Westport, CT: Praeger.

Fleming, J. (1984). *Blacks in college: A comparative study of students' success in black and white institutions.* San Francisco: Jossey-Bass.

Ford, D. Y. (1996). *Reversing underachievement among gifted black students: Promising practices and programs. Education and psychology of the gifted series.* New York: Teachers College Press, Columbia University.

Fordham, S., & Ogbu, J. (1986). Black students' school success: Coping with the burden of acting white. *Urban Review, 18,* 176–207.

Freeman, K. (1999). No services needed? The case for mentoring high achieving African American students. *Peabody Journal of Education, 74*(2), 15–26.

Fries-Britt, S. (1998). Moving beyond black achiever isolation: Experiences of gifted black collegians. *Journal of Higher Education, 69*(5), 556–576.

Fries-Britt, S. (2000). Identity development of high-ability black collegians. In M. D. Svinicki, R. E. Rice, & M. B. Magolda (Eds.), *New directions for teaching and learning: No. 82. Teaching to promote intellectual and personal maturity* (pp. 55–65). San Francisco: Jossey-Bass.

Fries-Britt, S., & Turner, B. (2001). Facing stereotypes: A case study of black students on a white campus. *The Journal of College Student Development, 42*(5), 420–429.

Fries-Britt, S., & Turner, B. (2002). Uneven stories: The experiences of successful black collegians at a historically black and a traditionally white campus. *The Review of Higher Education, 25*(3), 315–330.

Gurin, P., & Epps, E. G. (1975). *Black consciousness, identity, and achievement: A study of students in historically black colleges.* New York: Wiley Press.

Hope, R. O. (1996). Revitalizing minority colleges and universities. In L. I. Rendón & R. O. Hope (Eds.), *Educating a new majority: Transforming America's educational system for diversity.* San Francisco: Jossey-Bass.

Hummel, M., & Steele, C. (1996). The learning community: A program to address issues of academic achievement and retention. *The Journal of Intergroup Relations, 23*(2), 28–33.

Jencks, C., & Phillips, M. (1998). *The black-white test score gap.* Washington, DC: Brookings Institution Press.

Miller, S. L. (1995). *An American imperative: Accelerating minority educational advancement.* New Haven, CT: Yale University Press.

Mow, S. L., & Nettles, M. T. (1990). Minority student access and persistence and performance in college: A review of trends and research literature. In J. C. Smart (Ed.), *Higher Education: Handbook of theory and research* (Vol. 4, pp. 35–105). New York: Agathon Press.

Noldon, D. F., & Sedlacek, W. E. (1998). Gender differences in attitudes, skills, and behaviors among academically talented university freshmen. *Roeper Review, 21*(2), 106–109.

Ogbu, J. U. (1993). Differences in cultural frame of reference. *International Journal of Behavioral Development, 16,* 483–506.

Pascarella, E. T., & Terenzini, P. T. (1991). *How college affects students.* San Francisco: Jossey-Bass.

Roebuck, J. B., & Murty, K. S. (1997). Historically black colleges and universities: Their place in American higher education. In L. F. Goodchild & H. S. Wechsler (Eds.), *The history of higher education* (2nd ed., pp. 667–676). Boston: Simon and Schuster Custom Publishing.

Smedley, B. D., Myers, H. F., & Harrell, S. P. (1993). Minority-status stresses and the college adjustment of ethnic minority freshman. *Journal of Higher Education, 64*(4), 434–452.

Solano, C. H. (1987). Stereotypes of social isolation and early burnout in the gifted: Do they exist? *Journal of Youth and Adolescence, 16*(6), 527–539.

Sowell, T. (1972). *Black education: Myths and tragedies.* New York: David McKay.

Steele, C. M. (1992, April). Race and the schooling of black Americans. *Atlantic Monthly,* 68–78.

Steele, C. M. (1997). A threat in the air: How stereotypes shape intellectual identity and performance. *American Psychologist, 52*(6), 613–629.

Steele, C. M., & Aronson, J. (1995). Stereotype threat and the intellectual test performance of African Americans. *Journal of Personality and Social Psychology, 69*(5), 797–811.

Steele, C. M., & Aronson, J. (1998). Stereotype threat and the test performance of academically successful African Americans. In C. Jenks & M. Phillips (Eds.), *The black-white test score gap* (pp. 401–427). Washington, DC: Brookings Institution Press.

Willie, C. V. (1981). *The ivory and ebony towers.* Lexington, MA: Lexington Books.

Willie, C. V., & McCord, A. S. (1972). *Black students at white colleges.* New York: Praeger.

CHAPTER 11

Black Colleges and Universities in America and South Africa: Common Histories and Future Destinies?

Reitumetse Obakeng Mabokela and Gail E. Thomas

This chapter undertakes a comparison of two unique sets of institutions in higher education that are geographically isolated but closely linked regarding their political and historical context. The latter has shaped the missions, functions, and condition of these institutions and has left an indelible imprint on their development and present status. We refer specifically to the historically black colleges and universities in the United States and South Africa. We present findings and perspectives regarding the history, characteristics, and current status of these institutions, their students, and staff. The major question we address is the extent to which the challenges and future destiny of these institutions are similar. We hypothesize that given the strong and penetrating imprint of previous institutionalized segregation on black colleges and universities in the United States and South Africa, these institutions share similar characteristics and challenges. We conclude with projections about the future of these institutions.

OVERVIEW OF THE DEVELOPMENT OF HISTORICALLY BLACK COLLEGES AND UNIVERSITIES IN THE UNITED STATES AND SOUTH AFRICA

Black Colleges in the United States

Historically black colleges and universities (HBCUs) in America are those institutions established prior to 1964 whose major mission was the education of blacks that were legally excluded from attending most white colleges and universities. Thus, the historical mission, development, and function of these institutions were prescribed by societal norms and a social order that endorsed and enforced racial inequality and that restricted educational opportunity and social mobility for blacks. Initially, the Freedmen's Bureau, established after the Civil War to support recently freed slaves, provided the primary source of support for the education of black Americans. The bureau, along with members of the D.C. Congregational Church, founded Howard Normal and Theological Institute, which later became Howard University, one of the well known among U.S. black colleges and universities. Apart from Howard University, Cheney University, founded in 1830, and Lincoln and Wilberforce, founded in the 1850s (Hoffman, Snyder, & Sonnenberg, 1996), were the only existing black colleges and universities.

After the Freedmen's Bureau closed in 1873, there was no major alternative for the education of blacks until the passage of the Second Morrill Act in 1890. This act mandated that states establish separate public land-grant colleges for blacks and whites. The First Morrill Act of 1862 established public land-grant colleges for students of lower socioeconomic backgrounds. However, states used these funds exclusively to support white colleges (Hoffman, Snyder, & Sonnenberg, 1996).

With the exception of Howard, Fisk University, and Meharry Medical College, most black colleges only offered elementary- and secondary-level education (Hoffman, Snyder, & Sonnenberg, 1996). This restriction, along with the establishment and maintenance of separate black and white colleges, reflected the status quo of American society during the postslavery and Reconstruction era (Roebuck & Murty, 1993). The sentiments and attitudes of whites toward black colleges were consistent with the institutionalized norms and values prevailing in America during this time. For example, General S. C. Armstrong, a white who founded Hampton University, a black university, expressed and promoted the belief that "blacks were less competent than whites and should therefore receive a separate education that was of a lower caliber than that of whites" (Fleming, 1981). This ideology, and the establishment of separate educational and social institutions for blacks and whites, was legally upheld by the Supreme Court ruling in *Plessy v. Ferguson* (1896), which legalized the establishment of "separate but equal educational institutions for blacks and whites."

As a consequence of the passage of the Second Morrill Act, 19 black land-grant colleges were created as non-degree-granting institutions, with a curriculum that emphasized agriculture, industry, and mechanics. As a result of various contributions by private (mostly white) philanthropists and by some of the more well-established black churches, by 1927 there were approximately 80 black colleges and universities with a collective student enrollment of approximately 14,000 (Hoffman, Snyder, & Sonnenberg, 1996). While the student population at these institutions at this time was predominantly black, the administrative and teaching staffs were predominantly white. This persisted until the middle of the twentieth century when returning black veterans from World War II enrolled in large numbers at black institutions and demanded a greater representation of black staff and faculty at black institutions (Hoffman, Snyder, & Sonnenberg, 1996).

After the passage of the Second Morrill Act, some 33 black colleges were able to move beyond providing an elementary and secondary education to offering a college-level education (Fleming, 1981). Despite these gains, the public black colleges initially created for blacks were of poor quality, with inadequately trained teachers and facilities (Bowles & DeCosta, 1971). These colleges continued, however, to provide vocational and agriculture training for blacks while the private black colleges attempted to offer a more comprehensive liberal arts education geared toward careers in teaching and the ministry.

CHALLENGING AND DISMANTLING THE SYSTEM OF SEGREGATION

Under difficult political, financial, and social conditions, America's black colleges made progress in establishing themselves and in educating blacks. Some 40 private and 17 public black colleges were established between 1865 and 1890 (Fleming, 1981). Because of persistent segregation, these institutions could not obtain full membership in the Southern Association of Colleges and Secondary Schools (Fleming, 1981). This and other racially exclusionary practices became the fuel for black opposition and the subsequent challenge to the doctrine of "separate but equal." Booker T. Washington and his influence had died by this time. W. E. B. Du Bois, a prominent black scholar who advocated a liberal, more expanded, and equitable education for blacks, had gained popularity.

The National Association for the Advancement of Colored People (NAACP) rallied around Du Bois's ideology and formally challenged the doctrine of "separate but equal" when a black student was denied admission to a historically white American law school. In 1935 the organization filed a suit, in *Murray v. the University of Maryland,* on behalf of Donald Murray, the black student who was denied admission to the historically white university. The Supreme Court ruled in Murray's favor, and ordered that he be admitted to the program on the basis that the school had violated his right to equal protection under the 14th Amendment of the U.S. Constitution.

Four additional cases were filed in which the Supreme Court assumed the same posture and ruled against the doctrine of "separate but equal": *Missouri ex. Rel Gaines v. Canada* (1938), *Sipuel v. Board of Regents of Uni-*

versity of Oklahoma (1948), *Sweatt v. Painter* (1950), and *McLaurin v. Oklahoma State Board of Regents* (1950). The latter three cases involved the denial of admission to black students, on the basis of race, to traditionally white state and federally supported law schools. These four cases, coupled with *Murray v. Maryland*, laid the groundwork for the 1955 ruling in *Brown v. Board of Education of Topeka*. In this landmark case, the U.S. Supreme Court unanimously held that the doctrine of "separate but equal" was unconstitutional. The *Brown* decision addressed and targeted racial segregation in elementary and secondary education. Some 18 years later, in *Adams v. Richardson* (1973), the Supreme Court mandated that states that received federal funding desegregate their public colleges and universities. The *Adams* decision and the Higher Education Act of 1965 (which provided financial aid to disadvantaged students for postsecondary education) were the most important legal decisions impacting the educational attainment and achievement of black and other minority and disadvantaged students in higher education (Haynes, 1981).

Prior to higher education desegregation, black colleges awarded virtually all of the baccalaureate degrees that black students received in the United States. However, in 1994–1995, these institutions awarded only 29 percent of the bachelor's degrees, 15 percent of the master's degrees, 8.8 percent of the doctoral degrees, and 17.4 percent of the first professional degrees that black students received (Hoffman, Snyder, & Sonnenberg, 1996). Thus, given higher education desegregation and the broader opening of white public colleges to black students, U.S. black colleges and universities must now compete more effectively for black students, especially for the most academically talented. In addition, according to *Fordice*, they must justify their continued existence, as they now share the education of black students with a larger share of colleges and universities.

BLACK UNIVERSITIES IN SOUTH AFRICA

Historically black universities (HBUs) in South Africa, like their U.S. counterparts, were established primarily to provide postsecondary education to black students who were legally prohibited from admission to historically white universities (HWUs). All of the South African HBUs except for one were established in the 1960s or later, as a result of apartheid laws and policies. As the following discussion indicates, HBUs emerged and functioned under political and social conditions that were not supportive to their existence.

The Nationalist party government passed a number of laws that systematically entrenched racial segregation at all levels of society beginning in 1948 when the Nationalist party government took office. The Bantu Education Act of 1953 provided for the establishment of a racially differentiated system of education whose goal was to entrench the privileged position of whites[1] by providing inferior education to blacks (National Commission on Higher Education [NCHE] Report, 1996; Gwala, 1988; Kallaway, 1984). Racially and ethnically based universities were established for Africans, coloreds, and Indians under the provisions of the Extension of University Act of 1959. The University of the North was established for Sotho-, Venda-, and Tsonga-speaking Africans, the University of Zululand for Zulus, the University of the Western Cape for coloreds, and the University of Durban-Westville for Indians. The University of Fort Hare, the oldest black university, established in 1916, was designated for Xhosa-speaking Africans.

The creation of separate black universities fulfilled three primary goals: first, to legitimate and solidify the idea of separate racial and ethnic groups promoted by the National party government; second, to provide personnel to administer and support political structures in the newly created homelands (Subotzky, 1997; Gwala, 1988); and third, to maintain and reproduce the subordinate social and economic position of blacks (Christie & Collins, 1984).

All of the South African HBUs, like their U.S. counterparts, were established as teaching institutions whose responsibility was to prepare graduates who would be ready to enter the workforce after the completion of their bachelor's degrees. The 11 HBUs were classified into three broad categories based on their geographic location and the population group they were created to serve. The first group of black universities consisted of seven rural African universities. The universities in this category included the Universities of the North and Zululand, both established in 1960. The remaining five rural universities, often referred to as "bush universities," were created in the former independent homelands of Bophuthatswana, Ciskei, Transkei, and Venda. A branch campus of the University of the North was established in the self-governing homeland of Qwa-Qwa (Muller, 1991). With the exception of the University of Fort Hare, all other homeland universities were created during the late 1970s and early 1980s (Muller, 1991).

Urban universities comprised the second category of HBUs. These universities were characterized as urban versions of the bush universities, created to serve coloreds (University of Western Cape) and Indians (University of Durban-Westville) (Muller, 1991; Ashley, 1971). These universities received better funding and significantly better facilities relative to other HBUs.

The third group of HBUs included the two specialist universities: the Medical University of South Africa (MEDUNSA), established in 1978, and Vista University, founded in 1982. MEDUNSA was established as a response to the increasing demand for medical care within the black population. Vista was established as an urban black university with seven satellite campuses throughout the country. It was intended to serve primarily blacks in the urban areas (townships), and its academic programs focused on teacher education and improvement of teacher qualifications through an extensive system of distance education (Muller, 1991; Subotzky, 1997).

DISMANTLING APARTHEID

The discussion of U.S. HBCUs indicated that the courts played a pivotal role in dismantling segregation within U.S. higher education. While South African HBUs have a long history of student resistance against apartheid objectives (especially during the 1970s and 1980s), the process of dismantling the legal structures under which HBUs were established is a recent development. Since the change of government in 1994, there has been a concerted effort to transform the system of higher education from one marred with racial, gender, and class inequities to one more equitable. In 1995 President Mandela appointed a commission of inquiry to investigate the current conditions in postsecondary education and, on the basis of its findings, to offer recommendations for policy change in higher education. The National Commission on Higher Education's (NCHE's) report formed the foundation for the green and white papers[2] on higher education, and subsequently the Higher Education Act passed at the end of 1997.

The proposals for reform offered by the NCHE aroused a variety of responses from the various constituents. The strongest voice of opposition emerged from the HBUs and students. They charged that the NCHE report was irrelevant to the needs of HBUs and argued that if its recommendations were implemented, they would leave HBUs in a devastating position. They further argued that the NCHE report failed to offer recommendations that provided a coherent philosophy of education "derived from the national aspiration for liberation and justice" (Seepe, 1996, p. 15). Further, the report failed to critically evaluate the relationship between power and the production and dissemination of knowledge (Nkondo, 1996; Seepe, 1996). A "committee of 10," comprised primarily of senior administrators from HBUs and technikons (post-secondary education institutions that structurally and functionally fall between U.S. community colleges and traditional four-year colleges) was formed to lobby support against the NCHE report and to write an alternative report, the findings of which are unknown.

The preceding historical overview contextualized conditions under which HBUs emerged and functioned in the two countries. While the historical events in each country are clearly unique, HBUs in the United States and South Africa share one common thread: they emerged under political, social, and economic conditions that were hostile to their existence. In the following discussion, we examine the current characteristics of HBUs, their students, and faculty.

BLACK COLLEGES AND UNIVERSITIES: THEIR STUDENTS AND STAFF IN THE UNITED STATES AND SOUTH AFRICA

Currently there are 103 historically black colleges and universities in the United States. Forty of these institutions are public four-year colleges and 49 are private (Hoffman, Snyder, & Sonnenberg, 1996). The remaining 14 are two-year colleges: 10 public and 4 private. These institutions comprise 3 percent of the total number (n = 3,688) of U.S. colleges and universities, and on the average have smaller student enrollments than most U.S. colleges and universities (Vargas, 1996). In 1994, the average total student enrollment at U.S. black colleges was 2,719, compared to an average enrollment of 3,872 at white colleges (Hoffman, Snyder, & Sonnenberg).

In South Africa, the 11 HBUs constitute 50 percent of the 22 universities in the country. The remaining 11 universities include 6 Afrikaans-language universities, 4 English-language institutions, and 1 correspondence university. As in the case of the U.S. HBCUs, the average size of the South African HBU is smaller than that of the HWU. For example, in 1992 student enrollment at the smaller HBUs ranged from 2,045 students to 6,427, and the largest HBU had 14,340 students. In contrast, student enrollment at the HWUs ranged from 4,236 at the smallest university to more than 23,000 at the largest (Subotzky, 1997).

The majority of America's black colleges remain predominantly black in their student composition, and are undergraduate-degree-awarding institutions (Roebuck & Murty, 1993). In 1994, 85 percent of the students at these institutions were black, and 82 percent of the degrees awarded by these institutions were at the baccalaureate level (Hoffman, Snyder, & Sonnenberg, 1996). However, by 1995 four of the historically black institutions had become predominantly white in their student body composition, with 70 to 92 percent white student enrollment. Six had a 30 to 53 percent white enrollment, and an additional eight had 20 to 29 percent white enrollment (Vargas, 1996).

Enrollment data indicated that the majority of students in South African HBUs were (and still are) undergraduate students. With the exception of the Universities of Durban-Westville and the Western Cape, where enrollments in graduate programs were somewhat higher (17 percent), undergraduates comprised 90 percent or more of students enrolled at HBUs (Subotzky, 1997). The distribution of students by academic discipline indicated that the majority were enrolled in education (19 percent) and the social sciences (45 percent), with substantially lower enrollments in the natural sciences, medical sciences, and technical fields (Bunting, 1994). A similar trend exists in the United States regarding the distribution of black students by discipline; a much higher proportion are enrolled and graduate in education and the social sciences than in engineering and the natural sciences (Carter & Wilson, 1998).

A PROFILE OF STUDENTS AT HBUS

Studies have consistently shown that most students attending HBCUs in the United States enter with fewer family and academic resources than black and white students who attend predominantly white colleges and universities (Hoffman, Snyder, & Sonnenberg, 1996; Cross & Astin, 1981; Thomas & Hill, 1987; Wenglensky, 1997). Data by Nettles and Perna (1997) indicate that 39 percent of the black male students and 41 percent of the black female students at HBCUs had family incomes below $20,000, compared to 27 percent of the black male students and 35 percent of the black female students attending predominantly white colleges. These researchers reported further that compared to whites, black students who took the Standardized Achievement Test (SAT) scored on average 100 points lower on the math and verbal components of the test, had lower high school grades, had fewer years of academic study, had taken fewer honors courses, and were less likely to have parents who had received a college education. Many black colleges have prided themselves on being able to accept, educate, and graduate a high proportion of academically and economically disadvantaged students (Thomas & Hill, 1987; Thomas, 1991; Roebuck & Murty, 1993).

Students at South African HBUs exhibit similar characteristics to their counterparts in the United States. Black students enrolled at HBUs face a number of challenges. First, the academic training they received at the secondary school has not provided them adequate preparation to cope with university work. This problem of underpreparation is further exacerbated by the fact that the majority of black students, especially Africans, do not use English as a first language. Therefore, they not only face difficulties with the substantive content of the material but also with the language in which that material is taught.

Second, for some black students enrolled in HBUs, these institutions were not their first choice (Southern Region Education Board, 1990; Thomas, 1997). They would have preferred to attend a different university because HBUs are perceived as having lower academic standards and an inferior reputation. Therefore HBUs are confronted with students who do not particularly want to be there. Further, historically white universities in the United States and in South Africa often attract the cream of the crop among black students, further reinforcing the myth that HBUs are not academically competitive (Suggs, 1998; Dlamini, 1996).

Third, funding is a major impediment because most of the black students at HBUs come from disadvantaged backgrounds. South Africa's HBUs were funded on a formula that was based on criteria that were not favorable to their conditions—for example, student enrollment in graduate programs, although most HBUs were not designed to be postbaccalaureate institutions, and research output of faculty, although HBUs were specifically established to be teaching institutions that trained professionals.

Finally, the poor infrastructure and facilities at South Africa's HBUs and in the surrounding area presents a major impediment. The majority of the HBUs (with the exception of the University of the Western Cape and the University of Durban-Westville) were established in isolated parts of the country, in areas that lacked the most basic facilities such as schools, hospitals, and adequate transportation and accommodation. This restricted their active participation in the core of South African academic life (Gwala, 1988). Faculty at HBUs have been confronted by some of the same concerns as students. In the discussion that follows, we present a profile of faculty at these institutions and explore challenges they have to contend with.

FACULTY AND STAFF

In the fall of 1993, 66 percent of faculty in America's black colleges and universities were black (Hoffman, Snyder, & Sonnenberg, 1996). Because the major mission of most of the HBCUs remains teaching, faculty at these institutions are usually more heavily engaged in teaching than in research. Faculty at U.S. black colleges are also less likely to hold a doctoral degree than faculty at predominantly white universities and are more likely than their counterparts at predominantly white universities to hold the rank of associate and assistant professor rather than professor (Hoffman, Snyder, & Sonnenberg). In addition, faculty salaries are on the average lower at U.S. HBCUs than at the average predominantly white American university (Jackson, 1991; Thomas & Hill, 1987).

Black colleges and universities in America also employ a higher proportion of service and maintenance staff and a lower proportion of research assistants than other U.S. colleges and universities. The latter is attributed to the lower level of research activities at these institutions than at other institutions. A lack of adequate facilities to support research activities is also an inhibiting factor at many HBCUs in the United States (Kellogg Commission, 1997). A 1994 survey of research facilities at American colleges and universities indicated that only one in four facilities at the HBCUs was suitable for most highly developed scientific research and two in five were deemed unsuitable and in need of repair or renovation (Kellogg Commission, 1997).

According to the NCHE report, the distribution patterns of faculty at HBUs in South Africa do not reflect the demographic profile of the larger South African society. In a society in which Africans comprised 75 percent of the population in 1996, coloreds 7 percent, Indians/Asians 3 percent, whites 15 percent, and women 52 percent (Central Statistics Service, 1998), the most prestigious positions in higher education are predominantly occupied by white males. Blacks and women tend to be relegated to the lower rungs of the employment ladder, with a disproportionate number in service positions as opposed to academic or administrative positions. Similar patterns were observed among the administrative staff, where whites comprised 71 percent of the administrative staff, compared to Indians at 7 percent, coloreds 11 percent, and Africans 12 percent. With respect to service staff, whites constituted only 4 percent, while Indians comprised 3 percent, coloreds 22 percent, and Africans 71 percent (Bunting, 1994).

Gender inequities among faculty are also pervasive in South Africa. According to the NCHE report, 68 percent of the total research and teaching staff in 1993 was male. The distribution of women by rank points to more disparities, with the majority of female academics employed as junior lecturers or lecturers[3] (NCHE, 1996). White males constituted the majority of the permanent faculty at HBUs at their inception in the 1960s through the 1980s. However, since the early 1990s the proportion of African, colored, and Indian faculty has increased considerably—to the point where at some HBUs whites are no longer the majority. According to Subotzky (1997), whites comprised on average 52 percent of all full-time faculty members at the 11 HBUs in 1992; Africans were 32 percent, Indians 9 percent, and coloreds 7 percent.

Concerns have been raised about the quality of education and educators in South Africa's HBUs. There is a pervasive notion that academic standards at HBUs do not measure up to those of HWUs and that the quality of faculty is also inferior. Faculty at HBUs (and at other South African universities) are not always required to hold a Ph.D. or an equivalent terminal degree to be tenured (Subotzky, 1997). In 1990, 30 percent of faculty at HBUs held a doctorate, 36 percent a master's degree, and 34 percent had an honors or other postbaccalaureate degree, compared to 45 percent of faculty at HWUs with doctorates, 31 percent with a master's, and 24 percent with an honors or other postbaccalaureate qualification (Bunting, 1994; Subotzky, 1997).

The perceived underqualification of faculty at HBCUs and HBUs in the United States and South Africa, coupled with the persistent perception of black institutions as second-rate universities, presents challenges as these universities struggle to create a new identity and rid themselves of their historical marginal position.

FINANCIAL STATUS OF BLACK COLLEGES IN THE UNITED STATES AND SOUTH AFRICA

Government funding for American higher education has declined. However, America's black colleges continue to be more financially dependent on government funding than most other colleges and universities. In addition, they are more financially vulnerable than most of these institutions (Jones, 1993). Private black colleges rely on tuition to pay 54 percent of their expenses. Their remaining funding is derived from a combination of federal government, corporate sponsors, and the United Negro College Fund (Scott, 1998). Sixty-one percent of the revenues for public U.S. HBCUs—compared to 51 percent for other public colleges and universities—are derived from government funding (Hoffman, Snyder, & Sonnenberg, 1996). Because faculties at black institutions are more often engaged in teaching than in research, these institutions receive far less revenue from grants and contracts than do white colleges and universities.

Although the alumni of U.S. black colleges make valuable nonmonetary contributions in terms of moral support, public relations, and student recruitment, they contribute far less financially than alumni at the average white institution (Roebuck & Murty, 1993). Alumni giving at predominantly white institutions is $30,000 per student, compared to only $8,000 per student at predominantly black colleges (*Jet*, 1995). At Howard University, the largest and most comprehensive U.S. black university, only 7 percent of its 65,000 alumni made contributions to the college, compared to 20 percent of the alumni at most other colleges and universities (Suggs, 1998).

Citing data from recent U.S. censuses, Suggs (1998) noted that it is not surprising that American black alumni contribute less to their alma maters since there are seven times as many whites in America as blacks (220 million whites vs. 33 million blacks), and since whites are 23 more times likely than blacks to earn more than $100,000 annually. A ranking of the 460 U.S. colleges and universities with the highest endowments included only four HBCUs: Howard at $152 million, which ranked 128th; Spelman at $124 million, which ranked 156th; Hampton University at $97 million, which ranked 184th; and Dillard University at $32 million, which ranked 342nd. By contrast, the five universities (in descending order) with the highest endowments were predominantly white: Harvard, the University of Texas, Yale, Princeton, and Stanford. These five institutions had individual endowments between $3.8 billion and $7.0 billion (Suggs, 1998).

Between 1976–1977 and 1993–1994, increases in expenditures per student at public and private black U.S. colleges lagged behind increases at other public and private U.S. colleges and universities (Wenglinsky, 1996). President Clinton's administration provided $20 million to support and enhance America's black colleges (Wlotta, 1992). However, this amount has not kept pace with student enrollments at these institutions, or with the broad range of debts that many of these institutions incur (Wilson, 1998). Most of these institutions have experienced periods of extreme financial hardship. Recently, Howard University, one of the leading black colleges, was forced to fire or lay off more than 400 workers due to financial problems (Spence, 1998). Since 1977, at least 10 black colleges have closed because of financial problems.

South African HBUs have been similarly plagued by financial difficulties. The allocation funding has traditionally favored historically white universities over HBUs and technikons. South Africa's universities obtain their funding from government subsidies, tuition and fees, government research grants, private donations, and income from investments. Government subsidies comprised the largest proportion (50 percent) of university funds, followed by tuition and fees at about 20 percent (Sehoole & Wolpe, 1994). Prior to 1984, universities were funded by means of a subsidy formula that based the allocation of financial resources on criteria that were either very weak or nonexistent at HBUs. These included the number of students enrolled, the success rate of students at each institution, enrollment in the natural sciences as opposed to the humanities, graduate student enrollment, research output, and publications (Sehoole & Wolpe). The subsidy formula was amended in 1984 to restrict the number of undergraduate students for which subsidies could be claimed. Therefore, HBUs were locked out once again because their area of student growth was in the undergraduate sector.

The financial burden of South Africa's HBUs was further exacerbated by the fact that the majority of their students were (and still are) from disadvantaged socioeconomic backgrounds. Given that the government did not have an external system for providing student loans, HBUs had to allocate a significant proportion of their resources to student loans. Nonpayment of student loans is a problem that continues to plague many HBUs, resulting in a vicious cycle of student protests that characterize the beginning of each academic year (Naidu, 1997; Yoganathan & Lee, 1996).

The inability of black colleges to generate additional revenue and alternative funding will continue to create pressure and challenges for these institutions and limit their ability to compete more effectively for students, faculty, and staff. Therefore these institutions must continue their efforts to obtain what they perceive as a more adequate and fair share of state funding. Simultaneously, they must provide a quality education to students, many of whom cannot afford the current costs of attending these institutions, let alone any potential tuition increases that they might consider.

CONTRIBUTIONS AND STRENGTHS

The history as well as the present and the predicted future of black colleges and universities in the United States and South Africa has been and continues to be one of challenge: a challenge to exist, to persist, to thrive, and to chart a new course in the present era of desegregation, reduced funding, and increased accountability in higher education. Despite the multiple challenges that these institutions face, they have made (and continue to make) significant contributions to higher education in their respective countries and to the students who attend them. We now review some of the contributions and strengths of these institutions.

Black colleges in the United States and South Africa have built their legacy around the uncontested fact that they have provided higher education for a large proportion of low-income students who would not have otherwise attended college (Roebuck & Murty, 1993; Naidu, 1997). U.S. black colleges assumed responsibility for the higher education of most blacks, from the inception of these institutions up until 1950 (Wlotta, 1992). In addition, HBUs in South Africa, since their establishment in the 1960s, have graduated and continue to graduate the majority of black graduates. Both sets of institutions have historically trained and produced a sizeable proportion of black leaders. In America they including Martin Luther King Jr., Rosa Parks, Thurgood Marshall, Barbara Jordan, Toni Morrison, and Oprah Winfrey. In a recent study, Ehrenberg (1998) reported that approximately 80 percent of America's present black judges and 50 percent of its black lawyers received their initial education at HBCUs. Similarly, South African HBUs have trained prominent leaders such as Nelson Mandela and Robert Mugabe (president of Zimbabwe), both of whom graduated from the University of Fort Hare.

South African HBUs became important centers of opposition to apartheid ideology. For instance, the black consciousness movement in the 1970s, which was viewed as the catalyst for the 1976 Soweto student uprisings, found its roots among black university students (Marx, 1992). Additionally, the insistence by the Nationalist party government on keeping all postsecondary facilities separate resulted in the creation of facilities such as the Medical University of South Africa (MEDUNSA) for black students, an institution that some scholars contend has better facilities than some historically white universities (Subotzky, 1997).

Fleming (1984), Allen, Epps, and Haniff (1991), Thomas (1996), and Feagin, Vera, and Imani (1996) reported that an important contribution that U.S. black colleges have made and continue to make is their provision of a positive, supportive, and welcoming campus environment that fosters black students' satisfaction and success. These studies indicate that such environments are lacking at many of the predominantly white colleges that black students attend. Altbach and Lomotey (1991), Thomas (1996), Feagin (1996), and Allen (1991) and their colleagues reported that the negative climate and state of race relations for black students on predominantly white campuses in the United States is a problem that has not been adequately addressed. Although extensive research on the experiences of black students at South African HWUs is not available, Mabokela's (1998) research suggests that black students enrolled at HWUs feel marginal at best. They still do not perceive themselves as part of the HWUs' environment.

Feagin and his colleagues present evidence from their study that reveals that extensive discrimination exists against blacks in predominantly white institutions in a variety of forms, ranging from blatant racist actions to subtle and destructive practices such as racist jokes, hate messages, skits, and epithets. The authors note that the most damaging aspect for black students is the taking for granted by most white administrators, faculty, staff, and students on predominantly white campuses that "the campus is a white place in which blacks are admitted at best, as guests" (p. 11). Apart from being institutions that they can afford, black colleges offer students a sense of belonging and respect and the ability to interact with students and faculty who are of their own culture and who look like them; these are among the most common reasons that black students choose black colleges (Southern Region Education Board, 1990).

Studies in the United States have documented that while the enrollments of black students at U.S. predominantly white institutions have drastically increased, and have outpaced black student enrollments at HBCUs, black students at white institutions experience high attrition rates, lower levels of satisfaction, and lower rates of attending graduate school than their counterparts at predominantly black universities (Thomas, 1991; Jackson & Swan, 1991; Smith, 1991). Thomas (1991) also found that black colleges were more successful than predominantly white colleges in enrolling and graduating black students in the sciences and engineering, areas in which blacks are severely underrepresented. Wenglinsky (1996) recently reanalyzed the various claims reported in previous studies regarding the benefits to black students of attending black colleges. His findings confirmed past studies that have reported that: (a) predominantly black institutions are more financially accessible and affordable for black students, (b) more black students in black colleges than in white colleges aspire to and plan to pursue a postbaccalaureate degree, (c) black students in black colleges have higher persistence and graduation rates than black students in predominantly white colleges, and (d) black students at HBCUs are more often enrolled in science and engineering and pursue graduate degrees in these fields than black students in predominantly white institutions.

What appears clear is that apart from their traditional mission and legacy of educating blacks and producing many black leaders, America's and South Africa's black colleges and universities continue to assume a critical role in providing an affordable education and a positive and supportive environment that fosters black student access and success. In addition, U.S. HBCUs continue to provide U.S. graduate schools and the labor market with a disproportionate share of black baccalaureate degree recipients in the sciences and engineering (Carter & Wilson, 1998; Thomas, 1991).

CHARTING A FUTURE

Since the establishment of U.S. and South African black colleges and universities, much has changed regarding the nature and racial composition of higher education and the legal postures taken regarding the rights of blacks to participation in higher education. The major change that has had profound implications for black colleges and universities in both countries was the legal mandate (by court and/or by government) that race can no longer be a barrier to higher education access for blacks. In addition, in the United States courts have subsequently ruled in *Bakke* (1978) and more recently in *Hopwood* (1996) that achieving racial diversity and increasing minority student enrollment must not have an adverse effect on white student enrollment.

Based upon his interviews of U.S. black college presidents on more than 35 campuses, and with other individuals who work closely with these institutions, Suggs (1998) found that there appears to be consensus that many of these institutions will not survive in their present state and that some will have to "make themselves over or be forced to surrender their identity" (Suggs, 1998, p. 1). William Gray (1998), president of the United Negro College Fund, noted that many black colleges vary in their mission, and therefore must analyze their situation, define a clear niche, emphasize their strengths, and get rid of their weaknesses.

As previously noted, one of the strengths of black institutions in the United States and South Africa has been in providing the time, resources, and supportive teaching and learning environment to educate disadvantaged and at-risk students (Roebuck & Murty, 1993; Allen, 1992). Thus, documenting and publishing their techniques and marketing their strengths might prove to be a valuable investment for black colleges and universities. Also, given the concerns expressed by Boyer (1990) regarding the substandard quality of undergraduate and teacher education, some of these institutions might strengthen or redefine their niche in terms of becoming excellent citadels of undergraduate education and/or offering high-quality teacher education programs to prepare students to teach in an increasingly diverse society. In addition, they might form partnerships and ongoing working relationships with the local primary and secondary schools, especially those from which black colleges are likely to recruit future students. For example, some black colleges in the United States, such as Clark College in Atlanta, Georgia, have implemented an "adopt a future class" program which identifies promising elementary school students and commits to providing them with a scholarship upon successful entry to their college (*Black Issues in Higher Education*, 1996). These and other long-term recruitment activities might better enable black colleges to compete for students.

Suggs (1998) reported that some leaders at the more elite black colleges in the United States believe that they must establish admissions standards comparable to predominantly white colleges to recruit an adequate share of students. However, other advocates of black colleges (Wilson, 1998) contend that raising admissions standards could mean the death of many black public colleges that have thrived on enrolling and educating a large sector of academically and socioeconomically disadvantaged students. Capitalizing upon and extending their ability to recruit and graduate a higher proportion of black students in the sciences and engineering may provide an additional niche for black colleges and universities in the United States and South Africa.

Marketing and fund-raising, especially in the public black colleges, have been areas in which many black institutions have not had adequate experience or a competitive track record (Wilson, 1998). More innovative, visionary, and participatory leadership is an important prerequisite to black colleges and universities advancing in these areas (Suggs, 1998). Implementing and sustaining research as a major activity remains an additional challenge for black colleges in the United States and South Africa (Subotzky, 1997). Wlotta (1992) noted that over the past 20 years, the U.S. federal government has launched a variety of programs to build research capacity and infrastructure at black colleges. She noted further that much fear is expressed by faculty at these institutions that research will undermine teaching, and/or that the leadership at most of these institutions will not provide faculty with adequate time, resources, and rewards to effectively engage in research.

Given the long tradition of undergraduate teaching at black colleges and universities in both countries, we speculate that the transition to a prime research focus may not occur at some of these institutions and will occur only gradually at others. However, promising research activities and possibilities are already emerging at some of the better-established black colleges. For example, four of the black medical schools in the United States—Meharry, Morehouse, Howard, and Charles H. Drew—have formed a partnership with two medical universities in South Africa—the Medical University of South Africa in Pretoria and the University of Natal in Durban. The goals of the program are to help improve health care in South Africa and to address major health issues (i.e., infant mortality, AIDS) common to the black populations in both countries (*Jet*, 1995). These and other black institutions that are better positioned to conduct research might find it profitable to establish these types of partnerships. Involving their students and faculty in small-scale community projects to cultivate local partnerships, service learning, and mutually beneficial community research might be a promising approach for administrators and faculty at the smaller black colleges who wish to invest more in research.

Two final issues that black colleges and universities in the United States and South Africa must contend with in charting their future course concern their historical and cultural identity and their success in discarding their historical label as black second-class institutions tied to slavery and Reconstruction. The notion that black Americans are permanently, indelibly different is what Donald Horowitz (1985) has termed the "figment of the pigment," which means that the conspicuous and caste-like attribute of race is akin to "sealed compartments impervious to change" (p. 125). Historically and predominantly black colleges, like black Americans, are also quite conspicuous in their history, culture, and composition, and have been viewed in a similar manner. This is also true of South Africa's black colleges. The latter were historically known as "bush colleges"—rurally and geographically isolated institutions established to serve indigenous and previously colonized populations (Badat et al., 1994).

In Thomas's (1996) survey and interviews of students, professors, and administrators in South Africa's black colleges, many participants expressed the view that even if their universities were relocated to more central and urban areas, and substantially improved physically and financially, they would continue to be perceived as second-class institutions given a lack of substantial change in their predominantly black racial composition. While we do not have comparable data from respondents in American black colleges, findings by the Southern Regional Education Board (1990) indicate that the prevailing perception among black and white college students in the United States is that black colleges are inferior to white colleges and that independent of college grade performance, job access and mobility are more promising for students who attend white colleges than for those who attend black colleges. Thus, overcoming the stigma of race may still be an ongoing challenge for some of these institutions, as well as thriving and proving their viability in the current competitive arena of higher education.

Lastly, the question of what it means to be a black college (for those that still identify themselves as such) in present-day America and South Africa is an issue that some of these institutions and their students are still grappling with. While U.S. black colleges are highly diverse, and no single definition of "blackness" exists, many of these institutions take pride in and desire to maintain their historical and cultural identity (Spence, 1998). Some wish to maintain close ties with and provide service to the black communities in which they are located. As a result, emphasis on concepts such as cooperation, collective responsibility, community building, and self-determination have been integral to the historical mission of these institutions. However, as these institutions are increasingly forced to compete more effectively for students, staff, funding, and survival, it may be necessary for many of them to redefine or expand their cultural identity and their concept of local and global community.

The extent to which the latter moves U.S. and South African black institutions away from or closer to their cultural identity and original mission is unclear. Optimists who take the view that these institutions will not lose their identity or be compelled to make substantial alterations contend that those black colleges and universities with the skill to survive and strive will become stronger in their cultural identity and will continue to assume an important and unique role in American higher education (Suggs, 1998). Thus, it appears that becoming more competitive, marketable, and autonomous institutions may be one of the determining factors in preserving the cultural heritage and identity of U.S. and South African black colleges and universities. Their ability to attract a larger and more diverse pool of students and faculty is also an important factor.

CONCLUSION

In this chapter we set out to explore the similarities that exist between historically black universities and colleges in the United States and South Africa. Our findings support our hypothesis that these institutions share common characteristics and challenges that emanated from the strong imprint of institutionalized segregation and apartheid. In addition, our observations point to a number of areas of commonality: first, historically black colleges and universities in the United States and South Africa were created primarily as teaching institutions designed to serve the academic interests of a marginalized black population. Second, their infrastructure is poor and their financial base more vulnerable relative to traditionally white institutions. Third, although they have smaller student enrollments compared to white colleges and universities, they tend to have a higher proportion of students from economically disadvantaged backgrounds. Fourth, their students (as a group) tend to have lower academic performance on standardized tests and matriculation examinations (in South Africa) than other institutions. Fifth, their faculty may have lower academic credentials relative to their counterparts at white colleges and universities, thus fueling the perception of HBCUs as second-rate institutions.

Despite their ongoing struggles and challenges, however, historically black colleges and universities in the United States and South Africa continue to provide an academically supportive and socially and culturally relevant environment for their students. In America's black colleges, this translates into higher success and retention rates of black students in these institutions compared to their counterparts at predominantly white U.S. colleges and universities (Thomas & Hill, 1987; Thomas, 1996). To the extent that both sets of institutions remain successful in educating and supporting their students and can further attract and retain faculty and funding, they will continue to fill a critical niche in American and South African higher education.

NOTES

1. The racial classification terms used in this paper do not necessarily represent the author's position but are rather used to facilitate a clear and concise discussion. Although most of these terms are familiar they carry particular historical undertones specific to the South African context. African refers to people of indigenous ancestry; Coloreds are South Africans of mixed ancestry, usually Dutch, African, Malay and Khoison heritage; Indians/Asians are people of Indian descent; and Whites are people of European descent.

2. A Green paper is a government document that is the first step to the formation of a parliamentary bill. It is followed by a White paper, then a Higher Education bill that will be introduced and debated in parliament. A Higher Education Act will follow pending approval in parliament.

3. In the South African academic system the rank of faculty members is as follows: Professor, Associate Professor, Senior Lecturer, Lecturer, and Junior Lecturer.

REFERENCES

Adams v. Richardson 488 F.2d 1159 D.C. Circuit (1973).

Allen, W. R. (1992). The color of success: African-American college student outcomes at predominantly white and historically black colleges and universities. *Harvard Educational Review, 62*, 26–44.

Allen, W. R., & Haniff, N. Z. (1991). Race, gender and academic performance in U.S. higher education. In W. R. Allen, E. G. Epps, & N. Z. Haniff (Eds.), *College in black and white: African-American students in predominantly white and historically black public universities,* pp. 95–110, Albany: State University of New York Press.

Altbach, P. G. (1991). The racial dilemma in American higher education. In P. G. Altbach & K. Lomotey (Eds.), *The racial crisis in American higher education.* Albany, NY: State University of New York Press.

Altbach, P. G., & Lomotey, K. (Eds.). *The racial crisis in American higher education.* Albany, NY: State University of New York Press.

Ashley, M. J. (1971). The education of white elites of South Africa. *Comparative Education, 7*(1), 32–45.

Badat, S., Barron, F., Fisher, G., Pillay, P., & Wolpe, H. (1994). Differentiation and disadvantage: The historically black universities in South Africa. Bellville, South Africa: Education Policy Unit, University of Western Cape.

Bakke v. Regents of the University of California No. 76–811 (1978).

Black issues in higher education: Vol. 10. Ensuring the future. (1993). Arlington, VA: Cox, Matthews, & Associates, Inc.

Bowles, F., & DeCosta, F. A. (1971). *Between two worlds: A profile of Negro higher education.* New York: McGraw Hill.

Boyer, E. (1990). *Scholarship reconsidered: Priorities of the professorate.* Princeton, NJ: Carnegie Foundation for the Advancement of Teaching.

Brown v. Board of Education of Topeka. 347 U.S. 483: (1954).

Bunting, I. (1994). *A legacy of inequality: Higher education in South Africa.* Ronde-bosch, South Africa: UCT Press.

Carter, D. J., & Wilson, R. (1998). *Minorities in higher education.* Washington, DC: American Council on Education.

Central Statistics Service. (1998). *Men and women in South Africa.* Pretoria, South Africa: Author.

Christie, P., & Collins C. (1984). Bantu education: Apartheid ideology and labour reproduction. In P. Kallaway (Ed.), *Apartheid education: The education of black South Africans,* pp. 160–191. Johannesburg, South Africa: Ravan Press.

Cross, P. H., & Astin, H. S. (1981). Factors affecting black students' persistence in college. In G. E. Thomas (Ed.), *Black students in higher education,* pp. 64–75. Westport, CT: Greenwood Press.

De Clerq, F. (1991). Black universities as contested terrain: The politics of progres-sive engagement. *Perspectives in Education, 12*(2), 49–64.

Dlamini, J. (1996, September 18). Flocking to learn in former White Laagers. *Sunday Times,* p. 23.

Ehrenberg, R. G. (1998). *Historically black colleges and universities and the training of African-American lawyers and leaders of the legal profession.* Ithaca, NY: Cornell University.

Feagin J. R., Vera, H., & Imani, N. (1996). *The agony of education: Black students at white colleges and universities.* New York: Routledge Press.

Fleming, J. E. (1981). Blacks in higher education to 1954: A historical overview. In G. E. Thomas (Ed.), *Black students in higher education,* pp. 1–16. Westport, CT: Greenwood Press.

Gray, W. (1998). Black colleges chart course for next century. In E. Suggs (Ed.), *Fighting to survive: A look at America's historically black colleges and universities between October 1996 and February 1997,* p. 5. Durham, NC: Herald-Sun.

Gwala, N. (1988). State control, student politics, and the crisis in black universities. In W. Cobbett & R. Cohen (Eds.), *Popular struggles in South Africa.* Trenton, NJ: Africa World Press.

Haynes, L., III (1981). The Adams mandate: A format for achieving equal educa-tional opportunity and attainment. In G. E. Thomas (Ed.), *Black students in higher education,* pp. 329–335. Westport, CT: Greenwood Press.

Hoffman, C. M., Snyder, T. D., & Sonnenberg, B. (1996). *Historically black colleges and universities 1976–1994.* Washington, DC: National Center for Education Statistics.

Hopwood v. the University of Texas at Austin 116 Supreme Ct. 2581 (1996).

Horowitz, D. L. (1985). *Ethnic groups in conflict.* Berkeley: University of California.

Jackson, K. (1991). Black faculty in academe. In P. G. Altbach & K. Lomotey (Eds.), *The racial crisis in American higher education,* pp. 135–148. Buffalo: State Uni-versity of New York Press.

Jackson, K. W., & Swan, A. L. (1991). Institutional and individual factors affecting African-American undergraduate student performance: Campus race and students' gender. In W. R. Allen, E. G. Epps, & N. Z. Haniff (Eds.), *College in Black and White: African-American students in predominantly white and his-*

torically black public universities, pp. 127–144. Albany: State University of New York Press.

Kallaway, P. (Ed.). (1984). *Apartheid education: The education of Black South Africans.* Johannesburg, South Africa: Ravan Press.

Kellogg Commission. (1997). *Historically black colleges and universities.* Battle Creek, MI: Kellogg Foundation.

Logan, R. W. (1965). *The betrayal of the Negro from Rutherford B. Hayes to Woodrow Wilson.* New York: Collier Books.

Mabokela, R. O. (1998). *Black students on white campuses: Responses to increasing black enrollments at two South African universities.* Unpublished doctoral dissertation, University of Illinois Urbana-Champaign.

McLaurin v. Oklahoma State Board of Regents 339 U.S. 637 (1950).

Meyer, L. E. (1976). Oppression or opportunity inside black universities of South Africa. *Journal of Negro Education, 45*, 365–382.

Missouri ex. Rel. Gaines v. Canada 305 U.S. 337 (1938).

Muller, J. (1991). South Africa. In P. G. Altbach (Ed.), *International higher education: An encyclopedia.* New York: Garland Publishing.

Murray v. Maryland 182 A 590 (1935): 169 MD 478 (1937).

Naidu, E. (1997, March 14). Universities furious at "Apartheid perpetuating cuts." *Higher Education Review,* supplement in *New Nation*, p. 21.

National Commission on Higher Education (NCHE). (1996). *A framework for transformation.* Pretoria, South Africa: Author.

National partnership between U.S. and South African black colleges. (1995, March 20). *Jet.*

Nettles, M. T., & Perna, L. W. (1997). *The African-American data book: Vol. 3. The transition from school to college to work.* Fairfax, VA: Frederick D. Patterson Research Institute.

Nkondo, G. (1996, June 14). Defining a philosophy of education in South Africa. *Higher Education Review,* supplement in *New Nation*, p. 24.

Plessy v. Ferguson 163 U.S. 537 (1896).

Robbins, T. W. (1996, September 15). Foreign academics find top resources but poor results in South Africa. *Higher Education Review,* supplement in *New Nation,* p. 23.

Roebuck, J. B., & Murty, K. S. (1993). *Historically black colleges and universities: Their place in American higher education.* Westport, CT: Praeger.

Scott, G. (1998). An old-fashioned education: Tradition, character on the curriculum of single sex colleges. In E. Suggs (Ed.), *Fighting to survive: A look at America's historically black colleges and universities between October 1996 and February 1997*, p. 2. Durham, NC: Herald-Sun.

Seepe, J. (1996, May 3). Academics reject report. *Higher Education Review,* supplement in *New Nation*.

Sehoole, V., & Wolpe, H. (1994). *Draft policy proposals for the reconstruction and transformation of postsecondary education in South Africa.* Bellville, South Africa: Educational Policy Unit, University of Western Cape.

Sipuel v. Board of Regents of University of Oklahoma 322 U.S. 31 (1948).

Smith, A. W. (1991). Personal traits, institutional prestige, racial attitudes and African-American student academic performance in college. In W. R. Allen, E. G. Epps, & N. Z. Haniff (Eds.), *College in black and white: African-American*

students in predominantly white and historically black colleges and universities,
pp. 111–126. Albany: State University of New York Press.

Southern Education Foundation. (1998). *Miles to go.* Atlanta, GA: Author.

Southern Region Education Board. (1990). *Black and white students' perceptions of
their college campuses.* Atlanta, GA: Author.

Spence, K. L. (1998). *Black colleges should be black.* Ann Arbor: University of
Michigan.

Subotzky G. (1997). The enhancement of graduate programmes and research capacity at the historically black universities. Bellville, South Africa: Education Policy Unit, University of Western Cape.

Suggs, E. (1998). *Fighting to survive: A look at America's historically black colleges and
universities between October 1996 and February 1997.* Durham, NC: Herald-
Sun.

Sweatt v. Painter 339 U.S. 629 (1950).

Thomas, G. E. (1991). Assessing the college major selection process for African-
American students. In W. R. Allen, E. G. Epps, & N. Z. Haniff (Eds.), *College
in Black and White: African-American students in predominantly White and Historically Black Public Universities,* pp. 75–91. Albany: State University of New
York Press.

Thomas, G. E. (1996). *Race relations and campus climate for minority students at majority and minority institutions: Implications for higher education desegregation.*
College Station, TX: Race and Ethnic Studies Institute.

Thomas, G. E., Achmat, A., & Deedat, H. (1997). Students' voices from six South
African universities: Preliminary findings. Bellville, South Africa: Education Policy Unit, University of the Western Cape.

Thomas, G. E., & Hill, S. (1987). Black institutions in U.S. higher education. *Journal
of College Student Personnel,* 57–65.

United States v. Fordice 505 U.S. 717 (1992).

Vargas, A. (1996). *The historically black colleges and universities and nave are other
equal opportunity educational institutions.* Washington, DC: National Association for Equal Opportunity in Higher Education.

Wenglinsky, H. H. (1996). Educational justification for historically black colleges
and universities: A policy response to the U.S. Supreme Court. *Educational
Evaluation and Policy Analysis, 18*(1), 91–103.

Wilson, R. (1998). The scramble to survive. In E. Suggs (Ed.), *Fighting to survive, A
look at America's historically black colleges and universities between October 1996
and February 1997,* p. 2. Durham, NC: Herald-Sun.

Wlotta, E. (1992). Identity crisis: Teaching versus research. *Science, 258*(5085), 1223–
1225.

Yoganathan, V., & Lee, P. (1996, May 17). Campuses countrywide in crisis. *Higher
Education Review,* supplement in *New Nation,* p. 13.

APPENDIX A

Historically Black Colleges and Universities

Compiled by M. Christopher Brown II, Ronyelle Bertrand Ricard, and Saran Donahoo

Alabama

1. Alabama A&M University (1875)
   4900 Meridian Street
   Normal, AL 35762
   256-851-5000
   http://www.aamu.edu
   (four-year, public)

2. Alabama State University (1874)
   915 South Jackson Street
   Montgomery, AL 36105
   334-229-4100
   http://www.alasu.edu
   (four-year, public)

3. Bishop State Community College (1927)
   351 North Broad Street
   Mobile, AL 36603
   334-690-6801
   http://www.bscc.cc.al.us
   (two-year, public)

4. C. A. Fredd State Technical College (1965)
   202 Skyline Blvd.
   Tuscaloosa, AL 35405

   205-758-3361
   (two-year, public)

5. Concordia College (1922)
   1804 Green Street
   Selma, AL 36701
   334-874-5700
   http://higher-ed.lcms.org/selma.htm
   (two-year, private)

6. J. F. Drake Technical College (1961)
   3421 Meridian Street North
   Huntsville, AL 35811
   256-539-8161
   http://www.dstc.cc.al.us
   (two-year, public)

7. Lawson State Community College (1965)
   3060 Wilson Road
   Birmingham, AL 35221
   205-925-2515
   http://www.ls.cc.al.us
   (two-year, public)

8. Miles College (1905)
   5500 Myron Massey Boulevard

Fairfield, AL 35064
205-929-1000
http://www.miles.edu
(four-year, private)

9. Oakwood College (1896)
7000 Adventist Boulevard
Huntsville, AL 35896
256-726-7000
http://www.oakwood.edu
(four-year, private)

10. Selma University (1878)
1501 Lapsley Street
Selma, AL 36701
334-872-2533
(four-year, private)

11. Stillman College (1876)
3706 Stillman Boulevard
P.O. Box 1430
Tuscaloosa, AL 35403
205-349-4240
http://www.stillman.edu
(four-year, private)

12. Talladega College (1867)
627 West Battle Street
Talladega, AL 35160
http://www.talladega.edu
205-761-6212
(four-year, private)

13. Trenholm State Technical
College (1963)
1225 Air Base Boulevard
Montgomery, AL 36108
334-832-9000
http://tstc.cc.al.us
(two-year, public)

14. Tuskegee University (1881)
Kresge Center
Tuskegee, AL 36088
334-727-8011
http://www.tusk.edu
(four-year, private)

Arkansas

15. Arkansas Baptist College (1884)
1600 Bishop Street
Little Rock, AR 72202

501-374-7856
(four-year, private)

16. Philander Smith College (1877)
812 West 13th Street
Little Rock, AR 72202
501-375-9845
http://www.philander.edu
(four-year, private)

17. Shorter College (1886)
604 Locust Street
North Little Rock, AR 72114
501-374-6305
(two-year, private)

18. University of Arkansas at
Pine Bluff (1873)
1200 North University Drive
P.O. Box 4008
Pine Bluff, AR 71601
501-575-2000
http://www.uark.edu
(four-year, public)

Delaware

19. Delaware State University (1891)
1200 North Dupont Highway
Dover, DE 19901
302-739-4901
http://www.desu.edu
(four-year, public)

District of Columbia

20. Howard University (1867)
2400 Sixth Street, N.W.
Washington, DC 20059
202-806-6100
http://www.howard.edu
(four-year, mixed)

21. University of the District of
Columbia (1851)
4200 Connecticut Avenue, N.W.
Washington, DC 20008
202-274-5100
http://www.udc.edu
(four-year, private)

Florida

22. Bethune-Cookman College
(1904)

640 Dr. Mary McLeod Bethune
   Boulevard
Daytona Beach, FL 32114
904-252-8667
http://www.bethune.
   cookman.edu
(four-year, private)

23. Edward Waters College (1866)
    1658 Kings Road
    Jacksonville, FL 32209
    904-366-2500
    http://www.ewc.edu
    (four-year, private)

24. Florida A&M University (1877)
    400 Lee Hall
    Tallahassee, FL 32307
    904-599-3225
    http://www.famu.edu
    (four-year, public)

25. Florida Memorial College (1879)
    15800 N.W. 42nd Avenue
    Miami, FL 33054
    305-626-3604
    http://www.fmc.edu
    (four-year, private)

Georgia

26. Albany State College (1903)
    504 College Drive
    Albany, GA 31705
    912-430-4604
    (four-year, public)

27. Clark Atlanta University (1989)
    223 James P. Brawley Drive, S.W.
    Atlanta, GA 30314
    404-880-8000
    http://www.cau.edu
    (four-year, private)

28. Fort Valley State College (1895)
    1005 State College Drive
    Fort Valley, GA 31030
    912-825-6315
    http://www.fvsu.edu
    (four-year, public)

29. Interdenominational Theological
    Center (1958)
    671 Beckwith Street, S.W.

Atlanta, GA 30314
404-527-7000
(four-year, private)

30. Morehouse College (1867)
    830 Westview Drive, S.W.
    Atlanta, GA 30314
    404-215-2645
    http://www.morehouse.edu
    (four-year, private)

31. Morehouse School of Medicine
    (1975)
    720 Westview Drive, S.W.
    Atlanta, GA 30310
    404-752-1740
    http://www.msm.edu
    (four-year, private)

32. Morris Brown College (1881)
    643 Martin Luther King Jr. Drive
    Atlanta, GA 30314
    404-220-0100
    http://www.morrisbrown.edu
    (four-year, private)

33. Paine College (1882)
    1235 15th Street
    Augusta, GA 30910
    706-821-8230
    http://www.paine.edu
    (four-year, private)

34. Savannah State University
    (1890)
    P.O. Box 20449
    Savannah, GA 31404
    912-356-2186
    http://www.savstate.edu
    (four-year, public)

35. Spelman College (1881)
    350 Spelman Lane, S.W.
    Atlanta, GA 30314
    404-681-3643
    http://www.spelman.edu
    (four-year, private)

Kentucky

36. Kentucky State University (1886)
    East Main Street
    Room 201 Hume Hall
    Frankfort, KY 40601

502-597-6000
http://www.kysu.edu
(four-year, public)

Louisiana

37. Dillard University (1869)
2601 Gentilly Boulevard
New Orleans, LA 70122
504-283-8822
http://www.dillard.edu
(four-year, private)

38. Grambling State University
(1901)
P.O. Box 607
Grambling, LA 71245
404-679-4501
http://www.gram.edu
(four-year, public)

39. Southern University A&M
College (1880)
P.O. Box 9374
Baton Rouge, LA 70813
225-771-4500
http://www.subr.edu
(four-year, public)

40. Southern University at
New Orleans (1959)
6400 Press Drive
New Orleans, LA 70126
504-286-5000
http://www.suno.edu
(four-year, public)

41. Southern University at
Shreveport-Bossier City (1964)
3050 Martin Luther King Jr.
Drive
Shreveport, LA 71107
318-674-3300
http://www.susbo.edu
(two-year, public)

42. Xavier University of Louisiana
(1915)
7325 Palmetto Street
New Orleans, LA 70125
504-486-7411
http://www.xula.edu
(four-year, private)

Maryland

43. Bowie State University (1865)
14000 Jericho Park Road
Bowie, MD 20715
301-860-4000
http://www.bowiestate.edu
(four-year, public)

44. Coppin State College (1900)
2500 West North Avenue
Baltimore, MD 21216
410-383-5400
http://www.copp.edu
(four-year, public)

45. Morgan State University (1867)
1700 East Cold Spring Lane
Baltimore, MD 21251
443-885-3333
http://www.morgan.edu
(four-year, public)

46. University of Maryland—
Eastern Shore (1886)
1 Backbone Road
Princess Anne, MD 21853
410-651-2200
http://www.umes.edu
(four-year, public)

Michigan

47. Lewis College of Business (1874)
17370 Myers Road
Detroit, MI 48235
313-862-6240
http://207.91.252.4/lewis
(two-year, private)

Mississippi

48. Alcorn State University (1871)
1000 ASU Drive
Alcorn, MS 39096
601-877-6100
http://www.alcorn.edu
(four-year, public)

49. Coahoma Community College
(1949)
3240 Friars Point Road
Clarksdale, MS 38614
701-627-2571
http://www.ccc.cc.ms.us
(two-year, public)

50. Hinds Community College
    (1954)
    501 East Main Street
    Raymond, MS 39154
    601-857-3240
    http://www.hinds.cc.ms.us
    (two-year, public)

51. Jackson State University (1877)
    P.O. Box 17390
    1400 J. R. Lynch Street
    Jacksonville, MS 39217
    1-800-848-6817
    http://www.jsums.edu
    (four-year, public)

52. Mary Holmes College (1892)
    P.O. Drawer 1257
    West Point, MS 39773
    601-494-6820
    http://www.maryholmes.edu
    (two-year, private)

53. Mississippi Valley State
    University (1946)
    14000 Highway 82 West
    Itta Bena, MS 38930
    662-254-9041
    http://www.mvsu.edu
    (four-year, public)

54. Rust College (1866)
    150 East Rust Avenue
    Holly Springs, MS 38635
    662-252-8000
    http://www.rustcollege.edu
    (four-year, private)

55. Tougaloo College (1869)
    500 West County Line Road
    Tougaloo, MS 39174
    601-977-7730
    http://www.tougaloo.edu
    (four-year, private)

Missouri

56. Harris-Stowe State College
    (1857)
    3026 Laclede Avenue
    St. Louis, MO 63103
    314-340-3366
    http://www.hssc.edu
    (four-year, public)

57. Lincoln University (1866)
    820 Chestnut Street
    Jefferson City, MO 65101
    314-681-5042
    http://www.lincolnu.edu
    (four-year, public)

North Carolina

58. Barber-Scotia College (1867)
    145 Cabarrus Avenue
    Concord, NC 28025
    704-789-2900
    http://www.barber-scotia.edu
    (four-year, private)

59. Bennett College (1873)
    900 East Washington Street
    Greensboro, NC 27401
    910-370-8626
    http://www.bennett.edu
    (four-year, private)

60. Elizabeth City State University
    (1891)
    1704 Weeksville Road
    Elizabeth City, NC 27909
    252-335-3400
    http://www.ecsu.edu
    (four-year, public)

61. Fayetteville State University
    (1877)
    1200 Murchison Road
    Fayetteville, NC 28301
    910-672-1474
    http://www.uncfsu.edu
    (four-year, public)

62. Johnson C. Smith University
    (1867)
    100 Beatties Ford Road
    Charlotte, NC 28216
    704-378-1008
    http://www.jcsu.edu
    (four-year, private)

63. Livingstone College (1879)
    701 West Monroe Street
    Salisbury, NC 28144
    704-638-5505
    http://www.livingstone.edu
    (four-year, private)

64. North Carolina A&T State
    University (1891)
    1601 East Market Street
    Greensboro, NC 27411
    336-334-7500
    http://www.ncat.edu
    (four-year, public)

65. North Carolina Central
    University (1910)
    1801 Fayetteville Street
    Durham, NC 27707
    919-560-6100
    http://www.nccu.edu
    (four-year, public)

66. St. Augustine's College (1867)
    1315 Oakwood Avenue
    Raleigh, NC 27610
    919-516-4200
    http://www.st-aug.edu
    (four-year, private)

67. Shaw University (1865)
    118 East South Street
    Raleigh, NC 27611
    919-546-8300
    http://www.shawuniversity.edu
    (four-year, private)

68. Winston-Salem State University
    (1862)
    601 Martin Luther King Jr. Drive
    Winston Salem, NC 27110
    336-750-2041
    http://www.wssu.edu
    (four-year, public)

Ohio

69. Central State University (1887)
    1400 Brushrow Road
    Wilberforce, OH 45384
    937-376-6348
    http://www.centralstate.edu
    (four-year, public)

70. Wilberforce University (1856)
    1055 North Bickett
    Wilberforce, OH 45384
    937-376-2911

http://www.wilberforce.edu
(four-year, private)

Oklahoma

71. Langston University (1897)
    P.O. Box 907
    Langston, OK 73050
    405-466-2231
    http://www.lunet.edu
    (four-year, public)

Pennsylvania

72. Cheyney State University (1897)
    Cheyney and Creek Roads
    Cheyney, PA 19319
    610-399-2000
    http://www.cheyney.edu
    (four-year, public)

73. Lincoln University (1854)
    1570 Old Baltimore Pike
    P.O. Box 179
    Lincoln, PA 19352
    http://www.lincoln.edu
    (four-year, public)

South Carolina

74. Allen University (1870)
    1530 Harden Street
    Columbia, SC 29204
    803-376-5701
    http://www.scicu.org/allen/
    auhome.htm
    (four-year, private)

75. Benedict College (1870)
    600 Harden Street
    Columbia, SC 29204
    803-254-7253
    http://www.benedict.edu
    (four-year, private)

76. Claflin College (1869)
    700 College Avenue, N.E.
    Orangeburg, SC 29115
    803-535-5412
    http://www.claflin.edu
    (four-year, private)

77. Clinton Junior College (1894)
    1029 Crawford Road

Rock Hill, SC 29730
803-327-7402
http://www.clintonjr.college.org
(two-year, private)

78. Denmark Technical College
    (1947)
    P.O. Box 927
    Denmark, SC 29042
    803-793-3301
    http://www.den.tec.sc.us
    (two-year, public)

79. Morris College (1908)
    North Main Street
    Sumter, SC 29150
    803-775-9371
    http://www.morris.edu
    (four-year, private)

80. South Carolina State University
    (1896)
    300 College Street, N.E.
    Orangeburg, SC 29117
    803-536-7000
    http://www.scsu.edu
    (four-year, public)

81. Voorhees College (1897)
    P.O. Box 678
    Denmark, SC 29042
    803-793-3351
    http://www.voorhees.edu
    (four-year, private)

Tennessee

82. Fisk University (1867)
    1000 17th Avenue North
    Nashville, TN 37208
    615-329-8555
    http://www.fisk.edu
    (four-year, private)

83. Knoxville College (1875)
    901 College Street
    Knoxville, TN 37921
    615-524-6500
    (four-year, private)

84. Lane College (1882)
    545 Lane Avenue

Jackson, TN 38301
901-426-7500
http://www.lanecollege.edu
(four-year, private)

85. LeMoyne-Owen College (1862)
    807 Walker Avenue
    Memphis, TN 38126
    901-774-9090
    http://www.lemoyne-owen.edu
    (four-year, private)

86. Meharry Medical College (1876)
    1005 Dr. D. B. Todd Jr.
       Boulevard
    Nashville, TN 37208
    615-327-6111
    http://www.mmc.edu
    (four-year, private)

87. Tennessee State University
    (1912)
    3500 John Merrit Boulevard
    Nashville, TN 37209
    615-963-5000
    http://www.tnstate.edu
    (four-year, public)

Texas

88. Huston-Tillotson College (1876)
    900 Chicon Street
    Austin, TX 78702
    512-505-3000
    http://www.htc.edu
    (four-year, private)

89. Jarvis Christian College (1912)
    U.S. Highway 80
    Hawkins, TX 75765
    903-769-5700
    http://www.jarvis.edu
    (four-year, private)

90. Paul Quinn College (1872)
    3837 Simpson Stuart Road
    Dallas, TX 75241
    1-800-237-2648
    http://www.pqc.edu
    (four-year, private)

91. Prairie View A&M University
    (1876)

P.O. Box 188
Prairie View, TX 77446
409-857-2111
http://www.pvamu.edu
(four-year, public)

92. Saint Phillip's College (1927)
1801 Martin Luther King Jr.
   Drive
San Antonio, TX 78203
210-531-3200
http://www.accd.edu/spc/
   spcmain/spc.htm
(two-year, public)

93. Southwestern Christian College
(1949)
P.O. Box 10
Terrell, TX 75160
972-524-3341
http://www.swcc.edu
(four-year, private)

94. Texas College (1894)
2404 North Grand Avenue
Tyler, TX 75712
903-593-8311
http://www.texascollege.edu
(four-year, private)

95. Texas Southern University
(1947)
3100 Cleburne Avenue
Houston, TX 77004
713-313-7011
http://www.tsu.edu
(four-year, public)

96. Wiley College (1873)
711 Wiley Avenue
Marshall, TX 75670
903-927-3300
http://www.wileyc.edu
(four-year, private)

Virginia

97. Hampton University (1868)
P.O. Box 1000
Hampton, VA 23668

804-727-5231
http://www.hamptonu.edu
(four-year, private)

98. Norfolk State University (1935)
2401 Corprew Avenue
Norfolk, VA 23504
757-823-8600
http://www.nsu.edu
(four-year, public)

99. Saint Paul's College (1888)
115 College Drive
Lawrenceville, VA 23868
804-848-2636
http://www.saintpauls.edu
(four-year, private)

100. Virginia State University (1882)
P.O. Box 9001
Petersburg, VA 23806
804-524-5000
http://www.vsu.edu
(four-year, public)

101. Virginia Union University (1865)
1500 North Lombardy Street
Richmond, VA 23220
804-257-5600
http://www.vuu.edu
(four-year, private)

West Virginia

102. Bluefield State College (1895)
219 Rock Street
Bluefield, WV 24701
304-327-4000
http://www.bluefield.
   wvnet.edu
(four-year, public)

103. West Virginia State College
(1891)
P.O. Box 1000
Institute, WV 25112
1-800-987-2112
http://www.wvsc.edu
(four-year, public)

APPENDIX B

Predominantly Black Colleges and Universities

Compiled by M. Christopher Brown II, Ronyelle Bertrand Ricard, and Saran Donahoo

Alabama

1. Wallace Community College–
   Sparks Campus (1927)
   P.O. Drawer 580
   Eufaula, AL 36072–0580
   1-800-543-2426
   http://www.sstc.cc.al.us/
   (two-year, public)

2. John M. Patterson State
   Technical College (1962;
   originally charted in 1947)
   3920 Troy Highway
   Montgomery, AL 36116
   334-288-1080
   http://www.jptech.cc.al.us/
   (two-year, public)

3. Reid State Technical College
   (1963)
   P.O. Box 588
   Evergreen, AL 36401
   334-578-1313
   http://www.rstc.cc.al.us/
   (two-year, public)

California

4. Charles R. Drew University of
   Medicine and Science (1966)
   1731 E. 120th Street
   Los Angeles, CA 90059
   323-563-4800
   http://www.cdrewu.edu/
   (four-year, private)

5. Compton Community College
   (1927)
   1111 E. Artesia Blvd
   Compton, CA 90221
   310-900-1600
   http://198.188.134.9/
   (two-year, public)

6. Los Angeles Southwest College
   (1967)
   1600 Imperial Highway
   Los Angeles, CA 90047-4899
   323-241-5225
   http://www.lasc.cc.ca.us/
   (two-year, public)

7. West Los Angeles College (1968)
   4800 Freshman Drive
   Culver City, CA 90230
   310-287-4200
   http://www.wlac.cc.ca.us/
   (two-year, public)

District of Columbia

8. Southeastern University (1879)
   501 I Street, S.W.
   Washington, DC 20024
   202-488-8162
   http://www.seu.edu/
   (four-year, private)

Georgia

9. Albany Technical Institute (1974)
   1704 S. Slappey Boulevard
   Albany, GA 31701
   229-430-3500
   http://www.albanytech.org/
   (two-year, public)

10. Atlanta Metropolitan College
    (1974)
    1630 Metropolitan Parkway,
    S.W.
    Atlanta, GA 30310-4498
    404-756-4000
    www.atlm.peachnet.edu
    Also see: http://www.usg.edu/
    inst/atmetro.html
    (two-year, public)

11. Bauder College (1964)
    3500 Peachtree Road, N.E.
    Atlanta, GA 30326
    404-237-7573 or 1-800-241-3797
    http://www.bauder.edu/
    content_main.html
    (two-year, private)

12. Central Georgia Technical
    College (1989)
    3300 Macon Tech Drive
    Macon, GA 31206
    484-757-3400
    http://www.cgtcollege.org/
    (two-year, public)

13. Columbus Technical College
    (1961)
    928 Manchester Expressway
    Columbus, GA 31904
    706-649-1800
    http://www.columbustech.org/
    (two-year, public)

14. DeKalb Technical College (1961)
    495 N. Indian Creek Dr.
    Clarkston, GA 30021
    404-297-9522
    http://www.dekalb.tec.ga.us/
    (two-year, public)

15. Georgia Military College—
    Augusta-Fort Gordon
    Campus (1879)
    P.O. Box 7258
    Ft. Gordon, GA 30905
    912-445-2701
    http://www.gmc.cc.ga.us/
    (two-year, public)

16. Georgia Military College–Fort
    McPherson Campus (1879)
    1302 Cobb Street, S.W., Building
    179, Rm. 201
    Fort McPherson, GA 30330-1083
    404-464-2268
    http://www.gmc.cc.ga.us/
    (two-year, public)

17. Gupton Jones College of Funeral
    Service (1920)
    5141 Snapfinger Woods Drive
    Decatur, GA 30035-4022
    770-593-2257
    http://www.gupton-jones.edu/
    Pages/aframe.htm
    (two-year, public)

18. Herzing College–Atlanta (1949)
    3355 Lenox Road, Suite #100
    Atlanta, GA 30326
    404-816-4533 or 1-800-573-4533
    http://www.herzing.com/
    atlanta/home.htm
    (four-year, private)

19. Savannah Technical College
    (1929)
    5717 White Bluff Road
    Savannah, GA 31405
    912-351-6362 or 1-800-769-6362
    http://web.savannah.tec.ga.us/
    (two-year, public)

Illinois

20. Chicago State University (1867)
    95th Street at King Drive
    Chicago, IL 60628
    312-995-2000
    http://www.csu.edu/
    (four-year, public)

21. East St. Louis Community
    College (1969)
    601 James R. Thompson
    Boulevard
    East St. Louis, IL 62201-1101
    618-874-8700
    http://www.ivc.illinois.edu/
    Students/EastStLouis.htm
    (two-year, public)

22. East-West University (1935)
    816 S. Michigan Avenue
    Chicago, IL 60605
    312-939-0111
    http://www.eastwest.edu/
    (four-year, private)

23. Kennedy-King College (1935)
    6800 South Wentworth Avenue
    Chicago, IL 60621
    773-602-5000
    http://www.ccc.edu/
    kennedyking/
    (two-year, public)

24. Malcolm X College (1968)
    900 W. Van Buren
    Chicago, IL 60612
    312-850-7000
    http://www.ccc.edu/
    malcolmx/
    (two-year, public)

25. Olive-Harvey College (1970)
    10001 S. Woodlawn Avenue
    Chicago, IL 60628
    773-568-3700
    http://www.ccc.edu/
    oliveharvey/
    (two-year, public)

Indiana

26. Martin University (1873)
    P.O. Box 18567

Indianapolis, IN 46218
317-543-3235
Web page: None available
(four-year, private)

Kentucky

27. Simmons University [Bible
    College] (1873)
    1811 Dumesnil Street
    Louisville, KY 40210
    502-776-1443
    No university maintained site;
    see http://www.petersons.
    com/blackcolleges/profiles/
    simmons.html
    (four-year, private)

Maryland

28. Baltimore City Community
    College (1947)
    2901 Liberty Heights Avenue
    Baltimore, MD 21215
    410-462-8000 or 1-888-203-1261
    http://www.bccc.state.md.us/
    (two-year, public)

29. Prince George's Community
    College (1958)
    301 Largo Road
    Largo, MD 20774-2199
    301-336-6000
    http://pgweb.pg.cc.md.us/
    pgweb/web_directory.html
    (two-year, public)

30. Sojourner-Douglass College
    (1972)
    500 N. Caroline Street
    Baltimore, MD 21205-1898
    410-276-0306
    http://www.sdc.edu/
    (four-year, private)

Massachusetts

31. Roxbury Community College
    (1973)
    1234 Columbus Avenue
    Roxbury Crossing, MA 02120
    617-427-0060

http://www.rcc.mass.edu/
(two-year, public)

Michigan

32. Davenport University–Dearborn
    (2000)
    4801 Oakman Boulevard
    Dearborn, MI 48126-3799
    313-581-4400
    www.davenport.edu
    (four-year, private)

33. Davenport University–Flint
    (2000)
    488 N. Jennings Rd.
    Flint, MI 48504-1700
    810-789-2200
    www.davenport.edu
    (four-year, private)

34. Wayne County Community
    College (1967)
    801 W. Fort Street
    Detroit, MI 48226
    313-496-2600
    http://www.wccc.edu/
    (two-year, public)

Mississippi

35. East Mississippi Community
    College (1927)
    P.O. Box 158
    Scooba, MS 39358
    662-476-5000
    http://www.emcc.cc.ms.us/
    (two-year, public)

36. Mississippi Delta Community
    College (1927)
    Highway 3 and Cherry Street
    Moorhead, MS 38761
    662-246-6322
    http://www.mdcc.cc.ms.us/
    (two-year, public)

37. Natchez Junior College (1884)
    1010 N. Union Street
    Natchez, MS 39120-2875
    601-445-9702
    Web page: None available
    (two-year, private)

New Jersey

38. Bloomfield College (1868)
    467 Franklin Street
    Bloomfield, NJ 07003
    973-748-9000
    http://www.bloomfield.edu/
    (four-year, private)

39. Essex County College (1966)
    303 University Avenue
    Newark, NJ 07102
    973-877-3000
    http://www.essex.edu/
    (two-year, public)

New York

40. Audrey Cohen College (1964)
    75 Varick Street
    New York, NY 10013
    212-343-1234 or 1-800-33THINK
    http://www.audreycohen.edu/
    default2.html
    (four-year, private)

41. Fiorello H. LaGuardia
    Community College (1971)
    31–10 Thomson Avenue
    Long Island City, NY 11101
    718-482-5293
    http://www.lagcc.cuny.edu/
    (two-year, public)

42. Helene Fuld College of Nursing
    of North General Hospital
    (1945)
    1879 Madison Avenue
    New York, NY 10035
    212-423-1000
    Web page: None available
    (two-year, private)

43. Long Island College Hospital
    School of Nursing (1858)
    397 Hicks Street
    Brooklyn, NY 11201
    718-780-1952
    www.lich.org
    (two-year, private)

44. Medgar Evers College (1967)
    1650 Bedford Avenue

Brooklyn, NY 11225
718-270-4900
http://199.219.184.254/
    mecweb/default.htm
(four-year, public)

45. New York City Technical
    College (1971)
    300 Jay Street
    Brooklyn, NY 11201-2983
    718-260-5500
    http://www.nyctc.cuny.edu/
    (two-year, public)

46. York College (1966)
    94–20 Guy R. Brewer Boulevard
    Jamaica, NY 11451
    718-262-2000
    http://www.york.cuny.edu/
    (four-year, public)

North Carolina

47. Edgecombe Community College
    (1967)
    2009 W. Wilson Street
    Tarboro, NC 27886
    252-823-5166
    http://www.edgecombe.
    cc.nc.us/
    (two-year, public)

48. Roanoke-Chowan Community
    College (1967)
    109 Community College Road
    Ahoskie, NC 27910
    252-862-1200
    http://www.roanoke.cc.nc.us/
    (two-year, public)

Ohio

49. Cuyahoga Community College
    (1963)
    700 Carnegie Avenue
    Cleveland, OH 44115-2878
    216-987-8742
    http://www.tri-c.cc.oh.us/
    (two-year, public)

Pennsylvania

50. Peirce College (1865)
    1420 Pine Street
    Philadelphia, PA 19102-9919
    215-545-6400 or 1-877-670-9190
    http://www.peirce.edu/html/
    index.html
    (four-year, private)

South Carolina

51. Williamsburg Technical College
    (1969)
    601 Martin Luther King Jr.
    Avenue
    Kingstree, SC 29556-4197
    843-355-4110 or 1-800-768-2021
    http://www.williamsburgtech.
    com/
    (two-year, public)

Tennessee

52. Southwest Tennessee
    Community College (2000)
    P.O. Box 780
    Memphis, TN 38101-0780
    901-333-STCC or 1-877-717-
    STCC
    http://www.stcc.cc.tn.us/
    (two-year, public)

Texas

53. Bay Ridge Christian College
    (1962)
    P.O. Box 726
    Kendleton, TX 77451-0726
    979-532-3982
    Web page: None available
    May want to look at http://
    www.chog.org/Education/
    Schools.asp
    (two-year, private)

U.S. Virgin Islands

54. University of the Virgin Islands
    (1962)

2 John Brewer's Bay
St. Thomas, USVI
   00802-9990
340-776-9200
http://www.uvi.edu/pub-
   relations/uvi/home.html
(four-year, public)

Virginia

55. Virginia University at
    Lynchburg (1888)
    2058 Garfield Avenue
    Lynchburg, VA 24501
    434-528-5276
    learn@vuonline.net
    (four-year, private)

APPENDIX C

Further Reading on Black Colleges

Compiled by Timothy K. Eatman

Adams, K. R. (1993). Black College Blues. *Diversity and Division: A Critical Journal of Race and Culture, 2*(3), 8–11.

Adebayo, A. O., Adekoya, A. A., & Ayadi, O. F. (2001). Historically Black Colleges and Universities (HBCUs) as Agents for Change for the Development of Minority Businesses. *Journal of Black Studies, 32*(2), 166–183.

African American College Graduation Rates: Blacks Do Best at the Nation's Most Selective Colleges and Universities. (1999). *Journal of Blacks in Higher Education, 25*(Autumn), 122–127.

Allen, W. R., Epps, E. G., & Haniff, N. Z. (Eds.). (1991). *College in Black and White: African-American students in predominantly White and in historically Black public universities.* Albany, NY, US: State University of New York Press.

Ammentorp, W. (1999). Increasing the Number of Women of Color for Executive-Level Administration in Higher Education: A Focus on Strategies Used at Selected Historically Black Colleges and Universities (African-Americans). *Dissertation Abstracts International, Volume,* 60–04.

Annual report—National Advisory Committee on Black Higher Education and Black Colleges and Universities. (No. 0196–7665)(1977). Washington, D.C.: National Advisory Committee on Black Higher Education and Black Colleges and Universities.

Barrow, L. C., Jr. (1991). Black Colleges Still Not Sharing in the Gold. *Crisis, 98*(9), 15–19.

Billingsley, A., & Elam, J. C. (Eds.). (1986). *Inside black colleges and universities.* Chicago: Follett Press.

Black Issues in Higher Education. (1998). Charting a Black Research Agenda:An Interview with H. Patrick Swygert, Esq., President of Howard University. *Black Issues in Higher Education, 15*(1), 24–27.

Blacks in Higher Education: Some Solid Reasons for Hope and Cheer. (1994). *Journal of Blacks in Higher Education* (3), 43.

Bohr, L., et al. (1995). Do Black Students Learn More at Historically Black or Pre-dominantly White Colleges? *Journal of College Student Development., v36* (Jan–Feb 1995.), pp. 75–85.

Borden, V. M. H. (1998). The Top 100: Interpreting the Data. *Black Issues in Higher Education, 15*(10), 38–44, 46–58, 60–65.

Bowman, J. W. (1992). *America's Black colleges.* South Pasadena, Calif.: Sandcastle Pub.

Bowman, J. W. (1994). *America's Black & tribal colleges.* South Pasadena, Calif.: Sandcastle Pub.

Bowman, S. L., et al. (1995). *African American or Female: How Do We Identify Ourselves?* (No. ED409384). U.S.; Indiana.

Brown II, M. C. (1999). *The quest to define collegiate desegregation: black colleges, Title VI compliance, and post-Adams litigation.* Westport, CT: Bergin & Garvey.

Brown II, M. C. (2001). Collegiate Desegregation and the Public Black College. *Journal Of Higher Education, 72*(1), 46–62.

Brown II, M. C., Donahoo, S., & Bertrand, R. D. (2001). The Black College and the Quest for Educational Opportunity. *Urban Education, 36*(5), 553–571.

Burnett, I. E., Jr. (1995). *Second Chance Teachers Program Development in an Historically African-American University* (No. ED393804). U.S.; Louisiana.

California State Univ. Long Beach. Inst. for Teaching and Learning, & California State Dept. of Education Sacramento. (1989). *African American Educational Excellence. Planning Symposium Proceedings for the Development of the Center for Applied Cultural Studies and Educational Achievement (Long Beach, California, January 27, 1989)* (No. ED360424).

Carter, C. (1998). *The Moccasin on the Other Foot Dilemma: Multicultural Strategies at as Historically Black College* (No. ED421057). U.S.; Pennsylvania.

Carter, D. J., & Wilson, R. (1989). *Minorities in Higher Education. Eighth Annual Status Report* (No. ED320510). U.S. District of Columbia.

Chambers, F. (1978). *Black higher education in the United States: a selected bibliography on Negro higher education and historically Black colleges and universities.* Westport, Conn.: Greenwood Press.

Chambers, J. W., Jr., Kambon, K., Birdsong, B. D., Brown, J., Dixon, P., & Robbins-Brinson, L. (1998). Africentric Cultural Identity and the Stress Experience of African American College Students. *Journal of Black Psychology, 24*(3), 368–396.

Cheatle, L., Fischler, S., Sucher, J., Toub, M. D., Sante, L., Pacific Street Films., et al. (1999). From swastika to Jim Crow [1 videocassette (56 min.)]. New York, N.Y.: Cinema Guild [distributor].

Chenoweth, K. (1997a). Forthcoming ETS Report Proclaims the Importance of HBCUs. *Black Issues in Higher Education, 14*(16), 16–19.

Chenoweth, K. (1997b). Phenomenal Growth. *Black Issues in Higher Education, 14*(10), 34–36.

Chenoweth, K. (1998). African American College Presidents in Decline. *Black Issues in Higher Education, 15*(6), 20–25.

Coaxum III, J. (2001). The Misalignment Between the Carnegie Classification and Black Colleges. *Urban Education, 36*(5), 572–584.

Cohen, R. T. (2000). *The black colleges of Atlanta* (1st. ed.). Charleston, SC: Arcadia Publishing.

Constantine, J. M. (1994). The "Added Value" of Historically Black Colleges. *Academe, 80*(3), 12–17.

Constantine, J. M. (1995). The Effect of Attending Historically Black Colleges and Universities on Future Wages of Black Students. *Industrial & labor relations review, 48*(3), 531 (516 pages).

Corporation for National Service. (1996). *Learn and Serve America. Higher Education Program Descriptions, 1996* (No. ED403861). Washington DC.

Cowan, T., & Maguire, J. (1995). History's Milestones of African-American Higher Education. *Journal of Blacks in Higher Education*(7), 86–90.

Cross, T. L. (1993a). The Myth That Preferential College Admissions Create High Black Student Dropout Rates. *Journal of Blacks in Higher Education., 1* (Fall 1993), pp. 71–74.

Cross, T. L. (1993b). Vital Signs: The State of African Americans in Higher Education. *Journal of Blacks in Higher Education* (2), 29–39.

Cross, T. L. (1995). Vital Signs: The Current State of African Americans in Higher Education. *Journal of Blacks in Higher Education* (8), 49–55.

Cross, T. L. (1996a). The Progress of Admissions of Black Students at the Nation's Highest-Ranked Colleges and Universities. *Journal of Blacks in Higher Education* (13), 6–7.

Cross, T. L. (1996b). Vital Signs: The Current State of African Americans in Higher Education. *Journal of Blacks in Higher Education* (11), 61–65.

Cross, T. L. (1996c). Vital Signs: The Statistics that describe the present and suggest the future of African Americans in higher education. *Journal of Blacks in Higher Education* (13), 65–71.

Davis, E. B. (1993). Desegregation in higher education: Twenty-five years of controversy from Geier to Ayers. *Journal of Law & Education, 22*(4), 519–524.

Denes, R., & Highsmith, R. J. (1998). Keeping Score: Comparative Performance of Engineering Institutions in Creating Access, 1997–98. *Nacme Research Letter,* 22.

Department of Defense. (1996). *Infrastructure Support Program for Historically Black Colleges/Universities and Minority Institutions (HBCU/MI): Fiscal Year 1997.* Washington, D.C.: United States.

A directory of the historically and predominantly black colleges and universities (HBCUs). (1988). Washington, D.C.: U.S. Dept. of Health and Human Services Public Health Service Office of the Assistant Secretary for Health Office of Minority Health.

Drewry, H. N., Doermann, H., & Anderson, S. H. (2001). *Stand and prosper: private Black colleges and their students from the Civil War to the twenty-first century.* Princeton, N.J.: Princeton University Press.

Duncan, C. (2001). *A Survey of African American College Students: Reactions to the Terrorist Acts of September 11, 2001.* U.S.; Louisiana.

Edgcomb, G. S. (1993). *From swastika to Jim Crow: refugee scholars at Black colleges* (Original ed.). Malabar, Fla.: Krieger Pub. Co.

Edwards, A. (2000). *Thoughts on "Reconsidering the Washington-Du Bois Debate: Two Black Colleges in 1910–1911" and Thoughts on "Liberalism at the Crossroads: Jimmy Carter, Joseph Califano, and Public College Desegregation."* (No. ED445575). U.S. South Carolina.

Elbert, M. M. (1996). *The politics of educational decision making: historically Black colleges and universities and federal assistance programs.* Westport, Conn.: Praeger.

Euler, M. V. (1982). *Desegregation within institutions of higher education: What remedies does the law require?* Paper presented at the American Educational Research Association, New York.

Fairfax, J. (1991). *A Perspective on the Continuing Struggle for Equity* (No. ED349359). U.S. Georgia.

Fleming, J. (1984). *Blacks in college: A comparative study of students' success in Black and White institutions.* San Francisco: Jossey-Bass.

Fleming, J. (2001). The Impact of a Historically Black College on African American Students: The Case of LeMoyne-Owen College. *Urban Education, 36*(5), 597–610.

Fleming, J., & Garcia, N. (1998). Are Standardized Tests Fair to African Americans? Predictive Validity of the SAT in Black and White Institutions. *Journal of Higher Education, 69*(5), 471–495.

Foster, G. A. (1996). *Are Black colleges needed?: an at risk/prescriptive guide.* Kearney, NE: Morris Pub.

Foster, G. A. (2001a). *Is there a conspiracy to keep black colleges open?* Dubuque, Iowa: Kendall/Hunt Pub. Co.

Foster, G. A. (2001b). *Is there a conspiracy to keep black colleges open?* Dubuque, Iowa Kendall/Hunt Pub. Co.

Foster, L. (2001). The Not-So-Invisible Professor: White Faculty at the Black College. *Urban Education, 36*(5), 611–629.

Foster, L., Guyden, J., & Miller, A. (Eds.). (2000). *Affirmed Action: Essays on the Academic and Social Lives of White Faculty Members of Historically Black Colleges and Universities.* Lanham, MD: Rowman & Littlefield Publishers.

Freeman, K. (Ed.). (1998). *African American Culture and Heritage in Higher Education Research and Practice.* U.S. Connecticut.

Freeman, K., & Cohen, R. T. (2001). Bridging the Gap Between Economic Development and Cultural Empowerment: HBCUs' Challenges for the Future. *Urban Education, 36*(5), 585–596.

Frierson, C. L. (1993). *Perceptions of African American Educators toward Historically Black Colleges and Universities* (No. ED375193). U.S. Illinois.

Garibaldi, A.M. (1984). *Black colleges and universities: challenges for the future.* New York: Praeger.

Gather, B. (1996). *Revisiting Armenian art: works from historically Black colleges.* Katonah, NY: Katonah Museum of Art.

Gill, W. E. (1992). *The History of Maryland's Historically Black Colleges* (No. ED347887). U.S. Maryland.

Gilroy, M. E., & Duggan, A. E. (1995). The Hispanic Outlook in Higher Education, 1995–96. *Hispanic Outlook in Higher Education, 1–6,* 380.

Green, R. L. (1991). *The Progressive Role of Athletics in American Society: Past, Present, and Future* (No. ED346185). U.S. Ohio.

Greenlee, C. T. (2001). There's a Football Revival Goin' On. *Black Issues in Higher Education, 18*(12), 29–31.

Gurin, P., & Epps, E. (1975). *Black consciousness, identity and achievement: A study of students in historically black colleges.* New York: John Wiley and Sons.

Guy, T. C. E. (1994). *Africentrism—Perspective or Paradigm? Implications for Adult*

Education. Proceedings of the African American Adult Education Research Pre-Conference (Knoxville, Tennessee, May 18–19, 1994) (No. ED380533).

Hardin, J. A. (1989). *Hope Versus Reality: Black Higher Education in Kentucky, 1904–1954.* Unpublished dissertation, University of Mighigan, Ann Arbor.

Harrison, M. G. (2001, February 21–22, 2002). *Self Help/Self Care as a Prevention Strategy.* Paper presented at the Enhancing Outcomes in Women's Health Conference sponsored by the American Psychological Association, Washington, D.C.

Harvey, W. V. (2003). *Twentieth Annual Status Report on Minirites in Higher education* (No. 309560). Washington D.C.: American Council on Higher Education.

Hawkins, B. D. (1992). Black Faculty at HBCUs Becoming More Scarce. *Black Issues in Higher Education, 9*(18), 11–12.

Hawkins, B. D. (1993). Critics Question Process, Motives behind Naming of HBCU Presidents. *Black Issues in Higher Education, 10*(16), 23.

Healy, P. (1998). Education Department Pact With Florida Could Help Public Black Colleges. *The Chronicle of Higher Education, 45*(5), A44.

Heath, T. (1992, October 29–November 3, 1992). *Predicting the Educational Aspirations and Graduate Plans of Black and White College and University Students: When Do Dreams Become Realities?* Paper presented at the Association for the Study of Higher Education, Minneapolis, MN.

Hebel, S. (2001a). A New Push To Integrate Public Black Colleges. *Chronicle of Higher Education, 47*(39), A21–A22.

Hebel, S. (2001b). A Settlement and More Division in Mississippi. *Chronicle of Higher Education, 47*(34), A23–A24.

Hefner, D. (2001). Breathing New Life into Meharry. *Black Issues in Higher Education, 18*(11), 28–33.

Heintze, M. R. (1985). *Private Black colleges in Texas, 1865–1954* (1st ed.). College Station: Texas AM University Press.

Hewitt, T., Mullings, C., & Berlet, C. (Eds.). (1974). *Third World students.* Washington D.C.: United States National Student Association.

Higgins, R. D. (Ed.). (1994). *The Black Student's Guide to College Success. Revised and Updated Edition.* Westport, CT: Greenwood.

Himelhoch, C. R., Nichols, A., Ball, S. R., & Black, L. C. (1997, November 6, 1997). *A Comparative Study of the Factors Which Predict Persistence for African American Students at Historically Black Institutions and Predominantly White Institutions.* Paper presented at the ASHE Annual, Albuquerque, NM.

Historically Black colleges and universities: an assessment of networking and connectivity. (2000). Washington, D.C.: National Association for Equal Opportunity in Higher Education.

Hoffman, A. E. (1993). Federal Funding Upheaval: The Impact on Blacks. *Journal of Blacks in Higher Education* (2), 123–126.

Hoffman, C., Snyder, T. D., Sonnenberg, B., & National Center for Education Statistics. (1996). *Historically Black colleges and universities, 1976–1994.* Washington, D.C.: U.S. Dept. of Education Office of Educational Research and Improvement: For sale by the U.S. G.P.O. Supt. of Docs.

Hollis, B. J. (Ed.). (1984). *Swords upon this hill: preserving the literary tradition of Black colleges and universities: papers from the Ford-Turpin Symposium on Afro-American Literature.* Baltimore, Md.: Morgan State University Press.

Injay. (1999). *Black colleges & universities: charcoals to diamonds.* Huntsville, AL: SSSH! Enterprises.

Jackson, L. R. (1998, April 1998). *Examining Both Race and Gender in the Experiences of African American College Women.* Paper presented at the American Educational Research Association, San Diego, CA.

Janes, S. (1997, November 6). *Experiences of African-American Baccalaureate Nursing Students Examined through the Lenses of Tinto's Student Retention Theory and Astin's Student Involvement Theory. ASHE Annual Meeting Paper.* Paper presented at the Association for the Study of Higher Education, Albuquerque, NM.

Jaschik, S. (1994). Whither Desegregation? *Chronicle of Higher Education, 40*(21), A33, 37.

Jewell, J. O. (2002). To Set an Example: The Tradition of Diversity at Historically Black Colleges and Universities. *Urban Education 37, no, 1,* 7–21.

Jireh & Associates Inc. (1999). *HBCU admissions at-a glance: a pocket guide to admissions at HBCUs* (3rd ed.). Wilmington, DE: Jireh & Associates Inc.

Johnson, B. J. (2000, April 26). *Improving Faculty Socialization: Influences and Barriers and Historically Black Colleges and Universities.* Paper presented at the American Educational Research Association, New Orleans, LA.

Johnson, B. J. (2001). Faculty Socialization: Lessons Learned From Urban Black Colleges. *Urban Education 36, no, 5,* 630–647.

Johnson, K. V. (1996). Some Thoughts on African-Americans' Struggle to Participate in Technology Education. *Journal of Technology Studies, 22*(1), 49–54.

Johnson, R. C. (1992). *Providing African-American Students Access to Science and Mathematics. Research Report #2* (No. ED361456). Cleveland, OH: Urban Child Research Center, Levin College of Urban Affairs, Cleveland State University.

Jones, D. K. (1993). An education of their own: The precarious position of publicly supported black colleges after "United States v. Fordice". *Journal of Law & Education, 22*(4), 485–517.

Jones, L. (2002). *Making it on broken promises: leading Black male scholars confront the culture of higher education* (1st ed.). Sterling, Va.: Stylus Pub.

Kelley, G. A., & Kelley, K. S. (1994). Physical Activity Habits of African-American College Students. *Research Quarterly for Exercise & Sport, 65*(3), 207–223.

Kennard, T. H. (1995). *The handbook of historically black colleges & universities: comprehensive profiles and photos of black colleges and universities* (2nd ed.). Wilmington, DE: Jireh & Associates.

Kimbrough, R. M., Molock, S. D., & Walton, K. (1996). Perception of Social Support, Acculturation, Depression, and Suicidal Ideation among African American College Students at Predominantly Black and Predominantly White Universities. *Journal of Negro Education, 65*(3), 295–307.

King, S. H. (1993). The Limited Presence of African-American Teachers. *Review of Educational Research, 63*(2), 115–149.

Kujovich, G. (1994). Public Black Colleges: The Long History of Unequal Instruction. *Journal of Blacks in Higher Education*(3), 65–76.

Kunjufu, J. (1997). *Black College Student's Survival Guide.* Chicago, IL: African American Images.

Lamb, V. L. (1999). Institutional and Period Determinants of Baccalaureate Degrees from Historically Black Colleges and Universities: A Research Note. *Sociological Spectrum, 19*(2), 249.

Lang, M. (1992). Barriers to Blacks' Educational Achievement in Higher Education: A Statistical and Conceptual Review. *Journal of Black Studies, 22*(4), 510–522.

LaVeist, T. (1999). Top 50 Colleges for African Americans. *Black Enterprise, 29*(6), 71–80.

Leggon, C. B., & Pearson, W., Jr. (1997). The Baccalaureate Origins of African American Female Ph.D. Scientists. *Journal of Women & Minorities in Science & Engineering, 3*(4), 213–224.

Lehner, J. C., & United States. National Advisory Committee on Black Higher Education and Black Colleges and Universities. (1981). *A losing battle: the decline in Black participation in graduate and professional education: a report*. Washington, D.C.: The Committee.

Lindsay, B., & Justiz, M. J. (2001). *The quest for equity in higher education: toward new paradigms in an evolving affirmative action era*. Albany: State University of New York Press.

Locke, E. H., & Duke Endowment. (1985). *Prospectus for change: American private higher education: papers presented at colloquia in celebration of the sixtieth anniversary of the Duke Endowment*. Charlotte, NC: The Endowment.

Lockett, G. C. (1994, March 24, 1994). *Empowerment in HBCU's and PBCU's: Developing Microcosms of the Beloved Community through the Re-Definition of Social Institutions and the Learning and Application of Values*. Paper presented at the National Association for Equal Opportunity in Higher Education, Washington, D.C.

Logical Expression in Design. (1995). *The Murray resource directory and career guide to HBCUs* (Vol. 95 ed.-). Washington, D.C.: Logical Expression in Design.

López, G. R., & Parker, L. (2003). *Interrogating racism in qualitative research methodology*. New York: P. Lang.

Lusaka, J. (1999). Head, hand and heart: to serve and conserve. *Museum news, 78*(1), 40–45, 61.

Luti, A. N. (1999). When a door closes, a window opens: Do today's private historically black colleges and universities run afoul of conventional equal protection analysis? *Howard Law Journal, 42*(469).

Manzo, K. K. (1994). Database to Target HBCU Students: New Program Hopes to Increase Number of African American PH.D.s. *Black Issues in Higher Education, 11*(5), 26.

Matthews, C. M., & Library of Congress. Congressional Research Service. (1993). *Federal research and development funding at historically black colleges and universities*. [Washington, D.C.]: Congressional Research Service Library of Congress.

McAfee, S. R. W. (1974). *Organizational Variables and Educational Innovation in Selected Black Colleges and Universities: A Comparative Study*. Unpublished Ph.D., University of Michigan, Ann Arbor.

McDonough, P.M., Antonio, A. L., & Trent, J. W. (1997). Black Students, Black Colleges: An African American College Choice Model. *Journal for a Just & Caring Education, 3*(1), 9–36.

Mercer, J., & Morgan, J. (1990). Myths, Misunderstandings Often Keep Blacks, Asians Apart. *Black Issues in Higher Education, 7*(14), 13–15, 18–20, 22–24.

Merisotis, J. P., & O'Brien, C. T. (1998). *Minority-serving institutions: distinct purposes, common goals.* San Francisco: Jossey-Bass.

Miller, P. B. (1995). To "Bring the Race Along Rapidly": Sport, Student Culture, and Educational Mission at Historically Black Colleges during the Interwar Years. *History of Education Quarterly, 35*(2), 111–133.

Mitchell, R. (1993). *The Multicultural Student's Guide to Colleges: What Every African-American, Asian-American, Hispanic, and Native American Applicant Needs To Know about America's Top Schools.* New York: Noonday Press.

Mitchell, S. (2000). Affirmed action: Essays on the Academic and Social Lives of White Faculty Members of Historically Black Colleges and Universities. *Interchange, 31*(4), 455–456.

Mitchell, T. R. (1989). From Black to White: The Transformation of Educational Reform in the New South 1890–1910. *Educational Theory, 39*(4), 337–350.

Mohapatra, M. K., & McDowell, J. L. (1993). *Networking with Historically Black Colleges and Universities: Cultural Diversity in Public Administration Education at Indiana State University. A Final Report on a Cultural Diversity Innovation in Public Administration Education Project, 1992–1993* (No. ED363244). Washington, DC.: National Association of Schools of Public Affairs and Administration.

Mohr, P. (1975). *Black colleges and equal opportunity in higher education: a variety of papers advocating the retention of Black colleges and universities.* Lincoln, Neb.: Chicago-Southern Network Study Commission on Undergraduate Education.

More, T., Taylor, D., & Turner, D. (1998). African-American Youth Perceptions of Alcohol Advertisements: A Preliminary Analysis. *Challenge: a Journal of Research on African American Men, 9*(2), 67–82.

Moskowitz, M. (1997). The Status of Black Studies at the Nation's Highest-Ranked Universities. *Journal of Blacks in Higher Education* (16), 82–90.

Murray, C. (1994). HBCUs Gear Up to Produce Hospitality Managers. *Black Issues in Higher Education, 11*(13), 16–18.

Myers, S. (1986). *Economic issues and black colleges.* Chicago: Follett Press.

Myers, S. L., & National Association for Equal Opportunity in Higher Education (U.S.). (1986). *Economic issues and Black colleges.* Chicago: Follett Press.

NAACP photographs of schools and activities to eliminate segregation in education at the college and secondary levels. (1921). On *Visual Materials from the National Association for the Advancement of Colored People Records* [Visual]. Washington, D.C.: Library of Congress.

Nance, T., & Foeman, A. K. (1993). Rethinking the Basic Public Speaking Course for African American Students and Other Students of Color. *Journal of Negro Education, 62*(4), 448–458.

National Association for Equal Opportunity in Higher Education. (1975). *The National goal of equal opportunity and the historically Black colleges: a partnership for leadership in the development of a year 2000 plan for parity in education.* Washington, D.C.: National Association for Equal Opportunity in Higher Education.

National Association for Equal Opportunity in Higher Education (U.S.). (1989). *An Inventory of the capabilities of the historically black colleges and universities and other minority institutions (HBCUs/MIs): a NAFEO/DoD survey* (2nd ed. Vol. xi). Washington, D.C.: The Dept. of Health and Human Services.

National Association for Equal Opportunity in Higher Education (U.S.), & United States. Dept. of Health Education and Welfare. Region III. (1978). *Academic curricular developments in Black colleges and universities.* Washington, D.C.: U.S. Govt. Print. Off.

National Association of College Deans Registrars and Admissions Officers, & National Association for Foreign Student Affairs. (1973). *What's happening with U.S.—foreign student relations at predominantly Black colleges?* Washington, D.C.: National Association of College Deans Registrars and Admissions Officers (NACDRAO): National Association for Foreign Student Affairs (NAFSA).

National Task Force on Historically Black Colleges and Universities and Other Minority Institutions of Higher Education. (1999). *Making connections: findings and recommendations.* [Washington, D.C.?]: U.S. Dept. of Transportation Federal Highway Administration.

Needed system supports for achieving higher education equity for Black Americans: an analysis, report and recommendations for the establishment of national program objectives and system supports designed to support the achievement of equity for Black Americans in higher education. (1981). Washington, D.C.: National Advisory Committee on Black Higher Education and Black Colleges and Universities.

Nettles, M., Wagener, U., Millett, C., & Killenbeck, A. (1999). *Student Retention and Progression: A Special Challenge for Private Historically Black Colleges and Universities* (Vol. 108): Jossey Bass.

Nettles, M. T., Perna, L. W., Edelin, K. C., & Robertson, N. (1996). *The College Fund/UNCF Statistical Report, 1997.* Fairfax, VA: College Fund/UNCF.

Nettles, M. T., & Thoeny, A. R. (Eds.). (1988). *Toward Black Undergraduate Student Equality in American Higher Education.* New York: Greenwood Press.

Nettles, M. T. P., Laura W. Freeman, Kimberley Edelin. (1999). *Two Decades of Progress: African Americans Moving Forward in Higher Education.* Fairfax, VA: College Fund/UNCF, Frederick D. Patterson Research Inst.

Newby, J. E. (1982). *Teaching faculty in black colleges and universities: a survey of selected social science disciplines, 1977–1978.* Washington, D.C.: University Press of America.

Newman, K. A. (April 1994). *Researching Teachers in Residence: Bringing More Minority Teachers and Preservice Teachers into the Research Arena.* Paper presented at the American Educational Research Association, New Orleans, LA.

News and Views. (1996). *Journal of Blacks in Higher Education* (14), 14–74.

Nixon, H. L., & Henry, W. J. (1992). White Students at the Black University: Their Experiences Regarding Acts of Racial Intolerance. *Equity & Excellence, 25*(2–4), 121–123.

Nottingham, C. R. (1992). Psychological Well-Being among African American University Students. *Journal of College Student Development, 33*(4), 356–362.

Otuya, E. (1994). African Americans in Higher Education. *Research Briefs, 5*(3), 13.

Patel, N. H., & NAFEO Research Institute (U.S.). (1988). *Student transfers from white to black colleges.* Lanham, MD: University Press of America.

Payne, E. L. (1979). *America's Black colleges: roots, rewards, renewal.* Washington, D.C.: Delta Sigma Theta.

Pearson, W., & Fechter, A. (1994). *Who will do science?: educating the next generation.* Baltimore: Johns Hopkins University Press.

Perna, L. (1999). *The role of historically Black colleges and universities in preparing African Americans for faculty careers.* Montreal, Canada: Paper presented at the Annual Meeting of the American Educational Research Association.

Perna, L. W. (2001). The Contribution of Historically Black Colleges and Universities to the Preparation of African Americans for Faculty Careers. *Research in Higher Education 42, no, 3,* 267–294 (228 pages).

Pew Charitable Trusts., & Edgerton, R. (1998). *Historically black colleges & universities take a closer look at student retention: Dillard University, Fisk University, Hampton University, Howard University, Johnson C. Smith University, Morehouse College, Rust College, Spelman College, Tougaloo College, Xavier University.* [Philadelphia, Pa.]: Pew Charitable Trusts.

Phillip, M.-C., & Morgan, J. (1993). The Morehouse Mystique. *Black Issues in Higher Education, 10*(21), 16–19.

Poindexter-Cameron, J. M., & Robinson, T. L. (1997). Relationships among Racial Identity Attitudes, Womanist Identity Attitudes, and Self-Esteem in African American College Women. *Journal of College Student Development, 38*(3), 288–296.

Ponder, H., Freeman, M., Myers, S., United States. Dept. of Commerce, & National Association for Equal Opportunity in Higher Education. (2000). *Historically black colleges and universities an assessment of networking and connectivity.* Washington, DC: The Secretary of Commerce.

Posey, J. M., & Sullivan, O. R. (1990). *Wanted and Needed African-American Teachers* (No. ED323189). U.S. Mississippi.

Powell, R. J., Reynolds, J., Studio Museum in Harlem., & Addison Gallery of American Art. (1999). *To conserve a legacy: American art from historically Black colleges and universities.* Andover, Mass.

Preer, J. L. (1982). *Lawyers v. educators: Black colleges and desegregation in public higher education.* Westport, Connecticut: Greenwood Press.

Price, J. H., & Oden, L. (1996). African Americans in Health Education: Issues and Solutions. *Health Educator: Journal of Eta Sigma Gamma, 27*(2), 19–23.

Quarterman, J. (1996). African American Students' Perceptions of the Values of Basic Physical Education Activity Programs at Historically Black Colleges and Universities. *Journal of Teaching in Physical Education, 15*(2), 188–204.

Rankin, W. (1998). *German Language Instruction at Historically Black Colleges and Universities and the Future of German in (African) American Higher Education* (No. ED419392). U.S. Virginia: Hampton University.

Ratcliff, G. C. (1993). *An African-American Bibliography: Education. Selected Sources from the Collections of the New York State Library* (No. ED354905). New York.

Redd, T. M. (April 2, 1993). *An Afrocentric Curriculum in a Composition Classroom: Motivating Students To Read, Write, and Think.* Paper presented at the Conference on College Composition and Communication, San Diego, CA.

Richmond, P. A., Maramark, S., & United States. Office of Educational Research and Improvement. (1996). *On the road to economic development: a guide for continuing education programs at historically black colleges and universities.* Washington, DC: U.S. Dept. of Education Office of Educational Research and Improvement.

Roach, R. (1997). The Promise & The Peril. *Black Issues in Higher Education, 14*(2), 26–29.

Rodney, H. E., Tachia, H. R., & Rodney, L. W. (1999). The home environment and delinquency: A study of african american adolescents. *Families in society: the journal of contemporary human services, 80*(6), 551–559.

Rodney, L. W., & Rodney, H. E. (October 1–3, 1995). *National Conference Proceedings.* Paper presented at the Collaborating for Family and Community Violence Prevention, Atlanta, GA.

Roebuck, J. B., & Murty, K. S. (1993). *Historically black colleges and universities: their place in American higher education.* Westport, Conn. London: Praeger.

Roscoe, W. J., & NAFEO Research Institute (U.S.). (1989). *Accreditation of historically and predominantly Black colleges and universities.* Lanham, MD.

Sallie Mae. (1999). *Supporting the Historically Black College & University Mission: The Sallie Mae HBCU Default Management Program* (No. ED434559). Reston, VA: Sallie Mae.

Saving the African American child. A report of the task force on black academic and cultural excellence. (No. ED251538)(1984). Washington, D.C.: National Alliance of Black School Educators Inc.

Schnell, J., & Dates, J. (1993). *Promoting a More Inclusive Communication Curriculum Using Inter-University Faculty Collaboration as a Model* (No. ED358754). Ohio: Lilly Endowment, Inc.

Schwartz, R. A., & Washington, C. M. (1999a). African-American Freshmen in an Historically Black College. *Journal of the Freshman Year Experience, 11*(1), 39–62.

Schwartz, R. A., & Washington, C. M. (1999b). Predicting Academic Success and Retention for African American Women in College. *Journal of College Student Retention, 1*(2), 177–191.

Sims, S. J. (1994). *Diversifying historically Black colleges and universities: a new higher education paradigm.* Westport, Conn.: Greenwood Press.

Slater, R. B. (1994). Rating the Science Departments at Black Universities. *Journal of Blacks in Higher Education* (4), 90–96.

Smith, B. P. (1998). Two African American Women Who Spearheaded Early AAFCS Accreditation in Historically Black Colleges and Universities. *Journal of Family & Consumer Sciences, 90*(1), 34–37, 48.

Smith, D. H. (1993). Higher Education for Cultural Liberation. *Journal of Negro Education, 62*(2), 144–148.

Smith, D. H., & United States. National Advisory Committee on Black Higher Education and Black Colleges and Universities. (1980). *Admission and retention problems of Black students at seven predominantly White universities.* Washington, D.C.: National Advisory Committee on Black Higher Education and Black Colleges and Universities.

Smith, G. L. (1994). *A Black Educator in the Segregated South. Kentucky's Rufus B. Atwood.* Ithaca, NY: University Press of Kentucky.

Solorzano, D. G. (1995). The Doctorate Production and Baccalaureate Origins of African Americans in the Sciences and Engineering. *Journal of Negro Education, 64*(1), 15–32.

Southern Association of Colleges and Schools. Commission on Colleges and Universities. (1971). *Black colleges in the South; from tragedy to promise, an historical and statistical review.* Atlanta,: Southern Association of Colleges and Schools.

Spraggins, R. E. (1998). *Fly girl in the buttermilk: The graduate experiences at a predominantly white institution of black women who attended various undergraduate environments.* Unpublished Ph.D., Syracuse University, Syracuse, New York.

St. John, E. (1999). United We Stand: NAFEO, HACU, and AIHEC Have Formed a New Alliance To Improve Support for Students of Color. *Black Issues in Higher Education, 16*(11), 16–17.

Stephens, L. F. (1994). *Motivations for Enrollment in Graduate and Professional School among African American Students in HBCUs* (No. ED371064). U.S. South Carolina: Clemson Univ., SC. Houston Center for the Study of the Black Experience Affecting Higher Education.

Stewart, P. (2001). Why Xavier Remains No. 1. *Black Issues in Higher Education, 18*(11), 22–26.

Target date, 2000 AD: goals for achieving higher education equity for Black Americans. (1980). Washington, D.C.: National Advisory Committee on Black Higher Education and Black Colleges and Universities.

Taylor, E., & Olswang, S. (1999). Peril or Promise: The Effect of Desegregation Litigation on Historically Black Colleges. *The Western Journal of Black Studies, 23*(2), 73–82.

Taylor, R. A. (1996). Rainy Day Blues at UDC: Furloughs, Pay Cuts and Tuition Hikes at the University of the District of Columbia. *Black Issues in Higher Education, 13*(8), 8–11.

Terenzini, P. T., Yaeger, P. M., Bohr, L., Pascarella, E. T., & Amaury, N. (1997, May 1997). *African American College Students' Experiences in HBCUs and PWIs and Learning Outcomes.* Paper presented at the Association for Institutional Research (Orlando, FL, May, 1997), Orlando, FL.

Thomas, G. E., & Brown, F. (1981). *What Does Educational Research Tell Us About School Desegregation Effects?* Baltimore, MD: Johns Hopkins Univ., Baltimore, MD. Center for Social Organization of Schools.

Thomas, J. M., & Ritzdorf, M. (1997). *Urban planning and the African American community: in the shadows.* Thousand Oaks: Sage Publications.

Thompson, D.C. (1973). *Private Black colleges at the crossroads.* Westport, CT: Greenwood Press.

Thompson, T. (May 22–23, 1975). *Black colleges in educating and training health services administrators.* Paper presented at the Workshop sponsored by Health Services Administration Department, School of Business & Public Administration, Graduate Division, Washington, D.C.

Tollett, K. S. (1982). *Black Colleges as Instruments of Affirmative Action.* Washington, D.C.: Institute for the Study of Educational Policy.

The Tradition of White Presidents at Black Colleges. (1997). *Journal of Blacks in Higher Education* (16), 93–99.

Trent, W. T. (1984). Equity Considerations in Higher Education: Race and Sex Differences in Degree Attainment and Major Field from 1976 through 1981. *American Journal of Education, 92*(3), 280–305.

Turner, W. H. (March 31–April 4, 1985). *A critique of race relations theory as applied to public policy: The case of historically Black colleges.* Paper presented at the American Educational Research Association, Chicago, IL.

United States. Congress. House. Committee on Education and Labor. (1991). *Hearing on issues and matters pertaining to historically black colleges and universities hearing before the Committee on Education and Labor, House of Representatives, One Hundred First Congress, second session, hearing held in Washington, DC, December 16, 1990.* Washington: U.S. G.P.O.

United States. Congress. House. Committee on Education and Labor. (1991). *Hearing on issues and matters pertaining to historically black colleges and universities: hearing before the Committee on Education and Labor, House of Representatives, One Hundred First Congress, second session, hearing held in Washington, DC, December 16, 1990.* Washington: U.S. G.P.O.: For sale by the Supt. of Docs. Congressional Sales Office U.S. G.P.O.

United States. Congress. House. Committee on Education and Labor. Subcommittee on Postsecondary Education. (1988). *The unique role and mission of historically black colleges and universities hearing before the Subcommittee on Postsecondary Education of the Committee on Education and Labor, House of Representatives, One Hundredth Congress, second session, hearing held in Durham, NC, September 12, 1988.* Washington: U.S. G.P.O.

United States. Congress. House. Committee on Education and Labor. Subcommittee on Postsecondary Education. (1988). *The unique role and mission of historically black colleges and universities: hearing before the Subcommittee on Postsecondary Education of the Committee on Education and Labor, House of Representatives, One Hundredth Congress, second session, hearing held in Durham, NC, September 12, 1988.* Washington: U.S. G.P.O.: For sale by the Supt. of Docs. Congressional Sales Office U.S. G.P.O.

United States. Congress. House. Committee on Energy and Commerce. Subcommittee on Commerce Consumer Protection and Competitiveness. (1992). *Intercollegiate sports hearings before the Subcommittee on Commerce, Consumer Protection, and Competitiveness of the Committee on Energy and Commerce, House of Representatives, One Hundred Second Congress, first [and second] session.* Washington: U.S. G.P.O.: For sale by the U.S. G.P.O. Supt. of Docs. Congressional Sales Office.

United States. Congress. House. Committee on Energy and Commerce. Subcommittee on Commerce Consumer Protection and Competitiveness. (1992). *Intercollegiate sports: hearings before the Subcommittee on Commerce, Consumer Protection, and Competitiveness of the Committee on Energy and Commerce, House of Representatives, One Hundred Second Congress, first session, June 19, 1991—overview, July 25, 1991—academics and athletics, September 12, 1991—historically black colleges and universities.* Washington: U.S. G.P.O.: For sale by the U.S. G.P.O. Supt. of Docs. Congressional Sales Office.

United States. Congress. House. Committee on Natural Resources. (1993). *Historically Black Colleges and Universities Historic Building Restoration and Preservation Act report together with dissenting views (to accompany H.R. 2921) (including cost estimate of the Congressional Budget Office).* [Washington, D.C. ?: U.S. G.P.O.

United States. Congress. House. Committee on Resources. (1996). *Historically Black Colleges and Universities Historic Building Restoration and Preservation Act report (to accompany H.R. 1179) (including cost estimate of the Congressional Budget Office).* [Washington, D.C.]: U.S. G.P.O.

United States. Congress. House. Committee on Resources. Subcommittee on National Parks Forests and Lands. (1996). *Historic preservation oversight hearing before the Subcommittee on National Parks, Forests, and Lands of the Committee on Resources, House of Representatives, One Hundred Fourth Congress, second session, on H.R. 3031, a [sic] amend the act of October 15, 1966 (80 Stat. 915) as amended, establishing a program for the preservation of additional historic property through out the nation, and for other purposes; H.R. 563, to amend the National Historic Preservation Act to prohibit the inclusion of certain sites on the National Register of Historic Places, and for other purposes; H.R. 1179, to authorize appropriations for the preservation and restoration of historic buildings at historically black colleges and universities, March 20, 1996—Washington, DC.* Washington: U.S. G.P.O.: For sale by the U.S. G.P.O. Supt. of Docs. Congressional Sales Office.

United States. Congress. House. Committee on Science Space and Technology. Subcommittee on Science Research and Technology. (1988). *Federal science and technology support for historically black colleges and universities hearing before the Subcommittee on Science, Research, and Technology of the Committee on Science, Space, and Technology, House of Representatives, One Hundredth Congress, first session, October 9, 1987.* Washington: U.S. G.P.O.

United States. Congress. Senate. Committee on Energy and Natural Resources. (1994). *Historically Black Colleges and Universities Historic Building Restoration and Preservation Act report (to accompany H.R. 2921).* [Washington, D.C.?: U.S. G.P.O.

United States. Congress. Senate. Committee on Energy and Natural Resources. Subcommittee on Public Lands National Parks and Forests. (1994). *Cane River Creole National Historical Park a bill to restore and preserve historic buildings at historically black colleges and universities, and three public lands and national forests New Mexico bills: hearing before the Subcommittee on Public Lands, National Parks, and Forests of the Committee on Energy and Natural Resources, United States Senate, One Hundred Third Congress, second session, on S. 1509, S. 1975, S. 1897, H.R. 2921, S. 1919, S. 1980, April 21, 1994.* Washington: U.S. G.P.O.: For sale by the U.S. G.P.O. Supt. of Docs. Congressional Sales Office.

United States. Congress. Senate. Committee on the Budget. (1990). *Historically black colleges and universities of higher education hearing before the Committee on the Budget, United States Senate, One Hundred First Congress, first session, Atlanta, GA, November 13, 1989.* Washington: U.S. G.P.O.

United States. Dept. of Agriculture. University Affairs. (1981). *White House report: initiatives on historically Black colleges and universities.* Washington, D.C.: U.S. Dept. of Agriculture Office of Equal Opportunity University Affairs.

United States. Dept. of Health and Human Services. Division of Black American Affairs. (1983). *Historically Black colleges and universities fact book.* Washington, D.C.: The Division.

United States. Federal Interagency Committee on Education. (1969). Federal agencies and black colleges (p. v.). Washington: Federal Interagency Committee on Education: For sale by the Supt. of Docs. U.S. G.P.O.

United States. National Advisory Committee on Black Higher Education and Black Colleges and Universities. (1979). *Access of Black Americans to higher educa-*

tion: how open is the door? [Washington]: National Advisory Committee on Black Higher Education and Black Colleges and Universities: for sale by the Supt. of Docs. U.S. Govt. Print. Off.

United States. Office of Education. (1976). *Toward the maintenance of quality graduate education in historically black colleges and universities ; a report of the Office of Education working conference-meeting.* Washington: Dept. of Health Education and Welfare Office of Education.

Vital Signs: The Current State of African Americans in Higher Education. (1999). *Journal of Blacks in Higher Education* (23), 79–82.

Wagener, U., & Nettles, M. T. (1998). It Takes a Community To Educate Students. *Change, 30*(2), 18–25.

Walther, E. S. (1994). *Some readings on historically black colleges and universities* (Rev. ed.). Greensboro, NC: Management Information and Research.

Waltman, J. (1994). Assuring the Future of Black Colleges. *Chronicle of Higher Education, 40*(44), B1–2.

Watson, L., W. (1996). The Influence of Dominant Race Environments on Student Involvement, Perceptions, and Educational Gains: A Look at Historically Black and Predominantly White Liberal Arts Institutions. *Journal of College Student Development., v37*(n4 Jul–Aug 1996.), pp. 415–424.

White House Initiative on Historically Black Colleges and Universities. Corp Author(s): Department of Education, Washington, DC. (2002). U.S.; District of Columbia.

Whiting, A. N. (1991). *Guardians of the Flame: Historically Black Colleges Yesterday, Today, and Tomorrow.* Washington, D.C.: American Association of State Colleges and Universities.

Willie, C. V., & Edmonds, R. R. (1978). *Black colleges in America: challenge, development, survival.* New York: Teachers College Press.

Wilson, R. (1994). GI Bill Expands Access for African Americans. *Educational Record, 75*(4), 32–39.

Wilson, R. (1998). A Single Commencement Expands the Pool of New Black Ph.D.'s in Engineering. *Chronicle of Higher Education, 44*(36), A14–A16.

Wilson, R. (2001). A Battle over Race, Nationality, and Control at a Black University. *Chronicle of Higher Education, 47*(46), A8–A9.

Wintergreen/Orchard House Inc. (1995). *Historically Black colleges and universities.* New York, NY: Macmillan.

Wright, S. J., & United States. National Advisory Committee on Black Higher Education and Black Colleges and Universities. (1979). *The black educational policy researcher: an untapped national resource.* Washington, D.C.: National Advisory Committee on Black Higher Education and Black Colleges and Universities.

Index

About the Editors and Contributors

M. CHRISTOPHER BROWN II is the Executive Director and Chief Research Scientist of the Frederick D. Patterson Research Institute of the United Negro College Fund. He is on a continuing leave of absence from his appointment as Associate Professor of Education and Senior Research Associate in the Center for the Study of Higher Education at The Pennsylvania State University. His research addresses issues of higher education leadership and governance, postsecondary statutory and legal concerns, institutional history, and collegiate diversity. He is especially well known for his studies of historically black colleges, educational equity, and institutional culture. Dr. Brown is the author or co-author of more than 50 journal articles, book chapters, monographs, and publications related to education and society. His books include *The Quest to Define Collegiate Desegregation: Black Colleges, Title VI Compliance and Post-Adams Litigation* (1999), *Organization and Governance in Higher Education: An ASHE Reader* (2000), and *Black Sons to Mothers: Compliments, Critiques, and Challenges for Cultural Workers in Education* (2000, with James Earl Davis).

ALLISON N. CLARK is the Assistant Director of Digital Equity Initiatives at the National Center for Supercomputing Application (NCSA) located at the University of Illinois at Urbana-Champaign. Dr. Clark develops programs to create strategic relationships between the Alliance and members of underrepresented groups in the area of high performance computing. Her research interests include investigating culturally specific approaches to bridging the digital divide—specifically the combination of information technology with Hip Hop Culture.

SARAN DONAHOO is a doctoral candidate in Higher Education at the University of Illinois at Urbana-Champaign. Her research interests include history of higher education, international/comparative education, women in higher education, and higher education law.

TIMOTHY K. EATMAN currently works as a postdoctoral scholar in the Center for the Study of Higher and Postsecondary Education at the University of Michigan, School of Education. His research agenda centers on students from groups that are traditionally underrepresented in higher education and the impact that their participation in research opportunity programs has on career trajectory and quality of life. Dr. Eatman has published in various venues including the *Journal of Educational Finance, Readings on Equal Education*, and other book chapters and reports.

JACQUELINE FLEMING is currently the Director of the General University Academic Center at Texas Southern University in Houston, Texas. At TSU she has also served as Associate Professor of Education, Learning Specialist, and Retention Officer. She was also an Associate Adjunct Professor of Psychology at Barnard College, Columbia University, and a consulting psychologist in New York City where she was President of the Motivation Research Corporation. She has received three honorary degrees for her book *Blacks in College* (1984).

LENOAR FOSTER is an Associate Professor in the Department of Educational Leadership and Counseling Psychology in the College of Education at Washington State University. He holds joint appointments in Educational Leadership and in Higher Education and serves as the program coordinator for graduate programs in Higher Education. Previous to coming to Washington State University, he held tenured faculty positions at The University of Montana and at San Diego State University. He is the current editor of the Association for the Study of Higher Education Reader Series (Pearson Custom Publishing, Boston, MA) and serves as a member of the National Task Force on Principal Preparation, National Association of Secondary School Principals. His research interests and publications are in the areas of the secondary school principalship, school reform, distance education, and higher education administrative and faculty issues. Among his publications are *Affirmed Action: Essays on the Academic and Social Lives of White Faculty Members at Historically Black Colleges and Universities* (1999) and *Distance Education: Teaching and Learning in Higher Education* (2002).

KASSIE FREEMAN is the Dean of the Division of Educational and Psychological Studies and Professor of Education at Dillard University. Her research interests include cultural considerations related to African Americans and college choice, and comparative/international issues related to higher education and the labor market. She has edited two books titled, *The African American Culture and Heritage in Higher Education Research and Practice* and with M. Christopher Brown, II, *Black Colleges: New Perspectives on Policy and Practice*. She is also author of the forthcoming book titled, *African Americans and College Choice: The Influence of Family and School*. As a presidential appointee, she served on President Clinton's board of Advisors on Historically Black Colleges and Universities. She currently serves as President of The Comparative and International Education Society.

SHARON FRIES-RITT currently serves as an Assistant Professor in the College of Education at the University of Maryland, College Park. In 1998-1999 she was a visiting professor at the Harvard Graduate School of Education. Dr. Fries-Ritt's research focuses on high-achieving black collegians and their academic, social and psychological experiences. She has been an independent consultant for more than twenty years and has developed and implemented innovative training programs in the areas of multi-cultural relations and racial sensitivity for professional organizations in and outside of higher education.

PAUL GREEN is currently an Assistant Professor of education at University of California at Riverside. His major research areas and professional activity include Social Policy and the Law, urban policy and politics, politics of racial justice litigation, and political ecology of poverty and inequality. Dr. Green's professional activities include memberships in American Educational Research Association, Association for Public Policy Analysis and Management, American Political Science Association, Educational Law Association, South African Education Law and Policy Association, Comparative International Education Society, Association for the Study of Higher Education.

JANET A. GUYDEN is a Professor of Educational Leadership in the Department of Educational Leadership and Human Services at Florida A&M University, Tallahassee, Florida. She is actively involved in teaching, research, grant writing, and service. Dr. Guyden has been a secondary school teacher, the coordinator of an adult education program, and a counselor in both clinical and educational settings. At Paine College in Augusta, Georgia she served as director of the college counseling center and as Dean for admissions, recruitment, and financial aid. Dr. Guyden joined the faculty in the Department of Educational Policy Studies at Georgia State University in 1992 where she coordinated the Ph.D. program in higher education. Her research interests include the impact of organizations on individual functioning with specific interest in historically black colleges and teacher education reform.

BARBARA J. JOHNSON is an Assistant Professor of Education in the Department of Educational Leadership, Counseling and Foundations at the University of New Orleans. Her research interests include the experiences of students and faculty at historically black colleges and universities; the recruitment, development and retention of students and faculty in a variety of postsecondary institutions; and student affairs administration. Her recent publications have appeared in the *Review of Higher Education, Urban Education, Faculty in New Jobs, Diversity Issues in American Colleges and Universities* and *Women in Higher Education: An Encyclopedia.*

BRUCE ANTHONY JONES is currently Chair of the Division of Urban Leadership and Policy Studies at the University of Missouri at Kansas City. Dr. Jones developed a career in the field of philanthropy before beginning his academic career. He is the former director of the Consortium for Educational Policy Analysis housed at the University of Missouri at Columbia. Dr. Jones previously held a professorship at the University of Pittsburgh.

WYNETTA Y. LEE is Assistant Provost for Institutional Effectiveness & Research and Professor of Education at Dillard University. Dr. Lee has extensive experience in program development, implementation and assessment in higher education. Her primary research focuses on educational equity and academic success of special student populations in higher education (including minorities, women, academically under prepared students and community college transfer students). Her secondary research interests include impact assessments of higher education policies and programs (e.g., diversity initiatives and curriculum reform).

REITUMETSE OBAKENG MABOKELA is an Assistant Professor in the Higher, Adult, and Lifelong Education Program in the Department of Educational Administration at Michigan State University. Her research interests include an examination of race, ethnicity, and gender issues in postsecondary education; leadership issues among black female faculty and administrators; and organizational culture and its impact on historically marginalized groups. Dr. Mabokela is the author of *Voices of Conflict: Desegregating South African Universities* (2000); co-editor, with Kimberly Lenease King, of *Apartheid No More? Case Studies of Southern African Universities in the Process of Transformation* (2001); and co-editor with Anna L. Green, of *Sisters of the Academy: Emergent Black Women Scholars in the Academy* (2001). She has published articles in academic journals including *Comparative Education Review, American Educational Research Journal,* the *Journal of Negro Education,* and *The Review of Higher Education.*

NICOLE McDONALD is currently a Ph.D. student studying Education and Human Development at Vanderbilt University in Nashville, Tennessee. In addition to her studies at Vanderbilt, Nicole has worked as a Teaching Assistant in the Department of Leadership, Policy, and Organizations, and in student affairs administration at Vanderbilt and Emory Universities. Her research interests center on influences that impact the participation of students of color, particularly African American students, in higher education including the issues of access, college choice, and socialization.

RONYELLE BERTRAND RICARD is a doctoral candidate in Higher Education at The Pennsylvania State University. Her research interests include black colleges, student resiliency, and presidential leadership.

GAIL E. THOMAS is a Professor of Sociology at Soka University of America. Prior to joining the faculty at SUA, Dr. Thomas was Professor of Sociology and Founder and Director of the Race and Ethnic Studies Institute at Texas A&M University. She has also been a Visiting Professor at Harvard University and was Principal Research Scientist at the Center for Social Organization of Schools at John Hopkins University. Dr. Thomas is the editor of three books. Her most recent book is *Meeting the Challenge of U.S. Race Relations in America, 1990 and Beyond.* Her work has been widely published in sociological and educational journals, including the *Sociological Quarterly, Harvard Education Review, American Education Review Journal, International Journal of Higher Education,* and the *South African Journal of Higher Education.*